THE WORK ETHIC
IN BUSINESS

Aerial view of Bentley College, Cedar Hill, Waltham, Massachusetts.

The Work Ethic in Business

*Proceedings of the
Third National Conference
on Business Ethics*

Sponsored by
The Center for Business Ethics
Bentley College

Edited by
W. Michael Hoffman
Thomas J. Wyly
Bentley College

Oelgeschlager, Gunn & Hain, Publishers, Inc.
Cambridge, Massachusetts

Published in conjunction with
The Ethics Resource Center
Washington, D.C.

International Standard Book Number: 0-89946-068-2

Library of Congress Catalog Card Number: 80-22708

Printed in the United States of America

Library of Congress Cataloging in Publication Data

National Conference on Business Ethics, 3d, Bentley
    College, 1979.
    The work ethic in business.

    1. Work ethic—United States—Congresses.
    2. Labor and laboring classes—United States—
    1970-   —Congresses.   I. Hoffman, W. Michael.
    II. Wyly, Thomas J.   III. Bentley College.
    Center for Business Ethics.   IV. Title.
    HD8057.N23   1979   331'.01'3   80-22708
    ISBN 0-89946-068-2

Contents

List of Figures

List of Tables

Acknowledgments

The Third National Conference on Business Ethics and other activities of the Center for Business Ethics at Bentley College were made possible in part from grants from the following: Arvin Industries; Robert W. Brown, M.D.; The Council for Philosophical Studies (sponsored by the National Endowment for the Humanities); The General Mills Foundation; General Motors Corporation; Midland-Ross, Inc.; Motorola Foundation; The Raytheon Charitable Foundation; Rexnord, Inc.; Richardson-Merrill, Inc.; The Rockefeller Foundation; Semline, Inc.; Stop and Shop Manufacturing Companies; and F.W. Woolworth Company. On behalf of the Center, we wish to thank all these contributors and all the participants of the Third National Conference for sharing with us their support and ideas.

Our thanks also go to the Ethics Resource Center in Washington, D.C., for assistance in arranging the publication of this volume.

Finally, a special thanks must go to Theresa Armstrong, Susan Zimmerman, and Ellen Seale of the Center for Business Ethics, for the preparation and organization of these *Proceedings*.

W.M.H.
T.J.W.

Introduction

Thomas J. Wyly *

To everyone who proposes to have a good career, moral philosophy is indispensable.

Cicero, *De Officiis*, 44 B.C.

There is one and only one social responsibility of business . . . to increase its profits.

Milton Friedman, *Capitalism and Freedom*, 1962

[The United States needs] nothing less than a peaceful social revolution. The terms of the contract between industry and society are changing.

Henry Ford II, Ford Motor Company, 1973

In the long pull, nobody can expect to make profits—or have any meaningful use of profits—if the whole fabric of society is being ripped to shreds.

A.W. Clausen, President and Chief Executive Officer, the Bank of America, 1973

The survival of our economic system requires public confidence in the management and operation of business.

Gregory H. Adamian, First National Conference on Business Ethics, 1977

It is no longer possible—if it ever was—for any reasonable person to contend that "business is business," i.e., that business and ethics are intrinsically unrelated, or that many, if not most, business decisions do not also involve moral choices. Nor does it seem possible to assert that

*Executive Assistant to the President and Assistant Professor of English and Business Communications, Bentley College.

failure to consider aspects of business decisions beyond corporate financial advantage will be, in the long run, either tolerated by society or prudent for business itself. Both historians of business and ethical philosophers have clearly shown that business itself requires a moral environment in order to function—an environment, for example, in which contracts are honored, work honestly performed, and private property respected—and that to the degree such an ethical climate is lacking, business transactions are inevitably imperiled.

Business ethics today is perhaps the largest and most far-reaching branch of the maturing discipline of applied ethics, which in the past few years has commanded profoundly larger influence in virtually all the professions. The various scandals of the Vietnam–Watergate era, like previous revelations of abuse in our society, and others, spawned a crisis of confidence regarding many institutions, including politics and government, law, medicine, the media, the military, and religion, as well as business. American disillusion has been well documented by numerous studies and polls. Yet these revelations also gave impetus to many new efforts for correction and reform. Evidence of a deep and renewed interest in ethical study and practice is found not only in the proliferation of texts and courses in business ethics in the academic world, but also in the demand by business for such training, in the effort of many businesses to define standards of conduct against which to evaluate their activities, and in the reshaping of corporate structures to facilitate the discussion of ethical issues and increased regard of public opinion in corporate decisionmaking. There has also been substantial support for the study of business ethics from public and private foundations and from the government.

Persuasive evidence also exists that this concern for ethical business conduct will not diminish should news of misconduct recede from the headlines. It has become increasingly evident that business is inseparable from society's other institutions and its general culture, and that society will neither allow business to operate, nor will it judge business, on moral standards less stringent that those applied to our other institutions. Many forces have combined to shape this new accountability: the gigantic size of our larger corporations and the pervasiveness of business in modern life; the implications of advanced technology; the restraints and restrictions imposed over the past decade by government regulations, often in response to business abuses; the growing power of the consumerist and environmental movements; a more acute realization that energy must be used both conservatively and safely. All these developments strongly suggest that a watershed has been reached in the relationship of business to the rest of society, and that a general realization has taken place that moral questions concerning business activity are not of a transitory nature.

Yet the realization that business is not only financially, but also morally, inseparable from the larger social fabric, and that business has responsibilities to society other than its own financial success, is not a new departure, but rather a reshaping—conscious or not—of traditional principles that have long governed business-social relations. Only in the modern industrial age has the idea been advanced that a business enterprise fulfills its social obligations if it merely achieves a profit and breaks no law. Throughout the millennium of the Middle Ages, the social role of business was defined by the Church, which established a moral expectation of fair prices and living wages, and which regulated competition and adjudicated appeals. In the era of nation-state mercantilism, public interest was defined by sovereigns who unilaterally determined the contracts under which chartered corporations conducted their business; increasing the wealth of the state provided the wherewithal for the implementation of social policy. Only since the industrial revolution has business formed the philosophy that it served society best by serving itself, that social well-being emerged as a result of the prosperity of the entrepreneur or the corporation. This revolutionary thesis, it should be remembered, given full expression in Adam Smith's *The Wealth of Nations*, was from the first rejected by some as preposterous, if not evil.

Much of modern business has recognized, and is now struggling with, the challenge to incorporate into decision-making models consideration of the ethical dimensions of issues. Having learned the costly negative lessons that excessive regulation can result from violating civil rights, disregarding worker safety, despoiling the environment, and manufacturing unsafe products, and that declining productivity—and profitability—follow neglect of the quality of work life, corporations large and small are grappling with ways to assess hugely important influences on their affairs which, unlike other concerns, defy quantification, and which cannot be precisely related to the bottom line. Acknowledging that profit is not the only good even in a capitalist economy, business is now searching for ways to measure and act on values. Business now realizes that owners often have no more vested interest—and often less—than other constituencies, such as management, staff, suppliers, customers, and local communities. "Shareholder economics" is giving way to "stakeholder economics," yet we are just beginning to discover satisfactory socio-political processes to serve so many masters in a balanced way. Increasing shareholder wealth was a far simpler task than observing the diverse values represented by multiple "stakeholders."

One resource to which business has turned for assistance, and which can lend perspective and insight to such issues, is academia. What counsel should colleges and universities offer today's generation of corporate leaders, and what education should it provide the next generation in today's classrooms? Though both questions are being debated off and on the campus, some would suggest that the ethical dilemmas of business today are in many instances new and complex variations of old problems, and that one objective of educational institutions should be to equip modern businessmen and businesswomen with both historical knowledge and intellectual discipline in what has traditionally been called "moral reasoning," to *inform* students, and to provide them the opportunity *to form* their moral characters. Knowledge of what has traditionally been conceived of as right and wrong, and experience in examining difficult moral questions, will not necessarily move one to virtue, but will lead to a clearer recognition of the nature of moral choice and of the competing claims of rival values.

One contribution of higher education, then, should be to instruct students not only in the history of business, but also in the history of ethical thought, as well as modern applied ethics. It is well worth remembering that governments have found it necessary to regulate wages and prices as early as the Code of Hammurabi four thousand years ago; that the ethical theory of the ancient Greeks evolved from the dealings of their merchants and traders; and that Adam Smith, as well as his greatest ideological contrary, Karl Marx, began their careers as philosophers before they felt compelled to turn their mental powers to economic theory.

In truth, it seems that a modern businessman is conceptually ill equipped for the mounting challenges before him without a working knowledge of Adam Smith's "invisible hand" and Marx's contrary concern for wage depression and alienation from one's own labor; without examining the theories of human nature advanced by ethical and psychological egoists such as Hobbes in his *Leviathan*, and utilitarians like Hume, Bentham, and Mill; without an understanding of the indebtedness of industrial giants like Andrew Carnegie to Social Darwinists like Herbert Spencer; or without having compared Locke's defense of private property with Marx's view on class struggle. It is scarcely possible that such study and reflection, wedded to the application of ethical theory through such methods as case studies, will not ultimately enlarge one's moral decision-making power in the business arena, and develop the capacity for further growth through experience.

Such knowledge and study will surely lend perspective as one examines the presentations and discussions of these *Proceedings* of Bentley College's Third National Conference of Business Ethics, which center on two major themes: the quality of working life within the business world, and the role of government in the workplace. An introduction to the conference by Gregory H. Adamian, President of Bentley College, explains the raison d'etre of the Center for Business Ethics, i.e., to create a forum in which professional philosophers, business professors, executives, labor leaders, government representatives, leaders of public interest groups, and students can discuss and debate contemporary business ethics issues of major importance. Opening remarks at the conference by W. Michael Hoffman, Director of the Center, suggest the range and complexity of the variations on these themes explored in these pages. Presentations were followed by open discussion and debate, often with sharp differences of opinion, by major speakers and those in attendance. Both formal presentations and subsequent "Discussion" sessions are reproduced in full in these *Proceedings*. In editing this volume, Professor Hoffman and I have occasionally imposed some order and regularity on the language of these impromptu "Discussions," but much more we have preserved their extemporaneous quality, embodying a spirit of inquiry, controversy, and the exploration of practical solutions to business problems.

In Chapter 1, Leonard A. Wood, Executive Vice President of the Gallup Organization, presents the results of a special poll on *Changing Attitudes and the Work Ethic*, conducted especially for Bentley's Third National Conference on Business Ethics. The Gallup survey reveals a slightly improving attitude toward business in recent years, especially among the young and well-educated; a decline in the spirit of entrepreneurship in favor of a growing wish to work for an organization; an overwhelming desire among Americans for demanding work entailing responsibility and authority, rather than easy, unchallenging work; and a dominant belief that federal government regulation, rather than worker attitudes, welfare, labor unions, taxes, energy costs, or management practices, is the greatest cause of the slowdown in the rate of growth in American productivity over the past ten years.

Following this survey is a brilliant study by Michael Maccoby and Katherine A. Terzi of the Harvard Project on Technology, Work, and Character, entitled *What Happened to the Work Ethic?* This essay, enriched by a deep historical knowledge of work traditions in America, and extensive familiarity with contemporary work arrangements, traces the evolution of four different work ethics in America under changes brought on by urbanization and new technology and socio-economic systems. According to Maccoby and Terzi, the first of these ethics was Calvinist and Protestant; work was an expression of faith and salvation. The second was the Craft Ethic, described by Benjamin Franklin, emphasizing independence and the quality of workmanship. The third was the Entrepreneurial Ethic, dramatized by Horatio Alger, which held out the promise of creating one's own business. As America changed from a nation of self-employed farmers, craftsmen, and small businessmen to an organizational society, a fourth Work Ethic emerged: the new Career Ethic, which stresses that hard work will pay off in promotion to the top.

Against the framework provided by the Gallup survey and the historical perspective offered by Maccoby and Terzi, the *Proceedings* embark, in
Chapter 3, on an examination of *Various Corporate Approaches to
Quality of Work Life* programs. Steven H. Fuller, Vice President at
General Motors, discusses in "Becoming the Organization of the Future"
how a series of crippling strikes at GM, and the adversary environment
engendered, gave way in 1973, under management initiative, to a new
cooperative effort with the UAW. A joint National Committee to
Improve the Quality of Work Life brought about dramatic turnarounds
in plant efficiency through improvements initiated at the local level.

Next, Berth Jönsson first reviews the changing structure of the
Swedish work force, and then recounts and analyzes his company's
experience at its Kalmar plant since 1971 in "The Volvo Experience." By
redesigning the shape of an auto assembly plant and changing both hardware technology and work organization around the idea of production
teams, total production time was significantly reduced. Although such a
plant is 10% more costly to construct than a conventional plant of equal
capacity, the assignment of greater responsibility to workers led to fewer
supervisors and less supervision. Decreased turnover, reduced incidence
of sickness and absenteeism, and the entrepreneurial spirit generated by
these experiments made the Kalmar concept the driving force for changes
in production in other Volvo plants, both old and new. Jönsson stresses
that workers must participate fully in designing and implementing such
quality of work life programs, that such initiatives cannot be implemented from the "top down."

Last in this chapter, Rex R. Reed, Vice President for Labor Relations at
AT&T, reviews the history of his organization's "Work Itself" program.
Reed examines the lessons AT&T has learned from a quality of work life
program that was largely management designed, and which withered
after some initial successes.

These corporate views stand in marked contrast to the confessed
"personal cynicism" of Jerry Wurf, International President of AFSCME,
who insists that quality of work life is still most meaningfully measured
in terms of "wages, hours, and working conditions." Wurf asserts that
labor unions "have done more than any other institution in our society to
improve the quality of work life for everyone." In contrast to the
optimism over common interests and cooperative improvements
expressed by academicians like Maccoby, corporate leaders like Jönsson
and later in this volume, for example, by industrialist Sidney Harman
and UAW Vice President Donald F. Ephlin, Wurf contends that in a
democratic society labor-management relations are inescapably
adversarial, and that in the public sector the brutal imperative of political
advantage exploits workers even more severely than the imperative of

profit in private industry. Wurf contends that public sector labor relations are even "meaner," more irresponsible, tougher, and less accountable," and that collective bargaining can work only if it is recognized and conducted as a power struggle between equally strong opponents. The pointed controversy between Maccoby and Wurf that follows in the chapter's "Discussion" section illuminates the tension that often exists when quality of work life programs are introduced; where such programs have succeeded, they have increased both job satisfaction *and* productivity, but where management has taken the initiative in suggesting such approaches, over the bargaining table or elsewhere, labor has often been suspicious that such efforts were stepped-up productivity programs in disguise.

Chapter 5 introduces another major issue, *Affirmative Action and Equal Opportunity Employment*. Vivian Buckles, Regional Administrator of the Women's Bureau in the Department of Labor, details "The Progress of Women in the American Work Force," but notes that 80 percent of all women workers are still clustered in low-paying, traditional "women's jobs" averaging not more than $8,600 in salary per year. Further, women account for only 2.3 percent of those earning in excess of $25,000 per year. Two-fifths of all American women still work in only ten different occupations.

Marlene Gerber Fried, Professor of Philosophy at Bentley, next examines "Affirmative Action in a Declining Economy." Fried argues that in an era of diminished economic opportunity, increased competition constrains what can be accomplished through affirmative action, while bureaucratic watchdog agencies create the inaccurate impression that greater justice is being achieved. A declining economy leads to unproductive and unjust competition and charges of "reverse discrimination" when white males of ability cannot fulfill their career desires.

Finally, Kenneth I. Guscott, President of KGA Associates and a Director of the Boston branch of the NAACP, proclaims his faith in the capitalist system in "Affirmative Action as a Human Resource Tool." Guscott argues that there is greater financial profit in the full utilization of all human resources, regardless of race or sex, than in discrimination, and that educational systems must anticipate the nation's future economic needs so that young people may be prepared today for tomorrow's opportunities.

The ensuing "Discussion" in Chapter 5 brings to the fore many of the sharpest controversies surrounding affirmative action. Fried vigorously claims that since society and its institutions have made race and sex matters of relevance regarding educational and employment opportunity, remedies for past and current discrimination cannot be achieved without race- and sex-conscious selection procedures. Futher, Fried seems to argue that the inherent competitiveness of a profit-based economy results in a more unjust distribution of goods and services than other economic systems. She is strongly challenged on this point. Guscott, on the other hand, praises the competitiveness of the American system, provided all are given equal opportunity to compete. Buckles and Guscott also discuss the ironic problem that while study of the liberal arts often produces the most capable and productive workers, employers often shortsightedly do not employ or underemploy liberal arts graduates in favor of individuals with narrower, but more immediately useful, technical training. Both writers suggest that students combine liberal and professionally oriented studies to ensure career entry as well as capacity for professional and personal enrichment.

Chapter 6 offers three different perspectives on the theme of *Government Regulation and Intervention in the Workplace*. Eula Bingham, Assistant Secretary for Occupational Safety and Health at the Department of Labor, examines "Ethics and the Workplace." In an impressive explication of OSHA's mission, Bingham declares that a safe and healthful workplace is a basic human right. She discusses with specificity the difficulties involved in holding corporations accountable for worker safety and in obtaining full disclosure of health hazards. Bingham attacks the view of workers as capital and rebuts what she feels are distorted analyses of the costs of OSHA compliance.

Dennis Laurie, Manager of Public Affairs for ARCO Transportation, is less convinced of the need for federal workplace intervention, and inquires, "What Should We Do About Government Regulation?" He reports that the thirty largest federal regulatory agencies employ in excess of a quarter of a million people; that twenty new regulatory agencies were established since just 1970; and that some estimates of the cost of such regulations approach $120 billion per year. Laurie protests that many regulations are needlessly complex, overly simple, or contradictory. Although he concedes that federal regulations have achieved some improvements regarding equal opportunity and environmental protection, he nevertheless lashes out as the "shadow Congress" of bureaucrats and staff who have created a new industry of federal regulation. Laurie also calls for "sunset reviews" of regulatory legislation, and "economic impact statements" of proposed regulations.

Finally in this chapter, Marvin H. Kosters, Director of the Center for the Study of Government Regulation at the American Enterprise Institute, presents an interesting framework for "Cost-Benefit Analysis of Government Safety and Health Regulation." Kosters declares that despite the complexity of regulatory decisionmaking, considerable quantification of the costs and benefits of various OSHA regulations is possible, and that such analyses proceed most successfully as a step toward "systematic sensitivity" in identifying human values to be fostered in work environments.

Chapter 7 takes up another aspect of modern work, the *Extension of the Workplace into the Community*. First, Sloan K. Childers, Vice President for Public Affairs at Phillips Petroleum Company, traces the expanding notion of the work environment from the machine station to the entire community. This essay, "The Work Ethic in the Context of the Community," reviews possibilities for corporate social action that do not usurp functions traditionally belonging to city and town government.

Frederick G. Frost III, President and Chairman of the Board of A.T. Wall Company, then examines "Small Business Involvement in the Community." Frost attacks the myth that only major corporations can have major impacts on their localities. He declares that the typical businessman, who likely was born in the community, schooled there, resides there, and will probably retire there, has a much larger personal stake in his city or town than executives from larger enterprises.

Last, Fred K. Foulkes, Professor of Business Administration at Harvard Business School, attempts to construct "A Conceptual Framework for Business-Community Relations." Foulkes suggests that positive corporate impact on communities depends on the values of top management, particularly on an appreciation that the corporation is a guest of the community, and on the quality of staff assigned, full-time or part-time, to the community relations function. Foulkes urges that all line managers be trained to consider community relations as part of their job, and that many kinds of involvement produce, at least in the long run, benefits for the company as well as the municipality. Foulkes also indicates that smaller companies can unite to have a much larger joint impact than they would ever have singly. The "Discussion" section raises questions concerning the connection between community relations and employee relations, company pullouts, urban renewal and race relations, and shareholder attitudes.

The conference next examined *Some Aspects of Worker Dignity in the Corporation* (Chapter 8). Norman E. Bowie, Director of the Center for the Study of Values at the University of Delaware, posits that there exists a "Moral Contract Between Employer and Employee." Bowie reasons that employees, like employers, enter into work contracts as responsible, autonomous adults, and thus are moral agents responsible for respecting the rights of others and possessing rights that employers must respect. An employer's relationship with his company is thus not a purely economic one. Bowie therefore focuses his attention on the implementation of employee rights, particularly in conflict situations.

Bowie's remarks are followed by a provocative essay by Charles W. Powers, Vice President for Public Affairs at Cummins Engine Company, entitled "Individual Dignity and Institutional Identity: the Paradoxical Needs of the Corporate Employee." Powers discerns that individuals have paradoxically conflicting needs for a personal dignity and sense of self that are independent of work, *and* for an institutional role that provides a basis for action and participation in history. This conflict results in competing values in the organization, such as the right to employee privacy versus empathetic management based on knowledge of employee aspirations and problems; the right to equal treatment versus the right to hold and act on personal opinions regarding other people; and even the adoption of specific company regulations and ethical codes of conduct versus encouraging employee creativity, independence, and growth in making complex decisions. In sum, Powers focuses his attention on the contradictory natural needs of human character and personality, and how such needs and values must be carefully balanced in modern organizations.

Sidney Harman, in Chapter 9, presents *A Peace Plan for Workers and Bosses*. A Chief Executive Officer of Harman International, and former Undersecretary of the Department of Commerce, Harman analyses the extra costs entailed in adversarial labor-management relations, such as extra overtime in building up protective inventories, subsequent reduced work weeks, damaged relationships, and poor performance as prime attention is paid to hostile negotiations. At his own company, in Bolivar, Tennessee, where workers had historically played a major role in designing the plant production system and health and safety measures, both a deeper sense of worker responsibility and greater management respect for the attitudes and values of labor became apparent. Harman writes, "Some managers may not like to face it, but experience makes clear that workers possess an enormous untapped inventory of know-how. If they ever believed they were genuinely respected for what they know, were truly part of the action, they would jolt our economists, our pundits and our savants with what they would produce."

A labor leader, oil company executive, and federal mediator examine American work ethics in Chapter 10. Donald F. Ephlin, Vice President of the United Auto Workers, reports on the "Quality of Work Life in the Auto Industry." He compares GM assembly plants in Tarrytown, New York, where quality of work life is a flourishing success, and Framingham, Massachusetts, where neither management nor labor is interested in such efforts, and where grievances are much higher than in Tarrytown and productivity significantly lower. Unlike Jerry Wurf, Ephlin believes that quality of work life programs have worked best where they are separate from and complementary to the collective bargaining process. Ephlin, recalling Fuller's remarks, examines the history of local strikes that have occurred in his industry, even where economic conditions were very favorable, and concludes that such strikes resulted over quality of work life issues, although neither labor nor management realized it at the time.

John R. Hall, Vice Chairman and Chief Operating Officer of Ashland Oil, Inc., taking "A Business View of the Work Ethic," regards new demands by workers for personal satisfaction and job enrichment as part of the American heritage of each generation seeking a fuller life than that of its parents. He believes such demands are being frustrated by declining productivity, brought about by the stifling of capital formation and research and development by inflation and federal regulation. Hall concludes that addressing these causes of productivity decline will facilitate opportunities for making work more meaningful.

Finally in this chapter, Wayne Horvitz, Director of the Federal Mediation and Conciliation Service, explores "Confrontation Politics and Fundamental Issues in the Collective Bargaining Process." Horvitz, declaring that the workplace is an extension of the rest of society, suggests that there are many issues on which labor and management could act in collaborative partnership. The failure to do so, especially in approaching new issues, has resulted in the dramatic increase of federal regulation.

Stanley E. Seashore of the Institute for Social Research, University of Michigan, examines the famous Bolivar case as an instance of *Humanization of Work: Ethical Issues in Converting Ideology to Practice* (Chapter 11). Seashore concludes that work life programs are rarely bargained for in the traditional sense, but rather depend on larger capacities than traditionally found in labor and managements for mutual trust and a willingness to accept new risks. A greater recognition of economic and human interdependence is critical, Seashore suggests, for work life success.

In Chapter 12, Michael Brower and Richard Balzer, respectively the Directors of the American Center for the Quality of Work Life and the Massachusetts Labor-Management Center, conduct a *Workshop Discussion on Joint Labor/Management Activities*. Brower and Balzer specify fifteen lessons they have learned from extensive experience in many quality of work life settings, regarding such questions as the relationship of union and management leadership in such programs, the involvement of first-line supervisors and shop stewards, the pros and cons of using third-party professional consultants, and sharing the financial costs of program implementation. There is much to be learned from the wealth of knowledge and experience of these two individuals.

D. Richard Harmer, Professor of Management at Bentley College, declares in Chapter 13 that *The Work Ethic Is Alive, Well, and Living in Cleveland*. He presents perhaps the fullest examination to date of the remarkable Lincoln Electric Company, which, for nearly half a century, has consistently produced two to three times the sales volume product per employee as similar manufacturing organizations. Paying its employees annual bonuses that typically *equal* annual salaries, Lincoln's operating margins have nevertheless generally ranged between 25 percent and 30 percent of sales. Harmer presents Lincoln Electric as an alternative to traditional approaches to U.S. enterprise, and suggests that its portfolio of untraditional practices, including market strategy, approach to technological innovation, personnel policies, and management activities—all rooted in the industrial philosophy of the company's founder, James Lincoln—offers a pragmatic and workable model for other American companies in a variety of industries.

Finally, in Chapter 14, Paul E. Tsongas, junior Senator from Massachusetts, addresses *Work Ethics in an Era of Limited Resources.* Tsongas argues that there is no single culprit for the decline in American productivity, but rather a diversity of accomplices, and he cites less familiar causes such as two post–World War II phenomena, the mass entrance into the labor market of less experienced workers who were part of the baby boom, and the end of an era of transfer of workers from agriculture to highly productive manufacturing. He also claims that instances of "regulatory overkill" are the "predictable, inevitable result" of severe business abuses. Tsongas, like a surprising number of other speakers at the Third National Business Ethics Conference, calls for a new sense of cooperation and common interests by labor, management and government. Failure to overcome traditional attitudes of contention will make America even more vulnerable to international challenges from competitors and predators, and will inexorably lead to a further lowering of the U.S. standard of living.

Through the diversity of speakers and subjects at this Third National Conference, several important major themes emerge. Perhaps the clearest is a call from representatives from every sector of society to labor and management to temper traditional adversarial confrontation in their own and the national self-interest. Such an easing of tensions, and a cultivation of genuine trust, is a prerequisite for the implementation of successful quality of work life programs. Another theme is the multiple causation of America's decline in productivity, and hence the multiplicity of strategies needed to reverse this trend. A third common note is the persistent willingness of Americans to work—and to work hard and responsibly—despite stereotypes to the contrary. A fourth major theme is the wastefulness of discrimination of any kind, and the difficult complexities involved in attempting to achieve justice in the workplace through externally imposed remedies. And finally, government intervention is frequently viewed in these pages as principally the result of business abuse; if government regulation of the workplace is in some ways a detriment to economic growth, only wholesale reforms by industry regarding worker health and safety, civil and consumer rights, and environmental protection, will restore the marketplace to its previous state of semi-autonomy. In one very real sense, it is to the values of the free enterprise system, and to the freedom, dignity, and common humanity of all who labor to earn their living, that the Third National Conference on Business Ethics, and these *Proceedings*, have been dedicated.

Introduction to the Conference

*Gregory H. Adamian**

Bentley College's Center for Business Ethics was founded three years ago on the premise that a critical need existed to create a forum in which members of the academic and business communities could exchange ideas on timely subjects of practical and contemporary importance regarding business ethics. The Center came into being at a time when public opinion in the United States regarded business, government, and other American institutions as having largely departed from the ethical norms and values that we have traditionally considered at the heart of America's success as a nation and its stature as a world economic and moral leader. In the last few years we have experienced an era of reform in many of these institutions, but our heightened sensitivity to such matters has persuaded most observers that the ethical issues facing America are far more complex than previously imagined, and that only ongoing study and debate of these is-

*President, Bentley College.

sues as opposed to one-time solutions can succeed not only in defining and preserving a moral climate for decision making, but also in devising practical nuts-and-bolts solutions to some of the problems currently facing business enterprises.

Bentley College believes that the interchange at this conference between academic and business leaders strengthens instruction at Bentley and also improves the knowledge and perspective of all in attendance who occupy positions of responsibility in various business institutions.

This year's program, like those of previous years, brings together noted academicians, corporate executives, labor leaders, representatives from government, elected officials, and leaders of public interest groups, united by a commonality of interest, though certainly not of opinion. There are few opportunities for such a diverse gathering of individuals to debate and discuss business ethics issues. We are persuaded that this conference is making an important and unusual contribution. This year's special subject is "The Work Ethic." A review of the conference program suggests that the aspects of this theme are nearly as diverse as the list of panelists and speakers.

Whatever we might mean by "The Work Ethic" probably cannot be rightly understood without a grasp of the religious roots of American business ethics, especially but not exclusively in American Calvinism. New demands by workers for humanization and democratization of the workplace, the growing desire by members of a more affluent generation for more job satisfaction as well as job security, the alarming decline in the growth of American productivity, the complicated and enlarging role of government regulation and intervention regarding health and safety, affirmative action, and inflation control, as well as more familiar involvement, the resurrection of ethics in undergraduate and graduate curricula both in the professional schools and in the humanities; all these developments are issues that bear importantly on the conference theme and all are in one way or another inextricably related.

Behind any notion of the work ethic, however, must lie a fundamental acceptance of both individual and organizational responsibility. Bentley's active involvement in ethical concerns, both in sponsoring programs such as this one and imparting to our students a special and informed awareness of business ethics ultimately may benefit all the organizations represented and American society as a whole. The track record of our Center, its conferences, and publications have demonstrated how much all of us can profit from these endeavors. We ask for your continued participation and support. I know each of you will add something to this conference, and I hope all of you will find its deliberations enduringly worthwhile.

Opening Remarks

*W. Michael Hoffman**

Let me welcome you to our Third National Conference on Business Ethics, which this year has as its theme "The Work Ethic in Business." This conference is sponsored by the Center for Business Ethics, which was established at Bentley College in 1976 for the primary purpose of providing a nonpartisan forum to exchange ideas on business ethics in an industrial society, particularly as these ideas relate to the activities of corporations, labor, government, and the professions. The Center has previously sponsored two other national conferences, in 1977 and 1978, the *Proceedings* of which were published in two separate volumes that have been purchased by hundreds of organizations and individuals and are being used as texts in many business ethics courses throughout the country. In addition to these conferences and published *Proceedings,* the Center publishes a *Business Ethics Report* describing the highlights of the conferences, various bibliographies on business ethics, and collections of course syllabi in business ethics, and it serves as a general clearinghouse for ideas

*Director, Center for Business Ethics; Professor and Chair, Department of Philosophy, Bentley College.

and information concerning the field of business ethics studies. As a result of these activities, we trust that the Center has helped to promote the study of business ethics both here and abroad and to create a climate of greater understanding and trust among various constituencies and interest groups. We have also furthered our ultimate aim of establishing a better ethical framework within which to conduct business in general.

We have planned our conference around two major themes: first, the quality of working life within the business world, and second, the government role in the regulation of work and the protection of workers. I anticipate that some extremely timely and crucial questions will be raised at this conference. For example, what are the attitudes of workers today toward their jobs and careers? Are they satisfied or dissatisfied, and why? Has the work ethic lost its meaning, or are we passing through a new phase of work ethic, and, if so, how does it differ from our conception of the work ethic of the past? What is meant by quality of working life programs? Are they attempts by corporations truly to humanize the workplace, trying to make work more meaningful to employees, or are they smokescreens, as some in labor have alleged, through which corporations plan to exploit workers in an effort simply to increase productivity? For the most part, are labor unions supportive of quality of working life programs, or, as some corporate leaders have argued, are they antagonistic because they fear their role and purpose may be undercut if management and employers increase cooperation? In short, what is the mood of business and labor on this issue?

How closely related are these quality of working life programs to Europe's more radical attempts at worker democratization? Should workers have more participation in company policy decision making? If so, how should this be structured? For example, should worker representatives sit on corporate boards, or is this going too far? Should workers play a larger part in hiring supervisors and deciding on working conditions, or is this not going far enough? Should labor unions have a role in such restructuring, and, if so, what kind of role? How can or should government play any role in facilitating or regulating such attempts to improve quality of working life?

The conference is also designed to elicit such specific questions as the following: What effect has the emergence of women and minorities had upon work in America? Do affirmative action guidelines constitute justified preferential hiring or reverse discrimination? Have we arrived at equal opportunity employment in this country, or, if not, why not? What is the proper role of government regulation in the workplace? Has such intervention gone too far? For example, are

OSHA guidelines too rigid, and how do the workers themselves feel about such regulation? Are workers being properly informed about high-risk jobs? What specific independent actions are corporations taking to improve working conditions for their employees? What is the social responsibility of corporations regarding the community within which their workers reside? How can a corporation improve the community for its workers without dominating the community? Is this a proper use of stockholders' money? What is a corporation's responsibility to a community and its workers when it decides to leave the community? What does it mean to refer to the human dignity of workers, and what are corporations doing and what should they do to ensure such dignity? What are workers' rights, e.g., right of privacy, right of protection regarding whistle-blowing, right to equal opportunity, right to express views different from corporations?

I would hope that these questions, among many others, will be asked and that many ideas will be shared at this conference in an effort to explore some answers. Studs Terkel has said in his book on working that "Most of us have jobs that are too small for our spirit." The major question of this conference, I would suggest, centers around this thought. For if we believe that we are spiritually oppressed in our work, we must find ways to free ourselves by trying to make our work more meaningful. I hope ideas will emerge, through conferences such as this and others, which will provide such freedom and meaning, allowing our work truly to manifest the best of what it is to be a moral and human being.

CHAPTER 1

Changing Attitudes and the Work Ethic

*Leonard A. Wood**

Recent Gallup surveys would indicate that, while there has not been significant change in overall attitudes toward business, a slight shift toward a more favorable opinion can be discerned among the younger, better-educated groups. This trend could foreshadow a new direction in public attitudes toward business. Traditionally, change among the young, the better educated, and the more affluent segments of the population precipitates change throughout the population.

SIGNS OF POSITIVE CHANGE

In February 1977, respondents were asked to describe how their general attitudes toward business had changed over the past few years. About one in three, 35 percent, said that their attitudes had become more positive, while half (50 percent) described their attitudes as becoming more negative.

When this same question was asked in a later study, conducted in May 1978, the response was only slightly more favorable, with 38 per-

*Executive Vice President, The Gallup Organization, Inc.

Table 1. Positive Change in Attitudes Toward Business, by Age

	Those Who Felt More Positive		Net Change in % Points
	1977	1978	
	%	%	
Total	35	38	+3
Age			
18–34	37	46	+9
35–49	32	36	+4
50 and older	35	33	−2

Table 2. Positive Change in Attitudes Toward Business, by Education

Educational Attainment	Those Who Felt More Positive		Net Change in % Points
	1977	1978	
	%	%	
College	34	46	+12
High school	38	38	0
Grade school	26	28	+2

cent saying that they felt more positive and 46 percent saying that they felt more negative.

When the data are examined by age, we find a change among younger respondents, aged 18–34. In 1977, not quite two in five (37 percent) described a change in attitude toward a more favorable position. In May 1978, this proportion increased to almost *half* (46 percent). Less significant change was seen among those aged 35–49, going from 32 percent to 36 percent who reported having a better overall opinion. There was essentially no change among those aged 50 and older. (See Table 1.)

Change toward a more favorable attitude also seems to appear among the college educated. In 1977, about one in three (34 percent) college-educated respondents said that their attitudes toward business had improved in recent years. By 1978, this proportion was almost half (46 percent)—an increase of twelve percentage points. Those respondents with a high school education showed no change: the proportion in both surveys for this group was 38 percent. There was also no significant change among those with only a grade school education. (See Table 2.)

OVERALL ATTITUDE TOWARD BUSINESS

On both surveys, respondents were also asked to describe their general attitude toward business as being very positive, somewhat positive, somewhat negative, or very negative. Here, too, there appears to be a slight upward trend among the younger and the better-educated respondents, though again this change is not reflected on the surface of opinion.

In May 1978, 62 percent of all respondents described their general attitudes toward business as being very or somewhat positive. This proportion is almost identical to the proportion of 61 percent reported in February 1977.

By age, we again find evidence of a possible positive shift in opinion among young respondents. Of those aged 18–34 surveyed in February 1977, 59 percent said that their overall attitude toward business was very or somewhat positive. In May 1978, this proportion had risen seven percentage points to 66 percent. A very slight gain was noted among those aged 35–49. Among members of this age group, 60 percent cited a positive attitude in 1977, as did 62 percent of those interviewed in 1978.

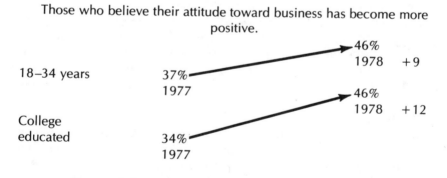

Those who believe their attitude toward business has become more positive.

18–34 years   37% 1977 → 46% 1978   +9

College educated   34% 1977 → 46% 1978   +12

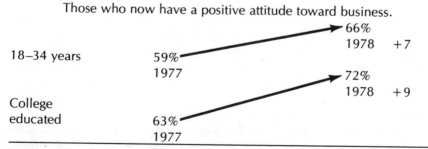

Those who now have a positive attitude toward business.

18–34 years   59% 1977 → 66% 1978   +7

College educated   63% 1977 → 72% 1978   +9

Figure 1. Shift in attitudes of young and well educated.

Table 3. Those with a Positive Overall Attitude Toward Business, by Age and Education

	Those with a Positive Attitude		Net Change in % Points
	1977	1978	
	%	%	
Total	61	62	+1
Age			
18–34	59	66	+7
35–49	60	62	+2
50 and older	64	55	−9
Education			
College	63	72	+9
High school	64	61	−3
Grade school	51	46	−5

These changes are offset by the apparently declining attitudes of those aged 50 and older. Among members of this age group surveyed in 1977, almost two in three (64 percent) said they felt very or somewhat positive toward business. However, in the May 1978 survey, the proportion had dropped to about half (55 percent).

There also seems to be an upward trend among the college educated. In 1977, about six in ten (63 percent) college-educated respondents reported having a positive attitude. This proportion increased to about seven in ten (72 percent) in 1978. There were slight declines among the high school–educated respondents (from 64 percent in 1977 to 61 percent in 1978) and grade school–educated respondents (from 51 percent to 46 percent in 1978).

An increasingly positive view of business by younger respondents can also be seen in a series of telephone interviews, each conducted with a nationally representative sample of about 1500 adults aged 18 and older. The first series was conducted in September and October of 1977, the second in late February and early March 1978, and the third in late April 1978. In all three, respondents were asked to rate their overall attitudes toward business.

Mentions of positive attitudes toward business among respondents aged 18–24 years showed a slight but steady gain over the period of the three studies. In the first study (October 1977), 63 percent of the members of this age group described their attitudes as being very or somewhat positive. A slight gain of three percentage points, rising to 66 percent, was seen in the second (late February 1978) study. By the time of the last series, in late April 1978, the proportion of all positive mentions had increased to 71 percent.

Table 4. Trend in Positive Attitudes Toward Business, by Age

Age	Those Who Were Very or Somewhat Positive			Net Change in % Points From I to III
	Wave I	Wave II	Wave III	
	%	%	%	
18–24	63	66	71	+8
25–34	61	66	65	+4
35–49	70	71	64	−6
50 and older	54	54	53	−1

A less significant increase was seen among members of the 25–34 year old age group. Over the period of the three studies, all positive mentions among members of this group increased from 61 percent to 65 percent. A decline in the percentage of positive mentions, from 70 percent to 64 percent, was noted among members of the 35–49 year old age group. There was virtually no change among those aged 50 and older.

THE DESIRE TO WORK

The great majority of American men and women say that they would continue to work, even if they no longer had to do so. The survey clearly points to a strong work ethic.

Very few men say they would stop working completely, even if they had enough money to do so. Asked, "If you had your choice, and money and child care were not a problem, which one of the following would you prefer to do: 'I wouldn't work, I'd work part-time, I'd work full-time'?" Only one man in ten, now currently employed, chose not to work at all. Three in ten would switch to part-time positions, while a majority (61 percent) would continue with full-time jobs.

This question was asked of a nationally representative sample of 1500 men and women interviewed in person during September 1979.

A different pattern emerges among women. For women working full-time, part-time employment is seen as the ideal—40 percent would choose working on a part-time basis. Fourteen percent would prefer not to work and 42 percent would continue working full-time if given the choice.

A part-time job represents the ideal compromise for many married women. A part-time job helps with family finances and provides them with an identity and interest outside the home. They are looked upon

Table 5.   Those Who Would Prefer to Work Full Time, Part Time, or Not Work

	Men Working Full Time	Women Working Full Time
	%	%
Work full time	61	42
Work part time	27	40
Wouldn't Work	10	14
Don't know	2	4

by others and can consider themselves "working women." But, by working part-time rather than full-time, they will have, at least in theory, more time for their children and home.

Many married women have been successful in finding part-time jobs. In fact, according to Department of Labor data, an increasing proportion of employed married women is working on a part-time basis. Since 1959, married women holding voluntary part-time positions increased some 130 percent, from about 2 million in 1959 to little under 5 million in 1977. During the same period, the number of married women with full-time jobs grew from about 8 million to 15 million, an increase of only 93 percent. Of all the married women working in 1977, 23.5 percent held part-time jobs. The proportion of part-time positions has been growing steadily since 1959, when the comparable figure was 20.5 percent. The survey results would indicate that this trend is likely to continue, if not accelerate.

ENTREPRENEURSHIP OR EMPLOYMENT

In a Gallup nationwide survey conducted in December 1977, those interviewed were asked whether, if given the choice, they would prefer owning their own business or working for someone else. This same question had previously been asked by the Gallup poll some thirty years ago, in 1947. At that time, going into business for oneself was an idea that appealed to most Americans. Almost seven in ten (68 percent) stated a preference for owning their own business compared to only about one in four (24 percent) who would want to work for someone else. Today far fewer Americans find the idea of their own business attractive. In the recent survey, opinion was divided, with some 48% opting for being self-employed and assuming the risks and an almost equal number—44 percent—preferring to work for someone else and letting them take the risks.

Table 6A. Those Who Prefer Own Business or Working for Someone Else

	June 1947	December 1977	Change '47-'77
	%	%	
Prefer			
Own business	68	48	− 20
Work for someone else	24	44	+ 20
No opinion	8	8	
Total	100	100	

Table 6B. Those Who Prefer Own Business or Working for Someone Else

	December 1977	September 1979	Change '47-'79
	%	%	
Prefer			
Own business	48	54	+ 6
Work for someone else	44	41	− 3
No opinion	8	5	− 3

Thirty years ago those in the professional and business occupations were most likely to want their own business, and this is still true today (81 percent in 1947; 59 percent in 1977). While the appeal of being self-employed has declined among all occupation groups, the decline has been the greatest among the white collar groups. Blue collar workers show a more modest drop. Working men were much more likely to want their own business than working women—67 percent among men versus 44 percent among women.

What is very interesting, however, is that virtually all the increase has taken place among working women. The proportion wanting their own business has increased from 44 percent to 54 percent, a ten percentage point increase. This question was repeated this past September. In this survey, the proportion expressing a desire to be an entrepreneur was 54 percent, a significant increase of six percentage points from the 48 percent in the 1977 study.

FACTORS INFLUENCING SUCCESS

A survey of young adults aged 18–24 years from eleven nations (including the United States) would indicate that great value is placed on the opportunities available for personal growth and autonomy. Although there are inevitable differences in opinion owing to the difference in cultural and economic backgrounds, there are some key points of agreement on issues concerning jobs and work, factors in becoming a success, and life goals.

Majorities see the ability to lead the kind of life they themselves idealize as being their life's goal, and would prefer the type of job that allows for the development of their individuality and skills. Further, most would welcome the chance for responsibility and authority in a job, rather than accepting a less pressured, easier one. Great personal effort and ability, rather than their educational or social background, are viewed as being the keys to success.

Approximately 2,000 interviews were conducted in each of the following countries: Japan, the United States, Great Britain, West Germany, France, Switzerland, Sweden, Australia, India, the Philippines, and Brazil.

The ability to develop one's individuality and capabilities is a prime factor to consider when choosing a job, according to a majority of the young adults in all but two countries surveyed. A high salary and a secure job were also considered to be valuable considerations. Less important to those surveyed were possible fame, short working hours, and the ability to serve society.

Almost eight in ten Swiss (79 percent), and seven in ten of those from Australia (70 percent), Sweden, Brazil (69 percent each), and the United States (68 percent) would choose a job through which they might develop their individuality and ability. Only two nations, India and the Philippines, had a proportion of mention of this aspect of less than half (India, 28 percent; Philippines, 38 percent).

High proportions would also look for a secure job, an aspect of seemingly particular importance to those from Sweden (64 percent), Australia (58 percent), Great Britain (54 percent), the Philippines (53 percent), and Japan (47 percent). Monetary reward was an important characteristic in the Philippines (52 percent), India (51 percent), and West Germany and Great Britain (49 percent each).

Somewhat less important in choosing a job was the opportunity it provided for helping society. This aspect was mentioned primarily by those in India (37 percent), the Philippines (36 percent), and Brazil (31 percent). One in five (20 percent) Americans felt this was an important consideration.

The results presented in Table 7 are taken from the "Second World Youth Survey," conducted by the Nippon Research Center, LTD, the Gallup affiliate in Japan. The survey was programmed and carried out for each country by stratified random sampling, between November 25, 1977 and January 6, 1978. Approximately 2,000 young adults,

Table 7. Factors in Becoming Successful

Country	Personal Effort	Personal Ability	Good Education	Social Position	Luck/ Fate	Don't Know
	%	%	%	%	%	%
Australia	77	55	39	11	9	2
U.S.A.	70	59	43	13	9	1
Japan	68	48	44	5	14	3
United Kingdom	64	65	37	11	17	1
Sweden	61	62	47	9	11	4
France	57	48	19	38	27	1
West Germany	57	61	11	22	31	3
Philippines	56	60	43	20	18	1
Brazil	52	52	30	36	23	1
Switzerland	52	53	35	27	24	1
India	45	37	48	23	38	2

aged 18–24 years, from each of the participating eleven countries were surveyed in personal interviews. (In India, illiterates and drop-outs from primary education were excluded. In Brazil, the sample was drawn from young adults in six major cities.)

RESPONSIBILITY AND AUTHORITY

When faced with a choice between a "tough, busy job" or a "job without responsibility and authority," the overwhelming preference in all but one country was the "tough, busy job". Half of young adults

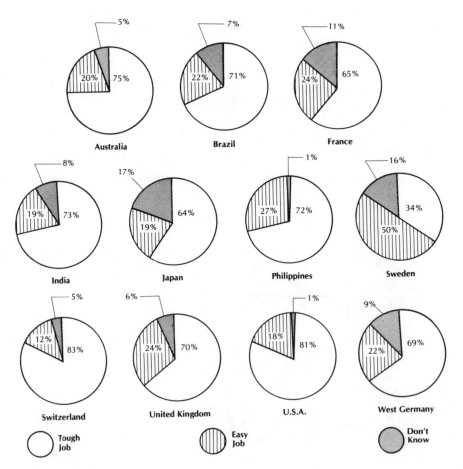

Figure 2. Type of job preferred.

interviewed in Sweden (50 percent) would choose the "job without responsibility and authority."

Those from Switzerland and the United States were the most likely to choose the more difficult position (83 percent and 81 percent respectively). Less than one in five (18 percent) of those from the United States opted for the lesser job.

ATTITUDES TOWARD PRODUCTIVITY

The decline in worker productivity—who or what is to blame?

A nationally representative sample of 1,000 top business executives were surveyed in the fall of 1978 concerning the reasons for declining productivity.

Those businessmen interviewed were given a list including fifteen possible factors and asked to say for each whether it has been a very important factor, an important factor, not very important, or not related at all to the lag in productivity growth.

"Federal government regulations" were way out in front, cited by 70 percent of respondents as a "very important cause." Another 25 percent said this has been an "important" cause, with only 3 percent saying that it was not an important factor.

Federal government regulations	70%
Worker attitudes	48%
Welfare, unemployment, and other income security benefits	45%
State government regulations	39%
General climate for business	38%
Labor union activity	37%
Capital gains taxes	33%
Inadequate plant and equipment investment	31%
Local government regulations	25%
Skill level of workers	22%
Corporate income taxes	21%
Energy cost or availability	20%
Inadequate research and development spending	18%
Personal income taxes	16%
Management attitudes	13%

Figure 3. Opinions about what has caused the slowdown in the rate of growth in productivity during the past ten years.

In a nationally representative telephone survey of 1,000 adults age 18 and older, those interviewed were asked to rate reasons for the decline in productivity.

> I am going to read you some things that have been mentioned as possible reasons for the decline. For each one please tell me whether you believe it is a very important reason, a somewhat important reason, not too, or not at all an important reason for the decline.
>
> a. We have not invested enough in new machines and equipment.
> b. Workers are not as conscientious and do not work as hard as in the past.
> c. New government rules and regulations make it harder to be efficient.
> d. Management is not as good as it should be.

As you can see in Figure 4, workers are most likely to blame themselves for the decline in productivity. Almost two-thirds (64 percent) thought "workers being less conscientious" was a very important reason for the decline in productivity. Management and government were next most frequently mentioned (45 percent management and 42 percent government regulations). Relatively few mentioned lack of investment in capital equipment as a very important reason.

In summary, businessmen blame government regulation for a decline in productivity, while workers blame themselves. Many recent surveys would suggest that workers have become more dissatisfied with their jobs than in the past. It is said that the new breed of worker expects more from his job than good pay and security. He believes working should provide an opportunity to develop, to do what he does best, to be respected, and to be treated fairly.

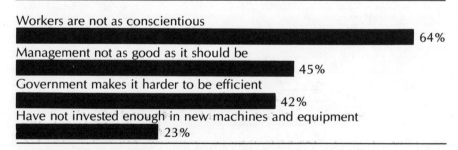

Workers are not as conscientious
64%
Management not as good as it should be
45%
Government makes it harder to be efficient
42%
Have not invested enough in new machines and equipment
23%

Figure 4. Ratings of very important reasons for decline in productivity.

Table 8. Proportion Expressing Satisfaction

Satisfied	1971	1979	Change '71-'79
	%	%	
With work	84	81	−3
With standard of living	78	71	−7
With housing	74	74	0
Children's education	60	53	−7
With future for you & family	58	52	−6
With way nation is being governed	37	23	14

SATISFACTION WITH WORK AND LIFE

A decline in job satisfaction is probably true and workers certainly have higher expectations from their jobs than in the past. Still, if work is put into perspective with other aspects of life, satisfaction with jobs is high.

In 1971, the Gallup poll asked a nationally representative sample of adults the extent to which they were satisfied with various aspects of their life.

> On the whole, would you say you are satisfied or dissatisfied with your housing situation? The work you do? Your children's education? The future facing you and your family? Your standard of living? The way this nation is being governed?

I repeated this series of questions this September. In both surveys those interviewed were most likely to express satisfaction with the work they do (84 percent in 1971, 81 percent in 1979). Satisfaction has declined only slightly (fewer than three percentage points).

Americans are less likely to express satisfaction with the other aspects of their life—standard of living, their future, their children's education, or the way the nation is being governed. And with the exception of housing satisfaction, levels have significantly declined. This is especially true for "how the nation is being governed."

LABOR UNIONS

A recent Gallup poll found that public support for labor unions had declined to an all time low. Since 1936 the Gallup poll has periodically asked nationally representative samples of Americans "In general, do you approve or disapprove of labor unions?" The latest survey conducted this past April shows 55 percent expressing approval of unionism. This follows an overall downward trend since 1957 when a high point in approval was reached—76 percent.

The results of this question reflect the growing erosion of support for unions that has been apparent for some time. Labor unions have been having trouble attracting and holding membership. According to

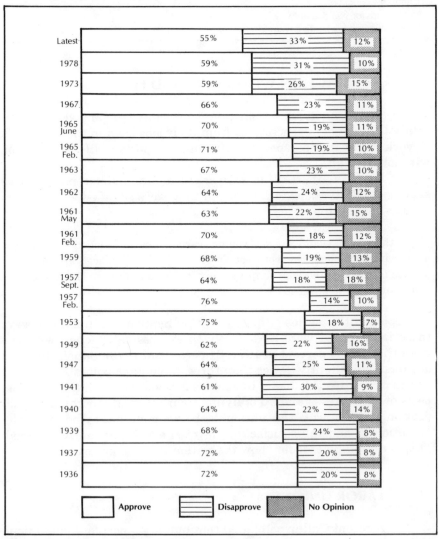

Figure 5. Rating of labor unions.

the National Labor Relations Board, unions in 1978 won less than half (46 percent) of their representation elections. This compares to a win rate of 57 percent ten years ago in 1968.

Even more indicative of their problems are the statistics on decertification elections, a vote on whether a union should continue to represent workers. In 1968, there were 239 such elections resulting in 156 decertifications—a 65 percent rate. In 1978, there were 803 elections and 594 decertifications—a 74 percent rate.

Much of the decline in union membership and the drop in public support can be blamed on changing times. White collar workers make up an increasingly large proportion of the work force and the service industry has grown tremendously. Workers in both these groups have traditionally been unreceptive to union representation. In addition to the changing composition of the work force, Americans have generally lost confidence in all institutions. Unions have undoubtedly been, to at least some extent, the victims of this loss of confidence.

The growing number of women in the labor force also has potential implications for labor unions. It has been said that unions dominated by men have not been responsive to the problems of women workers. As a consequence, many female workers have been slow to support representation.

While past Gallup surveys have found women in general to be less supportive of unionism than men, the most recent study found approval among both men and women to be about equal. However, an analysis by occupation groups does show some interesting differences. Because of the relatively small sample bases, one implication of the results would have to be thought of as speculative but still worth considering. Women in white collar jobs appear to be more supportive of unions than white collar male workers. Fifty-seven percent of the women white collar workers said they approved of unions in general, compared to 48 percent of the male white collar workers.

Among all male workers, blue collar workers are more likely to be supportive of unions than white collar employees (62 percent of blue collar men, versus 48 percent of white collar males, approve of unions).

The reverse seems to be true among women workers. Women in white collar positions appear to be somewhat more supportive of unions than blue collar women (57 percent white collar women approve of unions compared to 52 percent of blue collar women). Except for men in professional and business occupations, women with blue collar jobs appear to be the group of workers least supportive of unions.

Union membership now and in the past has been predominantly made up of blue collar workers. Very few white collar people have

Table 9. Worker Approval of Labor Unions

Labor Union	Working Women			Working Men		
	All Working Women	White Collar	Blue Collar	All Working Men	White Collar	Blue Collar
	%	%	%	%	%	%
Approve	55	57	52	55	48	62
Disapprove	32	34	30	36	43	30
No opinion	13	9	18	9	9	8
Number of interviews	(337)	(208)	(129)	(557)	(266)	(291)

16

belonged to labor unions although they have recently been very successful in attracting white collar government employees. Consequently, women in blue collar jobs would be much more likely than women in white collar positions to have first-hand dealings with a labor union or be a union member.

Could their apparent lack of support for unionism be the result of a lack of responsiveness on the part of unions to the needs and problems of women workers? The question is a particularly relevant one for labor unions. Women now make up 40 percent of the work force, and the proportion should continue to increase in the years ahead. Unions must have the support of women workers if they are to survive.

CHAPTER 2

What Happened to the Work Ethic?

Michael Maccoby* and Katherine A. Terzi**

As the country's productivity growth rate declines and inflation threatens economic stability, social scientists search for understanding. The growth of productivity helps make possible a rising
standard of living and keeps America's products competitive abroad.
Most economists agree with the Department of Commerce's view that
productivity growth requires more capital investment plus research
and development for new products and processes.[1] When machines
take over from people, or from less efficient workers, costs per unit
tend to decline. At best, however, experts insist that capital investment and research and development account for only a part of productivity increase. Beyond these inputs the issue is less clear, especially
in terms of the human factor. How do human attitudes affect productivity? Is the decline in productivity growth caused at least partly by a
change in attitudes toward work? Are Americans less motivated to
work productively now than in the past? Some observers think so.
They believe that there has been a decline in the work ethic, that
Americans no longer are impelled to work diligently.

If this view is correct, the implications are profound and threatening. It would mean that workers increasingly will try to give as little

*Director, Harvard Project on Technology, Work, and Character
**Administrator, Harvard Project on Technology, Work, and Character
Prepared for the use of the Special Study on Economic Change of the Joint Economic
Committee, Congress of the United States.

as possible to get as much as they can. Productivity is bound to deteriorate, as is quality—which demands caring and pride in workmanship. A disappearance of the work ethic implies that people will work hard only if forced to do so, or bribed by unrealistic wages and benefits. Costs would increase for policing, auditing, and control systems. Even then, who would watch the controllers who presumably would not escape the disintegrating work ethic? At the extreme, the decline in the work ethic would imply a significant change in the American character which would threaten our social system. As Erich Fromm has pointed out, each society must develop a social character that fits its productive system, so that people *want* to do what they *have* to do in order to keep the system functioning in the interests of all. Just as the work ethic has been a form of social cement for the American system, because it has expressed the productive strivings in the national character, its disappearance could weaken society.

We shall first define more precisely what is meant by the work ethic, and explore the historical transformations in this concept due in large measure to new technology, a changing socioeconomic system, and new challenges to traditional authority. Second, we shall review the current evidence of a decline in motivation to work in relation to different types of jobs and workers. And third, we shall interpret these findings in historical perspective and in terms of the challenges presented to leadership in America.

WHAT IS THE WORK ETHIC?

There is some confusion about the definition. Different observers define "the work ethic" differently.

For example, a *Washington Post* reporter visiting a typical midwestern city (April 22, 1979) writes about the "erosion of the work ethic" and quotes a union leader: "Guys used to have pride in work. . . . Not anymore."

The sociologist, Rosabeth Moss Kanter, has a different view: "The so-called work ethic of the past was really a 'progress ethic,' a conviction that hard work would pay off in future gains: a house in the suburbs, a crack at the move from mail room to management" *(New York Times,* January 28, 1979). Does the work ethic mean pride in performance, or the belief that hard work pays off, or both?

The difference is important inasmuch as it implies differences in social character. On the one hand, if the work ethic means *pride in workmanship,* this implies the character of a craftsman who wants to build products of the highest quality. Such an individual would be most alienated by a job which did not engage his pride in workmanship. He or she would resent an assembly line operation which allowed only a minute or so, for a repetitive task, and did not provide the satisfaction of building something and taking responsibility for its quality.

On the other hand, if the work ethic means payoff for hard work, the type of work done would matter less than would *chances for advancement*. The ambitious worker would become most alienated by a dead-end job. Such an employee might not mind an assembly line job for a while, if there were chances to move up in the hierarchy.

The difference between these two views of the work ethic implies significant differences in ways of organizing work to be most productive. The craft ethic would imply job enrichment, greater autonomy and responsibility for individual workers, and organizing production so that the individual worker can build a complete product. The career ethic might involve more rapid advancement and mobility within the firm, chances for training and counselling for career development. It might lead to a system of rank in person rather than job, based on level of skill and accomplishment. Which is closest to the truth?

The answer we believe is that both are accurate descriptions of what the work ethic means and has meant to some, but not all, workers. There is no way to study the distribution, historically, of different work ethics. The hypothesis presented here is an interpretation based on both history and our present-day studies of workers in both industry and government.[2] We have found that most workers do seek meaning in their work, especially the most productive and interested individuals. Some who appear to work merely for pay find meaning in unpaid work done outside of the workplace, for example, as parents or part-time farmers or craftsmen. In exploring American history, we can discern four definitions of the work ethic that represent changing socioeconomic periods, and a changing American character. At any time, there is probably a mix of ethics, with more than one existing side by side, but with one dominant.

The four are:

1. The Protestant Ethic
2. The Craft Ethic
3. The Entrepreneurial Ethic
4. The Career Ethic.

At the present, a fifth ethic, a self-development ethic, is emerging. The work ethic in America is changing, but it has changed before.

The Protestant Ethic

The Protestant ethic in America grew out of Calvinistic and Quaker individualism and asceticism. To some extent, this religious imperative to work at a calling for the glory of God was later secularized in the craft ethic of Benjamin Franklin which served as the ideal for generations of Americans.

The Puritan ethic supported a highly individualistic character, oriented to self-discipline and saving, antagonistic to sensuous culture, and oriented to deferred rewards. Unlike the Lutheran view of a calling as one's fate that should be accepted with good grace, the Calvinistic-Puritan view demanded constant work at one's "calling" as proof of one's faith and membership in God's elect. Citing the parable of the talents (Matthew 25), the Puritan was urged to prosper: "You may labor to be rich for God, though not for the flesh or sin."

As Max Weber points out in *The Protestant Ethic and The Spirit of Capitalism,* this appealed most to small farmers and craftsmen moving up in society and was functional for their success.[3] The Protestant ethic supported the development of a new man, with the individualistic character adapted to early capitalism in which the individual could control a farm, business, or workshop. Trust no man, repeated the Puritans. Only God should be your confidant. But there are no magical ways toward salvation through priestly intervention. Science and technology, combined with faith, and industry became the spirit of early America. The social character that supported this spirit was controlled, independent, and driven to overcome all doubts about salvation through work.

Later in American history, other religious traditions influenced attitudes to work. The Catholic sense of family and hierarchy and the Jewish belief in law and learning have contributed to forming the American character. But the Protestant ethic, expressed by the Puritans, provided the founding spirit, not altogether lost even in a modern, secular society.

The Craft Ethic

More than a century and a half after the Puritan colonization of America, Benjamin Franklin provided a rational ideology for this hoarding-productive character in his list of ideal virtues (traits) and in the sayings of Poor Richard. In so doing, he defined the craft ethic:

These names of virtues with their precepts were:
    1. *Temperance.* Eat not to dullness. Drink not to elevation.

2. *Silence.* Speak not but what may benefit others or yourself. Avoid trifling conversation.
3. *Order.* Let all your things have their places. Let each part of your business have its time.
4. *Resolution.* Resolve to perform what you ought. Perform without fail what you resolve.
5. *Frugality.* Make no expence but to do good to others or yourself; i.e., waste nothing.
6. *Industry.* Lose no time. Be always employed in something useful. Cut off all unnecessary actions.
7. *Sincerity.* Use no hurtful deceit. Think innocently and justly; and, if you speak, speak accordingly.
8. *Justice.* Wrong none by doing injuries or omitting the benefits that are your duty.
9. *Moderation.* Avoid extremes. Forbear resenting injuries so much as you think they deserve.
10. *Cleanliness.* Tolerate no uncleanness in body, clothes, or habitation.
11. *Tranquility.* Be not disturbed at trifles or at accidents common or unavoidable.
12. *Chastity.* Rarely use venery but for health or offspring—never to dullness, weakness, or the injury of your own or another's peace or reputation.
13. *Humility.* Imitate Jesus and Socrates. ("I cannot boast of much success in acquiring the reality of this virtue," wrote Franklin.)[4]

These traits served a society of independent craftsmen who rejected all bosses. We must "oversee our own affairs with our own eyes, and not trust too much to others," writes Franklin under the name of "Poor Richard Saunders." Unlike the Puritans, Franklin's craftsman no longer works for God's glory, but for himself. "In the affairs of this world, men are saved not by faith, but by the want of it," states Franklin, and he concludes: "God helps those who help themselves." The craft ethic was the basis for a nation of self-reliant, independent, and mobile individuals, no longer part of a religious community. The new character had negative as well as positive traits. Unlike Jefferson, who conceived of a developed heart as well as a disciplined mind, Franklin's list was that of a businesslike, male-dominated work force. It has no place for what have been considered feminine virtues of charity, love, kindness, compassion, tolerance, and generosity. The negative traits of the craftsman's character, not mentioned by Franklin, include obstinacy (the negative of resoluteness), stinginess (the negative of frugality), and the inability to cooperate (the negative of imperturbability, silence, and, in general, of the rugged individualism so admired in a young nation of refugees from authority).

Franklin's moderate, thrifty, independent craftsman distrusts the pursuit of quick wealth. Borrowing is to be avoided. "When you run in debt, you give to another power over your liberty." "There are no gains without pains." The essence of the work ethic for a nation in which 80 percent of the work force were self-employed, mainly as farmers and craftsmen, is Franklin's resolve:

> To apply myself industriously to whatever business I take in hand, and not divert my mind from my business by any foolish project of growing suddenly rich.[5]

The Entrepreneurial Ethic

In the beginning of the nineteenth century, a new spirit of the frontier and the industrial revolution began to infuse the nation's business. A combination of gambling and building, of egalitarianism and ambition, emerged in the America of Andrew Jackson.

Studying Americans in the 1830s, de Tocqueville questioned why the American shipping industry was able to navigate at a lower rate than those of the Europeans. The reason was not that they had cheaper ships or paid less for labor. American ships cost almost as much to build as European vessels, and pay for the American sailor was higher. "How does it happen, then, that the Americans sail their vessels at a cheaper rate than we can ours?" de Tocqueville asked. "I am of the opinion that the true cause of their superiority must not be sought for in physical advantages, but that it is wholly attributable to moral and intellectual qualities."[6] He continued, "The whole life of an American is passed like a game of chance, a revolutionary crisis, or a battle. As the same causes are continually in operation throughout the country, they ultimately impart an irresistible impulse to the national character."[7]

Francis J. Grund, a German visitor around the same time, was also impressed by the spirit of American business:

> There is, probably, no people on earth with whom business constitutes pleasure, and industry amusement, in an equal degree with the inhabitants of the United States of America. Active occupation is not only the principal source of their happiness, and the foundation of their national greatness, but they are absolutely wretched without it, and instead of the "dolce far niente," know but the horrors of idleness. Business is the

very soul of an American: he pursues it, not as a means of procuring for himself and his family the necessary comforts of life, but as the fountain of all human felicity; and shows as much enthusiastic ardor in his application to it as any crusader ever evinced for the conquest of the Holy Land, or the followers of Mohammed for the spreading of the Koran.[8]

The frontier offered dreams, hopes, and opportunities for the ambitious. The new entrepreneur had lost the craftsman's traits of caution and moderation. As de Tocqueville pointed out, Americans wanted to live well, and they were natural businessmen. After the Civil War, the acceleration of the industrial revolution, and the exploitation of technology and resources favored the rise of a new social character, new ideals, and the new version of the work ethic.

In the eras of the Puritan and craft ethics, technology could be created and employed by individuals. The individual craftsman, like Paul Revere, designed, built, and marketed his products, sometimes with the help of apprentices. Factories were essentially workshops in which craftsmen worked together. The first new entrepreneurs were merchants, not manufacturers, and the entrepreneurial ethic first emerged in a commercial rather than an industrial context. Then the creation and use of productive technology outgrew the reach of single individuals or groups of craftsmen. The entrepreneurs were able to organize and control the craftsmen. Through the division of labor and organized skills they were able to employ unskilled farm labor and the immigrants from Europe.

As Benjamin Franklin stated the craft ethic, so the heroes of Horatio Alger exemplified the entrepreneurial ethic for Americans, and became the models for success in a society increasingly dominated by rapidly growing business, and full of immigrants seeking employment. In contrast to the conservative, self-contained, and taciturn craftsmen, like Poor Richard, Alger's heroes, like Ragged Dick, are smart talking, tricky, entrepreneurial, and liberal spenders, with a taste for elegance. They are poor, but tough and honest, neither mean nor lazy. Dick works hard and charges more than the other boys for his shoe shines, because his service is better. In a way, the heroes of Horatio Alger represent the successful barons' version of an inner-directed climb from poverty that justifies their riches.[9] Real life Horatio Alger type success stories included Andrew Carnegie, John D. Rockefeller, and craftsmen-entrepreneurs like Thomas Edison, Henry Ford, and George Eastman. But small businessmen also identified with these entrepreneurial strivings.

However, as the frontier closed, the trend kept moving toward larger and more powerful business, and small businesses became less secure, less of a realistic possibility, particularly in areas in which entrepreneurs had created large technological systems. To document the degree of financial insecurity of small businesses, we tried to find exact statistics on the percentage of small businesses each year which succeed or fail. These precise figures are not available, but the Office for Planning, Research, and Analysis at the Small Business Administration (SBA) reports that for every nine or ten businesses that open each year, about eight go out of business. This is a discontinuance rate of about 80 to 90 percent and includes small businesses almost exclusively. One source attributed this high failure rate largely to mismanagement and inexperience in business.[10] Some people blame increasing government regulation, which is costly to small business and which calls for administrative rather than entrepreneurial abilities. However, another source at the SBA reported that many proprietors go out of business in order to earn better livings as salaried employees. This seems to us the more likely reason to close down shop because today, even with experience and good management, a small retail business will succeed against the competition of chain stores only if it is particularly favored in location or if the entrepreneur is exceptionally innovative. Even then, he may be stymied by other factors.

The entrepreneurial ethic, the idea that a person with the right attitude could make it on his own, became a justification for inequality, and an answer to those who complained about submitting to the discipline of organizations. Auto workers interviewed by Ely Chinoy as late as the early 1950s dreamed of opening up their own gas stations or garages.[11] Yet, during the period 1800 to 1970 the number of self-employed in America fell from 80 to 8 percent of the work force.

This trend implies that it is harder and harder for an individual entrepreneur to prosper. Although some opportunities still remain, such as in advanced technology, special services, or the leisure industries, the competition is tough. The scientist-engineer must have a brilliant idea, be able to raise enough capital, learn how to market his product, and to administer according to government regulations. The restaurant owner needs a special attraction or elegance, since new "greasy spoons" cannot compete with the technology and organization of McDonalds.

Furthermore, the small businessman must be able to handle increasingly costly and complicated government regulations. Character traits that used to serve a certain type of independent small businessman in the market are no longer so adaptive when he has to compete with large corporations. The willingness to work long hours and keep the store open on Sundays and holidays used to contribute to success.

But what is the use of such sacrifice and durability when large chains such as Safeway decide to remain open on Sundays? In this market, self-employment becomes a realistic possibility only for the very brilliant entrepreneur, not for the average American whose work future more often centers in a large organization.[12]

Although the self-employed are still, on the average, more satisfied with work than wage earners, an increasing percentage of the self-employed themselves perceive disadvantages to self-employment in excessive responsibility, long hours, and economic insecurity, as compared to a career in organizations.[13]

The Career Ethic

As the economic system changed, and with it the traits necessary for success, the entrepreneurial ethic no longer expressed the strivings of many of the most talented and highly motivated individuals. At the same time, new technological systems required increased division of labor and complex organizational hierarchies. Success in the large organization depended on administrative rather than entrepreneurial skills. Business schools began to train managerial technicians with a new managerial-career ethic, replacing the entrepreneurial ethic. Rather than hoping to establish their own businesses, these people sought jobs in the large organizations in business, government, and the nonprofit sector. Their goal was to move up in the organization, toward increased responsibility and organizational status. In the 1950s, the career ethic seemed a managerial ethic in organizations; in the 1970s, it appears to some observers as *the* work ethic.

The career ethic implies technology that is less craftlike, more dependent on codified and systematized knowledge which can be applied somewhat independently of a specific organizational context. In entrepreneurial business, cumulative experience pays off, whereas in organizations using new and changing technology, theoretical knowledge becomes more significant than experience, especially experience within a particular organization.[14]

This ethic belongs especially to "the new class" of professionals and technicians who make their living by their ability to solve problems, to apply the latest information, and to manage.[15]

As more young people enter the work force with high school and college educations, aspirations for careers emerge in traditionally blue collar workers. These people expect the work place to be a meritocracy: anyone who demonstrates the indicated skills and abilities should be able to rise up the organization. Talent and hard work should earn success and promotion.

The meritocracy implies a system based on opportunity and fairness. Rights in the work place are guaranteed. The element of chance and luck should be eliminated. Daniel Bell and Daniel Yankelovich have written about the way in which educated people feel that they are entitled, not only to a job, but also to a chance for advancement. The meritocracy fosters a new "psychology of entitlement,"[16] especially for those who pass the tests. Those with the credentials who do not move up fast enough feel cheated. Those who fail to make the grade become resentful and turned off to work.

Rosabeth Moss Kanter writes:

> Connected with this stronger rights consciousness is the frustration younger workers express about not getting more and further faster. The apocryphal story of the Harvard Business School MBA who expects to go from entry-job to the executive suite in six months now has its counterpart at every level of the organization. My colleagues and I surveyed 150 factory workers at a leading manufacturing company to learn about current reactions to their jobs, as the first step in a process of change. One of the most significant findings was the overwhelming sense of disappointment most of them had about not having enough opportunities for development and advancement. The workers thought advancement occurred too slowly, if at all. Yet this company is one that is well known for promoting people at all ranks relatively rapidly.[17]

Career has become the central concern for an increasingly large number of people. As long as there is a payoff, careerists are motivated to prepare for positions and to do what is necessary to move up. However, the career ethic has the negative consequences of narrowing intellectual development. Brighter individuals subordinate their learning to the requirements of career, suppressing natural curiosity in college to take courses they will do well in and that will pay off in the work place.

Each work ethic implies a different social character, different satisfactions and dissatisfactions at work, and a different critique of society. The Protestant ethic implies a character driven to work, consciously to show membership in the elect, unconsciously to overcome any doubts about faith. The Puritan worked for the glory of God, and his own salvation and reward in heaven. His goal was a community of the elect needing neither kings nor bishops, and he would not tolerate unethical and undisciplined behavior.

The craft ethic implies a hoarding-productive character oriented to saving and self-sufficiency, to independence and self-control, and to rewards on earth. The craftsman is most satisfied by work which he controls, with standards he sets. He believes that only he is close enough to the details of technology to make the right decisions about what should be built and how. But industrial organization is designed to enable ideas conceived by talented people to be carried out by ordinary people. The craftsman's critique is of bosses, either entrepreneurs or company men, who tell him what to do, and threaten his independence. He distrusts bigness and power, even though technology has grown too large to be created or controlled by individuals.

The entrepreneur implies a bold, risk-taking character, with an orientation toward exploiting opportunities and using people. The entrepreneur is most satisfied by the opportunity to build his own business. Some entrepreneurs are satisfied with economic independence; others seek wealth and are motivated by the gambling spirit. The entrepreneur's critique is of a society that strangles free enterprise and individual initiative. He is critical of bureaucracy, red tape and regulation, and of people who choose security ahead of adventure. He dislikes unions, which, he feels, destroy his relationship with employees.

The career ethic implies an other-directed, ambitious, marketing character. Such an individual is most satisfied by work which gives him the chance to get ahead; he seeks to develop himself in a way which fits the requirements of career, to become a more attractive package worth more in the market. In an organization, the entrepreneur demands complete loyalty from his helpers, and in return rewards and protects them; he turns against them only if they are disloyal. The careerist expects fair play in his assigned role; and wants to know the rules of the game—what is expected of him and what he will receive in return. His critique is of a system that blocks him, leaves him stuck in dead-end jobs, powerless to move ahead or develop himself. The career ethic challenges both unionism and paternalism with their emphasis on seniority and loyalty because moving ahead to the careerist is based on winning a game with fair rules.

More than the other types, the career ethic thus involves a critique of the whole organization and its principles. This critique can call for changes in the organization of work, to increase fairness in promotions, and to provide opportunities for learning and development. The careerist may recognize that to enjoy greater freedom to make decisions, he must move up the ladder. Failure to do so may also mean loss of respect from others and self-respect.

On a deeper level, many successful careerists suffer from anxiety, guilt, and depression. They are anxious about constantly being judged and evaluated and worried about saying or doing the wrong thing.

They feel guilty about giving in too much to others, having to judge others, betraying their own beliefs, including a craftsmanlike sense of integrity, and stretching the truth in order to look good. And they are depressed about the competitiveness and unfriendliness of organizational life.[18] The extent of self-alienation resulting from the career ethic has driven many individuals to question its value. Even some who have reached the top criticize the costs of careerism in family life and the underdevelopment of the emotions.

Recent surveys indicate that a concern with both life outside of work and intrinsic aspects of work is challenging the career ethic.[19] Jerome M. Rosow reports that only 21 percent say that their work is more important than leisure activities.[20] The 1977 Michigan Survey found that one third of married workers feel that their jobs interfere with family life,[21] and more than half complain they lack time for leisure activities.[22]

Surveys by both Yankelovich and the University of Michigan indicate that a large percentage of Americans want work that is challenging and/or allows the opportunity for self-expression and growth.[23] This would seem to contradict the flight from work to leisure activities, unless we assume that a reason for turning away from work is the lack of opportunity for growth, and/or that people want challenge, but not so much as to make work all-absorbing.

Yankelovich believes that the work ethic is being challenged by what he calls a "self-fulfillment" ethic. A growing number, especially the younger, more educated, and affluent are concerned with personal growth and enjoyment of life both at work and leisure.[24] When these strivings take priority over considerations of career, large organizations which count on the career ethic are in trouble. The career ethic implies that employees will strive for promotions and perform even when their work is not particularly interesting or satisfying. Driven by anxiety and their desire to prove their own worth by symbols of success and validation by the organization, they will sacrifice other satisfactions (family life, vocational interests, even integrity), overcoming their guilt to adapt themselves to organizations. But what would happen if the career ethic lost its grip on America?

Is there a fifth work ethic of self-fulfillment or self-development? Does it imply a change in the American character? Is it adaptive to changing technology and work? Before considering the meaning and implications of "self-fulfillment" in the context of change in technology and the socioeconomic system, we shall examine the evidence of whether or not Americans are less motivated to work today than in the past.

IS THERE LESS MOTIVATION TO WORK?

Are Americans less motivated to work now? What is the evidence of a decline in motivation to work? One approach to answering this question is to examine changes in attitudes to work. Another is to examine objective indicators of motivation, such as absenteeism and turnover. Studies over the last quarter century share one conclusion: the issue is complex and confusing. Some groups are satisfied with certain aspects of work and not others. Some groups report high levels of satisfaction and others low levels. From our point of view this is not surprising. For example, we would expect individuals with a strong career ethic to be satisfied with work if they felt they were moving up organizational hierarchies, and dissatisfied if stuck, but not really greatly concerned about the substance or meaning of the work itself or its social value. We would expect those with the craftsman's ethic to be satisfied, if they had the opportunity to perform skilled work with good pay, and dissatisfied, if they did not. But surveys do not provide information on the fit between work ethics and social character in relation to job characteristics. Rather, we can only infer these relationships by focusing on distinctions between different socioeconomic, occupational, and cultural subgroups in relation to work attitudes and satisfaction.

What follows is an attempt to summarize what is known and not known about attitudes to work and their changes over time. The data is of two kinds: *objective indicators* of dissatisfaction (absenteeism, poor quality products, turnover); and *attitudinal studies*. We will briefly touch on what is known about work attitudes from objective indicators and the relationship between work attitudes and productivity. Then we will concentrate on attitudinal studies, reviewing the trend data as a whole, focusing on differences between groups according to demographic characteristics.

Objective Indicators

What is the evidence from objective economic indicators that Americans are losing the motivation to work? Objective indicators do not form a conclusive pattern supporting the hypothesis of a decline in motivation, but there is evidence from cases that when leadership understands and respects the goals and values of different employees, productivity increases.

Although unscheduled absences have until recently been on the rise, this may have been due to more liberal personnel policies rather than a change in work attitudes. Strikes over working conditions have increased, but they cover a wide spectrum of issues making generalizations difficult:

> Other indicators give little or no support to any decline in the work ethic: the absence of any long-term trend in the quit rate, the rebound in the rate of productivity improvement, and the relative stability of labor relations activity ... In summary, Americans may be more unhappy at work, but there is very little evidence to show that this has affected their economic performance.[25]

Although the above was written in 1974, before the lag in productivity growth was as apparent as it is now, the *AFL-CIO American Federationist* concurs with this point of view. The decline in productivity gains, they report, has been exaggerated, and is due mainly to a recession, not to a decline in the work ethic or labor's productivity:

> The contention the work ethic has declined is a generalization refuted by the healthy productivity gains in many industries. In several industries, productivity rose more than 5 percent per year from 1972 through 1977. These include telephone communications, synthetic fibers, bottle and canned soft drinks, and corn milling. Motor vehicle and several other industries had productivity growth rates of about 3 percent. And for manufacturing as a whole, productivity grew a healthy 3.5 percent in the year 1978. The workers in high productivity industries are no different than those in low productivity industries—so there's simply no support for the notion of a fundamental decline in the 'work ethic.'[26]

Where technology is highly developed and workers are at a high level of technical skill as in telephone communications, jobs are more likely to fit the career ethic or the craft ethic. Here productivity is in general increasing, although there are industries like coal mining where health and safety measures limit productivity. But in service jobs where new technology is not a controlling factor, productivity gains have been low. The *Federationist's* statement that workers in high productivity industries are the same as those in low productivity industries may not be true. In parts of the service and retail sectors, the attitude of the worker, and relationships among people, carry greater leverage for improving productivity, even though investment in automated systems may in the future lower labor costs.

Even in workplaces more bounded by advanced technology (for example, the Bell System) there have been significant gains in productivity when installation and repair workers have been actively involved in analyzing their work and proposing, implementing, and evaluating changes in it.[27] If we were to move towards emphasizing greater durability and repairability of goods in order to save materials and energy, productivity of repair services and maintenance will become increasingly important, requiring not only new technology, but also more involvement of this kind.

The Commitment to Work

For most people the issue is not: Do I still want to work? as much as: Does my job turn me off? Surveys show a consistently strong affirmation of the value of work for three-quarters of the population. When asked if they would continue to work even if they could live comfortably for the rest of their lives without working, most people choose to work. This holds constant throughout several surveys, the percentage choosing to work ranging from 67.4 percent (1969, University of Michigan), 71.5 percent (1977, University of Michigan), 73 percent (1974, Yankelovich, *The New Morality*), to 75 percent (1978, Renwick & Lawler).[28] About the same proportion don't think they would be happier if they "didn't have to work at all": 76.3 percent (1977, University of Michigan). A full 84 percent of college-age youth in 1973 believed it was "very important to do any job (one was doing) well."

The American commitment to hard work has been reaffirmed in other studies as well, although as we shall note there is growing criticism about the quality of work and fairness of rewards. Between 1969 and 1973, the percentage of college students rejecting the statement: "(I) would welcome less emphasis on working hard in the future" grew from 41 percent to 50 percent (Yankelovich, in Rosow, et al., 1974), perhaps indicating the weakening of the ideology of the 1960s with its appeal to "dropping out."

"Young adults' [20–24 age group] commitment to the labor force, once about equal to that of the population as a whole, is now far stronger. On average, 3 of 4 young adults were working or seeking work in 1977. Their civilian labor force participation nearly matched that of those age 25–44—the group that is most committed to the labor force."[29]

The labor force continues to grow at an increasing rate as many people not previously employed, in particular women and the old, try to enter the world of paid jobs. Eli Ginzberg considers: "The rapid entry of women into the labor market is the single most outstanding phenomenon of the century."[30] From a little less than 29 percent of the labor force in 1948, women have increased their share to the point of nearly 42 percent in 1978.[31] The demand for paid jobs is not likely to let up soon. Columnist Ellen Goodman reported a particularly striking statistic from a national survey aiming to assess future educational needs: in 1973–74 only 3 out of 100 (3 percent) 17-year-old girls claim "housewife" as their number one career choice. Clearly they intend to take a job rather than stay home.[32]

The proportion of women who are in the labor force has also increased, from 32.7 percent in 1948 to 50 percent of women in 1978; and the Bureau of Labor Statistics estimates that by 1990 the percent of women who are in the labor force will increase to between 53.8 percent and 60.4 percent of all women.[33] The exception to increased labor force participation is that of older men, age 55 to 64, which actually declined, from 89 percent in 1947 to 80 percent in 1977. (Is this decline voluntary? How much can be attributed to the rate of technological change, displacing workers too old to learn a new occupation?)

If we accept the premise that Americans still believe in the value of work well done and most want the chance to work, how can we understand indications of dissatisfaction? The first explanation is that while working remains important, other arenas of life—leisure, family—are also gaining in importance. The second explanation, which we will explore now, concerns dissatisfaction, not with work per se, but with the actual jobs that people hold and the nature of supervision. Do existing work patterns, rewards, and incentives engage and motivate employees? Or, do they cause people to withdraw, disaffected, perhaps focusing their productive energies outside of work? One observer put it well:

> That the work ethic—that collection of beliefs, attitudes and aspirations about work—is changing, I have no doubt. Whether it is eroding—in the sense that individuals are losing the commitment to, and pride and satisfaction in, work—remains to be seen . . . If in the face of changing work values, employers attempt to continue the traditional patterns and habits of organizing, managing and motivating people, they will be on a collision course with the future and the work ethic will most surely be eroded.[34]

There is evidence to suggest some jobs are less satisfying despite a still high motivation to work. One item on the University of Michigan survey supports this view. When asked: "If you were free to go into any type of job you wanted, what would your choice be?" the results were:

	1969	*1973*	*1977*
The job he or she now has:	49.2	43.7	38.1%
Retire and not work at all:	6.3	4.6	1.9%
Prefer some other job to the job he or she now has:	44.4	51.7	60.0%
		15.6% increase	

Here we see a striking shift with implications for motivation to work.

In this connection it is important to note that 50 percent of those questioned by the Gallup poll said they "could accomplish more each day if they tried." Those dissatisfied with their job tended to say they could do more if they tried.[35] The Harris poll asked whether people would be "very willing to work harder under certain conditions." Between 46–64 percent were very willing to work harder, depending on the reward. Pay came out ahead (64 percent) but was closely followed by "more to say about the kind of work you do and how you do it" (61 percent); additional schooling or training (59 percent); and being able to work more independently (58 percent).[36]

There is little agreement on the relationship between attitudes, and productivity, and other economic indicators. However, in many work places, individuals do not share ideas for improving productivity due to lack of trust that they will be listened to, or will share equitably in productivity gains.[37]

Studies also indicate a growing crisis of legitimacy, confidence, trust, authority: a crisis of leadership. While reaffirming the importance of work to individual well-being, most people no longer expect to be rewarded equitably, according to their efforts. Between 1967 and 1975, the number of students who believed "Hard work always pays off" was nearly reversed, from 69 percent agreeing in 1967 to 75 percent saying "no" in 1975.[38] A survey undertaken by the American Council of Life Insurance asked a similar question with similar results. Between 1968 and 1978, the percent agreeing with the statement: "Hard work will always pay off if you have faith in yourself and stick to it" declined, from 58 percent to 44 percent. This finding suggests that a key belief which is consistent with both the traditional craft ethic and the career ethic is dissolving.

Daniel Yankelovich also reports a "growing feeling of social injustice—84 percent of the public now believes that those who work hard and live by the rules are not getting a fair break."[39] In a country that so highly values fairness and equity, such disaffection may express resentment and withdrawal. It may be related to the general decline in trust of authority and institutions, especially since the Vietnam War and Watergate, combined with an increasing level of education. It may support an attitude of looking out for number one and beating the system.

Job Satisfaction: General Data

Job satisfaction implies some fit between motivation and work. Most experts agree that in all surveys, over time, and in all subgroups, general job satisfaction has been and still is high, although there is growing dissatisfaction expressed with specific aspects of work.

Eighty-eight point four percent (1977, University of Michigan) report being "very" or "somewhat satisfied" "all in all" with their job, up slightly from 85.5 percent in 1969.[40] People appear more satisfied in response to a single question, such as: "All in all, how satisfied would you say you are with your job?" in contrast to indexes composed of several such questions. Thus, if you use a global index composed of several general measures of job satisfaction rather than the single measure quoted above, you will find a slight, though significant decline in job satisfaction between 1969 and 1977. The single measure, in contrast, shows a slight increase in satisfaction during this same period. There is also general agreement that a higher percentage are positive about job satisfaction in general than about specific aspects of work, such as chance to use one's abilities, good supervision, resources available to do the job, and good pay. In the same survey (University of Michigan) in which global satisfaction with work increased between 1973 and 1977, satisfaction with specific job characteristics declined by between 11–43 percent. Further discussion of the methodology of job satisfaction surveys is needed here, because the findings are contradictory and hence questionable.

Specific aspects of job satisfaction are assessed differently from overall job satisfaction. People surveyed are asked to rate selected job characteristics (e.g., chance to develop skills and abilities, pay, friendly coworkers) in either or both of two ways

how *important* that aspect is to the respondent (in 1969 and 1973);
how *true* the respondent considers that aspect to be of his/her own
   job (in 1969, 1973, 1977).

The difference or congruence is sometimes used as a measure of job dissatisfaction or satisfaction in 1969 and 1973. This is a complex and somewhat confusing procedure. Asking whether the respondent's job provides "too little," "too much," or "just the right amount" of each job attribute would be more direct and easier to interpret. Sometimes the rating of "how true" various characteristics are is used by itself as a measure of job satisfaction, even though that aspect of work may not be important to a person. In the 1977 University of Michigan Survey only the "how true" ratings were used; the "how important" question was for some reason omitted. This makes sense for some of the job characteristics which by their wording imply satisfaction/dissatisfaction (e.g., "I am not asked to do *excessive* amounts of work," our emphasis). However, for most aspects, a rating of how *true* does not automatically imply how satisfied one is. For example, if an individual considers it very true he is "given a lot of freedom to decide how I do my own work," does this mean he is *satisfied* with this situation? Perhaps he would prefer more direction be given him as to how he should carry out a difficult job. We don't know, because he was not asked. When used to gauge job satisfaction, this particular measure carries certain implicit values on the part of the researchers which may or may not be shared by the workers interviewed.

Even with these limitations, the data reveal some interesting trends. Let's look first at what's important to people at work.[41] Then we will consider how actual jobs measure up to expectations. There is growing evidence to suggest they do not. Specifically, what is important to people at work? Has this been changing?

The University of Michigan surveys in 1969 and 1973 asked this question. There were significant differences in 1969 between white collar and blue collar workers which make further general statements misleading. (Those differences will be considered further later on in this paper.) To summarize, white collar workers put interesting work at the top of their list, with "opportunity to develop my special abilities" second. Information (3), authority (4), help and equipment (5), friendly coworkers (6), and three other attributes all came in ahead of good pay (10), job security (12), and fringe benefits (17).

Blue collar workers rated traditional rewards as far more important: good pay came first; job security, third. Help and equipment (2), information (4), and friendly coworkers (5) were more important than interesting work (6). More recent surveys suggest the differences between white collar and blue collar workers are diminishing.[42]

By 1973, the picture was not very different. Interesting work still headed the list. Opportunity to develop special abilities; friendly and helpful coworkers; information; and a competent supervisor ranked higher in importance in 1973 and 1969; while good pay; good job security; help and equipment; and authority ranked lower in the same four-year period.

How do jobs measure up to these standards? We do not have importance ratings to compare with job characteristics for 1977, but we can compare 1973 importance ratings with 1973 and 1977 job evaluations (University of Michigan Survey). Selecting out certain job characteristics relating to both self-development and financial rewards, we find gaps between what is wanted and what is found at work, indicating pressure points for job dissatisfaction. For example, in 1973, almost 15 percent more people said interesting work was very important to them than considered it very true of their own jobs. Similar gaps were reported in 1973 for the following job characteristics:

opportunity to develop special abilities	(25.8% "gap")
chance to do what I do best	(17.8%)
good pay	(23.4%)
fair promotions	(27.7%)
good chance for promotions	(36.3%)

Desires for good fringe benefits (9.6 percent gap); good job security (1.1 percent); and enough authority to do the job (3.9 percent) were almost satisfied in 1973. Since we lack importance ratings for 1977 we cannot compare them with "true" ratings for 1977. But when 1977 true ratings are compared with 1973 importance ratings, even greater satisfaction gaps appear, due to the generally lower true ratings in 1977: interesting work shows a 23 percent gap. Good fringe benefits and good job security, although mainly satisfied in 1973, show much larger gaps in 1977, up to 20.8 percent and 20.2 percent, respectively. Other items showed increased dissatisfaction as well:

opportunity to develop special abilities	(36.9% gap)
chance to do what I do best	(28.0%)
enough authority	(14.9%)
good pay	(36.9%)
fair promotions	(40.2%)
good chance for promotions	(40.8%)

Importance ratings aside, it is significant that, taking evaluations of job aspects between 1973 and 1977, the proportion of people reporting these aspects as "very true" of their own jobs *declined for every aspect but one.* [43] There was a significant and consistent decline of about 11 percent in key indicators. If expectations at work just held constant during this period, this would imply a drop in satisfaction at work (unless these aspects were undesirable to the worker). The average drop between 1973 and 1977 was 8.8 percent. The largest declines were reported for:

1. good pay	declined by	13.5%
2. promotions handled fairly		12.5%
3. enough help and equipment		11.9%
4. can forget my personal problems		11.3% [44]
5. good fringe benefits		11.2%
6. good job security		11.1%
7. problems hard enough		11.1%
8. opportunity to develop my special abilities		11.1%
9. enough authority		11.0%
10. responsibilities clearly defined		11.0%

The remaining twenty-three aspects declined by less than 11 percent each.

Considering results of various studies, we conclude that no single factor is responsible for satisfaction with work for everyone.[45] To understand the meaning of satisfaction requires a different kind of study, a more exploratory, anthropological method than the survey instruments generally used, one which takes account of differences in both social character and types of work.[46]

These findings appear to indicate a general disaffection with organizations, especially a feeling of inequity. While this may be the result of organization and management that does not sufficiently engage the work ethic, it also appears that an increasingly educated and ambitious workforce is dissatisfied with jobs that do not allow them to use their knowledge. This latter conclusion is supported by responses to two questions in the University of Michigan Survey:

> Do you have some skills and training from your experience and training that *you would like to be using in your work* but can't use on your present job? (emphasis ours); and

> What level of formal education do you feel is needed by a person in your job? What is the highest grade of school or level of education you completed?

More than a third (35.6 percent) of respondents in 1977 have skills and training they want to use at work but can't. This is an increase of 10.5 percent over 1973 (25.1 percent). Turning to formal education, nearly as many (32.2 percent in 1977) had more formal schooling than their jobs required—an increase of 4.5 percent over 1973 (27.7 percent). These responses clearly point to considerable underutilization of skills, training, and education, and this at a time when our productivity growth is on the decline.

Job Satisfaction: Demographic Differences

Although studies of satisfaction at work do not differentiate social character types, they do categorize workers in terms of age, sex, race, occupation, income level and education. The University of Michigan Survey report states:

> In any case, the search for single, simple, and universally relevant explanations for changes in job satisfaction, and other outcome measures, is likely to be fruitless. The explanatory factors may be complex, and

may well be quite different for the various subpopulations that make up the American labor force.[47]

Who is most dissatisfied? Who is most satisfied? Whose attitudes are changing most? Do we know why? There is general agreement that the most dissatisfied sectors of the labor force are young (under 30), black, and low income (under $10,000). The most satisfied are older (over 50), in professional/managerial occupations or self-employed. Dissatisfaction has been increasing most for those with some high school education or a college degree, those in the 21–29 age bracket, the wage and salaried, men, professional/administrative/managerial employees, operatives, and nonfarm laborers.

Beyond these sketchy generalizations, the picture gets cloudy. Different studies report contradictory conclusions, which is not surprising since demographic categories lump together different types of people in terms of character and competencies. Despite these limitations, we will review suggestive demographic differences, pointing out areas of agreement and controversy. The categories most often referenced and used for drawing distinctions in terms of work attitudes are:

*age
*income level
*race
 sex
 educational attainment
*occupation (particularly blue-collar—white-collar, and nonman-
   agerial—professional/managerial differences)

Those demographic groups which account for clear differences in attitudes to work have been marked with an asterisk (*). The other major groups (sex and education) do not account for clear differences when other demographic characteristics are held constant.

1. Age: Numerous reports in newspapers, journals, and television programs have alerted us to a growing unrest of young workers, and surveys support these reports. It is generally agreed that the young (under 30) are among the most dissatisfied workers, while older people (over 50) are among the most satisfied.[48]

What contributes to this widespread malaise? Is it really a new phenomenon? Now, as always, the young begin their working lives in entry-level jobs which are usually less interesting, less responsible, and lower-paid than the jobs reserved for those with more experience and training. They are apprentices who are expected to follow orders. However, today more than ever before, young people resent autocratic authority.

What is new is that today's youth have grown up in a socioeconomic context significantly different from that of their parents and grand-parents. Most are not immigrants, either from foreign lands, or newly arrived from rural areas to cities almost as alien to them as to their foreign-born counterparts. Unions and government have established basic conditions of employment as rights incorporated into law. Affirmative action and equal access have become rights. The shadow of a major economic depression does not linger in the memories of young workers, and most grew up in a period when rising living standards from year to year came to be taken more and more for granted. With the exception of pockets of hopelessness in the inner cities and rural outposts, few people live with the expectation of long periods of unemployment and hardship. Thanks to government programs, such as unemployment and workmen's compensation, and unions' negotiated supplementary benefits, most workers and their families are protected against at least the worst effects of joblessness. These changes have, of course, had an impact on the population as a whole. But the young, with no other experience, have been most affected by these conditions, which they take as a matter of course and a matter of right. Changes in society have changed the social character so that it is less frightened and submissive, more self-affirmative and critical of inequity. There is no evidence that large numbers of young people are trying to avoid work. However, their reasons for working and the terms on which they will work show changing values. If these values are frustrated at work, young workers may increasingly seek to disengage themselves from their jobs.

2. Income: Of course, low income contributes to job dissatisfaction.[49] The growing concern for nonmaterial rewards at work does not replace the wish for material rewards. Concern for good pay, job security, a decent living, and the opportunities it affords does not exclude a concern for interesting, self-fulfilling work. Those who feel their compensation is inequitable or who feel stuck in low-paying jobs are dissatisfied.

3. Race: Blacks are consistently less satisfied with their jobs than are whites. This is true of all categories except one: neither white nor black workers over 44 are comparatively dissatisfied.[50] Young blacks are especially unhappy about their employment situation, their work *and* lack of it. Estimates of black youth unemployment range from 46–60 percent.[51] When they manage to find a job, it tends to be both low-paid and low in intrinsic rewards. When young blacks find employment, it is usually in jobs noted for high job dissatisfaction: as unskilled laborers or as operatives. It is not surprising, then, to learn that this group—young, low-paid, black workers—reports the "highest levels of depression," gauged from questions such as "How often do you feel down-hearted and blue?"[52] The revitalization of these down-hearted, written-off sectors of the population is one of the most complicated and serious challenges facing America. It requires understanding the social character of these young people in relation to their opportunities, and developing social policy which brings out the best in them.

4. Occupation: Operatives and nonfarm laborers are the two least satisfied occupational groups by most accounts. They are also the groups with the sharpest *declines* in satisfaction between 1969 and 1977.[53] Service workers and clerical workers are the next most dissatisfied groups. In general, blue-collar workers appear more dissatisfied than white-collar workers, but when professional/managerial white-collar employees are excluded, the rest (the clerks, typists, etc.) increasingly resemble blue-collar workers. Professional and managerial employees, in contrast, are among the most satisfied groups, but they are also becoming more dissatisfied.[54]

Overall, professional, managerial, highly skilled, or self-employed workers are most satisfied, while the unskilled, clerical, sales, or service workers are least so. A recent *Harvard Business Review* article calls this the "hierarchy gap," and points to an increasing similarity of attitudes between lower-level employees regardless of collar color, when compared to their professional and administrative higher-ups. They conclude:

> The distinctions that once clearly separated clerical and hourly employees are becoming blurred. Both groups value and expect to get intrinsic satisfactions from work (e.g., respect, equity, and responsiveness), which were formerly reserved for managers. The work force itself and what it demonstrably values are indeed changing: all parts of the work force are beginning to overtly articulate their needs for achievement, recognition, and job challenge.[55]

5. Educational Attainment: Level of formal education by itself does not appear to appreciably determine job satisfaction. On the whole, those with most (graduate level) and least (8 years or less) schooling are more satisfied than the vast majority who have some high school education up through an undergraduate degree.[56] Satisfaction has dropped in all categories (except graduate level). The largest numerical increases in the labor force come in precisely those groups who are comparatively less satisfied; that is, those with some high school up to college graduates. This category is growing: between 1948 and 1972, the average educational attainment of the labor force increased from 10.6 years to just beyond high school (12.4 years). The increase in education of the American population is striking. Between 1950 and 1975, the percent of Americans aged 25 and over with a high school diploma almost doubled, from 34 percent to 63 percent.[57] As we have noted, many of these people are experiencing dissatisfaction with work that does not ask enough of them. The combination of low income and some college is a sure formula for discontent.

Daniel Yankelovich's comparative studies of youth (noncollege, college, some college education) offer evidence for the view that a general change in social character (and the work ethic) is occurring. He concludes that young people without a college education want the same sorts of personal satisfactions and opportunities in their work as do their college-educated peers, but they have little hope of attaining them in a labor market where *one-third* already say they are overeducated for their jobs.[58]

6. Sex: Differences between men and women regarding job satisfaction are not conclusive. Some studies report higher satisfaction on the part of men; some by women; and some no significant differences.[59] Although there was not much difference between men's and women's attitudes in the 1977 University of Michigan Survey, male job satisfaction did show a significantly greater *decline* between 1969 and 1977 than did that of women.[60] Most observers agree that the increase of women in the work force has profound consequences for the organization of work, but there is less agreement on the nature of these consequences. Clearly the desire for flexible working hours was initiated and fueled by the entry of women into the work place. Still primarily responsible for home and children but anxious to work outside the home, women are seeking flexible hours in hopes of balancing demands of family and work.

What do we know about why women are seeking paid employment in unprecedented numbers? What satisfies and dissatisfies them? And, how does work compare in importance to home and family?

Clearly there are many reasons why women take jobs. First, economic needs. Many married women consider a second income necessary to maintain their standard of living. In 1977, 21 percent of those surveyed said their family income was inadequate for meeting monthly expenses. For 57 percent of those same respondents, this posed a "sizeable" or "great" problem.[61] Also, as divorce becomes commonplace, women can no longer depend on their husbands for support.

The combination of inflation's erosion of household income, expectations of a comfortable standard of living, and changing attitudes of women and men towards working mothers, as well as availability of child care, have contributed to a dramatic change in the American household. According to Rosabeth Moss Kantor: "The traditional nuclear family—husband as breadwinner, wife not in the paid labor force—now accounts for *fewer than 20 percent of all American families.* The number of single-parent households has risen dramatically" (our emphasis).[62]

Second, independence and self-development are goals which some women try to achieve by taking paid employment. Desiring more egalitarian relationships with their husbands, they want to contribute directly to their family income; or they want their own income separate from their husbands', and not subject to male control.

When they take a job, are they likely to find it satisfying? On a number of counts, they may find it wanting: pay, status, intrinsic interest, responsibility, authority.

Despite affirmative action programs and gains by women in recent years in advancing to managerial levels and in entering occupations formerly the sole province of men, women remain concentrated in lower-level, lower-paid, and lower-status jobs in a few sectors, mainly clerical and services (52.9 percent in 1974). In 1970, over a third of working women were concentrated in only seven occupations; secretary, retail saleswoman, household worker, elementary schoolteacher, bookkeeper, waitress, or nurse. Half of all women workers were concentrated in only twenty-one occupations, in contrast to a much broader distribution of men over sixty-five occupations. The segregation of women into relatively few sex-specific jobs is further illustrated by the fact that in 1960 over half of working women held jobs where 70 percent or more of their co-workers were also women.[63]

These are also sectors where dissatisfaction is concentrated and increasing. However, most surveys do not find significantly greater dissatisfaction on the part of women over men. The exception is women with preschool children (under 6 years old). They register higher job dissatisfaction for reasons which we can only speculate about: perhaps juggling child-rearing responsibilities with a job; perhaps they have lower-paying jobs;[64] or perhaps they would prefer to spend more time with their children.[65] More in-depth studies are needed to understand the causes of such reported dissatisfaction and to understand the goals of women at work.

Summary: Sorting out reports of demographic characteristics, a general profile emerges of the most and least satisfied sectors of the labor force:

Most Satisfied	Least Satisfied
Middle-aged or older	Under thirty years
White	Black
Graduate education	Some high school through college degree, especially if overeducated for jobs
Professionals/managers/ administrators	Unskilled laborers or operatives
	Low income (under $10,000)

Declines in job satisfaction, however, are reported across-the-board for most sectors of the labor force. Demographic differences show some trends, but many researchers consider that they are "not generally the best indicators of job satisfaction."[66] How else can we understand differences between groups of people? Very few studies are available that focus on understanding differences in job satisfaction based on character and culture.[67] Yet many reports allude to such differences. All descriptions of a "new breed" of worker, the "new narcissism," the "me generation," and soon refer to a change in the American character. Following these observers, we find evidence of such an attitudinal change emerging, from the career ethic to the self-fulfillment, self-development ethic.

No work ethic fits all Americans, but most Americans are motivated to work. For some, work is an expression of religious belief. For some, it is craftsmanship. Some are driven by entrepreneurial dreams. Some strive to climb the corporate ladder to success or at least to a position of "status." Some seek a form of self-fulfillment through service.

A great many individuals who are motivated to work are dissatisfied with employment that blocks their strivings for self-fulfillment and that does not fit their work ethic. The frustrated craftsman forced into monotonous work may become angry and careless. The hardworking careerist "stuck" in a dead-end job that allows neither learning nor promotion may become bitter. Many of those who feel bored and powerless at work lose interest and look for satisfactions outside.

These can be either self-developing activities—childrearing, community service, gardening, crafts, sports—or activities that support an escapist, consumer attitude, encouraged by television images of enjoyment. The evidence from studies indicates, however, that unfilling work stimulates escapist, rather than self-developing leisure, and that it is difficult to develop and maintain an active attitude to life when one is continually turned off at work.[68] This issue of human productivity is not limited to the workplace. Rather, it is an issue of national character and national vitality. Unless leadership in business, government, and unions understands what motivates people, it is likely to bring out the worst rather than the best in a changing national character.

CONCLUSION: THE CHANGING AMERICAN CHARACTER

To understand the changes in the American character that have caused increased dissatisfaction with work, we need to examine two broad interrelated historical currents.

One current is the transformation of traditional rural to modern urban values based on innovations in technology, increased education, and the disappearance of a sense of independence rooted in self-employment and the entrepreneurial ethic. The other is the decline of patriarchal authority based on new demands for human rights and the changed role of women, such as equality in the work place. These are, of course, trends. Although some people, especially in rural areas, are still rooted in the older patterns, and different social character types (e.g., craftsmen and careerist) express these changes differently, the trends affect everyone.

One of the most significant social changes in America in this century has been the migration from farms and small towns to the cities. Traditional rural values included fundamentalist religious belief and an ascetic ethic of self-sacrifice, either for personal salvation or for family welfare. Unlike in farm society, the unity of family and religious community is no longer necessary for survival. The majority today must adapt to a different reality of large organizations, where success depends on technical or professional competence and the ability to cooperate with different types of people. Although Americans are still more religious than many West Europeans, the modern urban individual is more skeptical about religion and beliefs that separate people than his rural counterpart, and more oriented to self-fulfillment rather than to God or family. Technological advances have lessened the need for hard physical work and stimulated new desires for entertainment. Technology for the home as well as telecommunications and personal transportation have freed women from housework and isolation in the household. Education has encouraged more people to aspire to higher status. Freed somewhat by technology and affluence from the tyranny of necessity, individuals of all classes have broken old taboos and sought experiences that, in the past were the exclusive property of the rich. From a psychoanalytic point of view, both sexual liberation (based on new contraceptive technology and the erosion of traditional values) and the media's message to consume rather than save, which in the expansive 1950s and 60s appeared economically positive, has undermined the main mechanisms of the traditional, uptight, hoarding character. The negative traits of the new character are narcissistic modes of self-fulfillment, self-centeredness, greediness, and lack of concern for others. The positive traits are increased concern and personal responsibility for self-development and personal health, freedom to learn and experiment.

The disappearance of self-employment is, in large measure, a result of the demise of the family farm and the small town services that supported it, and the growth of corporate forms of organization, aided by innovations in telecommunication and data processing. Gone with self-employment is the comforting idea that if one does not like work in the organization, he can always go out and start his own business. Increasingly, the sense of independence is rooted in technical, professional, and managerial skills, rather than ownership of a farm or a business. The negative traits that have resulted are those of careerist self-marketing, the need to sell oneself, to become an attractive package at the expense of integrity. The positive traits are those of flexibility and tolerance, and the need to understand and cooperate with strangers.

The decline in patriarchy has resulted both from urban values, from a science and information based technology, and from many challenges to the domination of the father and the boss. Unions, welfare and unemployment payments, the civil rights movement, the women's movement, and protest against the great wars of twentieth century have enlarged the concept of human rights and destroyed the automatic respect for authority traditionally held by the autocratic patriarchal figure in both business and government. The decline of patriarchy results in the demand for rights, as opposed to protection by a powerful figure (although, like adolescents, some people want both).

For organizations, the negative side of this trend has been the crisis of authority. Lacking respect for traditional bosses and institutions, employees become cynical, rebellious, and expert at beating the system. The positive side is a critical, questioning attitude. This is combined with the wish for mutual respect and involvement in an organization run on principles of equity and concern for individual development that is based on voluntary cooperation rather than submission.

In other words, the rebellious spirit can either undermine authority or transform the authority structure. How will this transformation take place? Union-Management Cooperative Projects to change work in Bolivar, Tennessee (Harman-UAW) and Springfield, Ohio (city management-AFSCME) have been achieved through collective bargaining, but they have required managers able to act as resources rather than bosses.

These projects and others have demonstrated that the primary tasks of leadership at work are to understand different attitudes, different strivings for self-fulfillment, and to establish operating principles that build trust, facilitate cooperation, and explain the significance of the individual's role in the common purpose. What brings out the worst in employees, including middle and lower levels of management, is a sense of powerlessness due to size and anonymous authority that treats everyone like a part in a large machine and denies individuality. Insecurity, suspicion, rumor, and a sense of injustice grow in organizations where employees do not understand the reasons for decisions and do not have a say in how work is organized and evaluated.

Our experience in projects to improve work in both industry and government is that only a small minority of workers have a negative character structure that is immune to good leadership and the resulting peer pressure to cooperate. This is a generation prepared to communicate, and responsive to reasonable explanations. Leadership will bring out the best in the emerging American character only by welcoming the positive aspects of that character, the needs for involvement, personal development, including life-long learning at work and equity. This becomes a necessity in an era of limits when concern for the common good must temper the career ethic.

How will future technology affect these changes? Changing technology in both industry and offices provides possibilities for involving employees in the organization of work, but only if leadership is able to develop the trust and involvement necessary.[69] In an information-based society, there are increasing needs for service, but again, the quality of service will depend on the quality of leadership. Some of the most talented college graduates seek self-fulfillment by making a meaningful social contribution through public service, believing that business is not an institution that serves society. Often, they are disappointed by the lack of orientation to service in government as opposed to policing and control. Real opportunities for service are, in fact, great in both government and business, but again, this requires leadership sensitive to bringing out the best in people by a commitment to ethical as well as economic values.

Is this leadership a new form of benevolent patriarchal authority? That is unlikely, since in most large organizations, managers are employees also. Trust depends, not on the owner's good faith, but on a "constitutional" system of rights and obligations. However, even within such a system managerial leadership concerned about people as well as profit is necessary to bring out the best in people.

If leadership in business, unions and government does not help to establish a new work ethic of self-development and service by appealing to the positive elements in the American character, it is likely that the traditional work ethics will be replaced by a negative search for "self-fulfillment." This ambiguous ethic can mean either greedy cravings to have more for oneself, or it can mean demands for employment that serves both personal growth and social welfare. It can mean development of one's authentic interests in the arts, sciences, and professions; or it can mean a drive to win at any price.[70] As long as we do not distinguish ethically based self-development from other modes of self-fulfillment, and organize work to support what is most productive in the American character, the new ethic may contribute to undermining the motivation to work.

NOTES

1. Office of the Chief Economist, U.S. Department of Commerce. "The Decline in Productivity Growth: Its Causes and Approaches to Remedial Actions." Unpublished paper submitted to the National Productivity Council, Washington, D.C., April 1979.
   The contribution of workers to productivity gains is generally not considered as a major factor determining increasing productivity. Even in the services and retail trade where the work is not machine-paced and worker's attitudes are more important, the workers' contribution to productivity is considered only in terms of the degree of experience and training they have. A less experienced work force is less productive. However, our research and experience with work places where work has been improved through the participation of workers and managers shows that productivity can be increased significantly when the workers are engaged in improving their own working conditions.
2. See reports from The Harvard Project on Technology, Work and Character:

   Maccoby, "Changing Work: The Bolivar Project," *Working Papers,* Summer 1975.
   "The Bolivar Project of Joint Management-Union Determination of Change According to Principles of Security, Equity, Individuation, and Democracy," May

1973–January 1974, *Final Technical Report* to the National Commission on Productivity, February 1974 (with W. E. Upjohn Institute for Employment Reasearch).

Maccoby, Margaret Molinari Duckles, and Robert Duckles, "Study Project to Improve the Quality of Work Life at the Department of Commerce," July 1, 1977–October 31, 1978.

Maccoby, "The Bolivar Project: Productivity and Human Development," *Human Futures,* Winter 1978.

Barbara Lenkerd, "Why Is It Frustrating To Work At ACTION Headquarters? or Attitudes Toward Work At ACTION Headquarters," unpublished report.

3. Max Weber, *The Protestant Ethic and The Spirit of Capitalism,* New York: Charles Scribner & Sons, 1930.
4. Jesse L. Lemisch, *Benjamin Franklin: 'The Autobiography' and Other Writings* (New York: New American Library, 1961), p. 95.
5. Ibid., p. 183.
6. Alexis de Tocqueville, *Democracy in America* (New York: Vintage Books, 1958), p. 441.
7. Ibid., p. 443.
8. Francis J. Grund, *The Americans in Their Moral, Social, and Political Relations* (Boston: Marsh, Capen & Lyon, 1837), p. 202.
9. In the works of Horatio Alger there is the beginning of the career ethic, since successful entrepreneurs like Ragged Dick are often recognized and promoted by a paternal industrialist.
10. Dun & Bradstreet cites similar causes for failures of businesses in general, regardless of size. Dun & Bradstreet, Inc., *The Failure Record Through 1970* (New York: Dun & Bradstreet, 1971), pp. 11–12.
11. Eli Chinoy, *Automobile Workers and the American Dream* (Boston: Beacon Press, 1955).
12. Michael Maccoby and Katherine Terzi, "Character and Work in America." Reprinted from Phillip Brenner, Robert Borosage, Bethany Weidner (eds.), *Exploring Contradictions: Political Economy in the Corporate State* (New York: David McKay, Inc., 1974).
13. The University of Michigan 1977 Survey reports figures on the declining appeal of self-employment between 1973 and 1977:

	1973	1977	Differ-ences
There are only advantages to self-employment	42.1%	31.9%	-10.2%
There are both advantages and disadvantages to self-employment	56.3%	63.5%	+7.2%
Type of *advantage* independence	41.9%	38.6%	− 3.3%
Type of *disadvantage*			
excessive responsibility	19.2%	26.6%	+ 7.4%
excessive hours	15.2%	22.6%	+ 7.4%
economic insecurity	11.6%	16.2%	+ 4.6%

Robert P. Quinn and Graham L. Staines, The 1977 Quality of Employment Survey (hereafter *The 1977 Survey*) (Ann Arbor, Michigan: Survey Research Center, Institute for Social Research, University of Michigan, 1977).
14. See Daniel Bell, *Coming of The Post-Industrial Society* (New York: Harper & Row).

15. In 1974, Daniel Yankelovich wrote "The professional managerial and technical categories are the fastest growing occupational groupings in the country . . . increasing numbers of young people are heading straight for these upper-level niches, their eyes fixed on the goal marked 'successful career.' " *The New Morality: A Profile of American Youth in the Seventies* (New York: McGraw-Hill, 1974), p. 22.
16. Daniel Yankelovich, "The Meaning of Work," in Jerome M. Rosow, ed., *The Worker and the Job.* (Englewood Cliffs, N.J.: Prentice-Hall, Inc., 1974), p. 30.
17. Rosabeth Moss Kantor, "A Good Job is Hard to Find," *Working Papers,* May/June, 1979.
18. Michael Maccoby, *The Gamesman: The New Corporate Leaders* (New York: Simon & Schuster, 1976).
19. The following responses from the 1977 Michigan Survey strongly support this conclusion (p. 245).

The most important things that happen to me involve:	% in agreement
my job	49
family life	95
leisure activities	45

20. Jerome M. Rosow, "The Workplace: A Changing Scene," *VocEd,* (February 1979), p. 23.
21. Beatrice Walfish, "Job Satisfaction Declines in Major Aspects of Work Says Michigan Study; All Occupational Groups Included," *World of Work Report,* vol. 4, no. 2 (February 1979) pp. 1, 14–15.
22. Robert O. Quinn and Graham L. Staines *The 1977 Quality of Employment Survey,* pp. 264, 276.
    Is this new? Is family leisure more important now than in the past? We do not have trend data. On the one hand, there are examples of companies like McDonald's for the first time giving workers longer paid vacations rather than a bonus *(Washington Post,* June 27, 1979). On the other hand, in the nineteenth and early twentieth century, fears were expressed that Americans preferred consumer enjoyments to work and that the fruits of their industry were undermining the work ethic. (See Daniel T. Rodgers, *The Work Ethic in Industrial America 1850-1920.* [Chicago: University of Chicago Press, 1978].)
23. Yankelovich writes: "Despite some difference in future outlook there are remarkably few differences in the job criteria of blue-collar, white-collar, and college-trained, professional young people. While blue-collar workers as a group place greater emphasis on good pay (blue-collar 65 percent, white collar 60 percent, professional/executive 53 percent), they are only slightly less committed to meaningful and interesting work than other young workers."
    The top job criteria for the majority of all young working people include:
    Friendly, helpful coworkers (70 percent).
    Work that is interesting (70 percent).
    Opportunity to use your mind (65 percent).
    Work results you can see (62 percent).
    Pay that is good (61 percent).
    Opportunity to develop skill/abilities (61 percent).
    Participation in decisions regarding job (58 percent).
    Getting help needed to do the job well (55 percent).
    Respect for organization you work for (55 percent).

Recognition for a job well done (54 percent).

Daniel Yankelovich, *The New Morality: A Profile of American Youth in the 70's* (New York: McGraw-Hill Book Company, 1974).

24. Evidence of the importance of nonwork time is available in several studies. A few examples will suffice:

62 percent say their main satisfaction in life does *not* come from their work (1977, University of Michigan, p. 239).

Between 35 and 60 percent would like to spend less time working and more time with their family, even if it meant earning less money (1977, University of Michigan, p. 268).

Only 21 percent say work is more important to them than leisure (Jerome Rosow, "The Workplace: A Changing Scene," *VocEd,* February 1979, p. 23).

Unfortunately we lack trend data to see how much of a change this is. "There is evidence to suggest that this phenomena is occurring in other countries as well. A Canadian study finds similar work attitudes among Canadian youth, namely a desire to work but not at just any job. To be satisfying the job should offer a chance to develop oneself, participate in decisions, and share in responsibility. If they can't find it, they may prefer unemployment to a job they find alienating." (Robert Lefebvre, "Young People Want to Work, but . . .," *The Quality of Working Life: The Canadian Scene,* Winter 1979.)

"A Swedish study reportedly arrived at comparable findings. Swedish men asked in 1955 and 1977: "which gives your life the most meaning - your family, your work or your leisure?" showed a pronounced shift towards leisure and away from work. In 1955, 33 percent chose work; 13 percent leisure; 45 percent family. By 1977 it shifted to just 17 percent work; 27 percent leisure; and 41 percent family." (Jerome M. Rosow, "The Workplace: A Changing Scene," *VocEd,* February 1979, p. 23.)

25. Peter Henle, in Rosow, op. cit., p. 141. Compatible findings are reported also in Sar A. Levitan and William B. Johnston, *Work is Here to Stay Alas,* Salt Lake City, Ut.: Olympus Publishing Company, 1973. And in Robert P. Quinn, Graham L. Staines, and Margaret R. McCullough, *Job Satisfaction: Is There a Trend?* Manpower Research Monograph no. 30, document no. 2900-00195, Washington, D.C., U.S. Government Printing Office, 1974.

26. Bill Cunningham, "Bringing Productivity Into Focus," *The AFL-CIO American Federationist*, May 1979, vol. 86, no. 5, p. 5.

27. This has been documented at Ohio Bell (personal communication).

28. Daniel Yankelovich, *The New Morality* (New York: McGraw-Hill Book Co., 1974), surveyed college-age youth only; Renwick and Lawler surveyed readers of *Psychology Today* (May 1978); the University of Michigan Survey of Working Conditions was a nationwide statistical sampling of all employed persons.

A 1955 study suggests this may have declined. In 1955, between 58 percent (unskilled workers) and 91 percent (sales workers) of employed men studied chose to continue working. Figures are not available as totals, only detailed by occupation and class. Comparability with the more recent studies is further reduced since they surveyed both men and women while the 1955 study included only men. However, additional evidence of a decline comes from the University of Michigan 1969 Survey which reports that a 1960 sample of employed men responded 80 percent in favor of working, up from 78 percent in 1950 (Weiss and Kahn). The 1969 Michigan Survey reported only 73.3 percent of men would continue working, a decline of about 7 percent (University of Michigan Survey, 1969, p. 45), in male workers' attraction to work in general. N.C. Morse and R.S. Weiss, "Function and Meaning of Work and the Job," *American Sociological Review,* vol. 20, no. 2, April 1955, p. 197. Cited in: Robert S. Weiss and David Riesman, "Social Problems and Disorganization in the World of Work," *Contemporary Social Problems,* Robert K. Merton and Robert A. Nisbet, eds. (New York: Harcourt, Brace & World, Inc., 1961).

29. Carol Leon, "Young Adults: A Transitional Group With Changing Labor Force Patterns," *Monthly Labor Review,* vol. 101, no. 5, May 1978, p. 4.
30. TAP 17, *The Changing Nature of Work* (Washington, D.C.: American Council of Life Insurance, n.d., p. 3.
31. BLS *Current Population Survey* figures for women aged 16 years or older in the labor force.
32. Ellen Goodman, *Washington Post,* November 23, 1976, " 'Happily Ever After'," reporting on the 1973–74 National Assessment for Education Progress survey.
33. BLS Report 551, No. 4 Fourth Quarter 1978. BLS Current Population Survey figures on women aged 16 years and older.
34. Ian H. Wilson, "Here Comes Change, Ready Or Not," *Mainliner Magazine,* vol. 23, no. 5, 1979.
35. Gallup Opinion Index, *Job Satisfaction and Productivity,* report no. 94, Princeton, N.J.: Gallup Opinion Index, April 1973.
36. Louis Harris and Associates, "The Public's General View of Productivity," October 1972.
37. At the Harman auto parts plant in Bolivar, Tennessee, before management and the UAW instituted a Work Improvement Program 75 percent of the workers stated they had ideas to improve work but kept them to themselves. Michael Maccoby, "Changing Work: The Bolivar Project," *Working Papers,* Summer 1975, pp. 43–55.

    The majority of a small sample of fifty-eight businesses involved in "job enrichment programs" reported improved productivity in terms of better resource utilization, lower absenteeism and turnover, and better quality. Antone F. Alber, "Job Enrichment Programs Seen Improving Employee Performance, But Benefits Not Without Cost," *World of Work Report,* January 1978, vol. 3, no. 1, pp. 8–9, 11.
38. Rosow, "The Workplace." Clark Kerr, who takes this as a statement of the work ethic cites a study by Trow showing that most people still believe that "Hard work always pays off." *Work In America, The Decade Ahead,* Clark Kerr and J.M. Rosow, (eds.), (New York: Van Nostrand Reinhold, 1979) p. xiii.
39. Daniel Yankelovich, address to the Public Agenda Foundation, March 1979.
40. "Very satisfied": 1969—46.4 percent; 1977—46.7 percent;
    "Somewhat satisfied": 1969—39.1 percent; 1977—41.7 percent.
41. Some items can be compared only between 1969 and 1973 since the 1977 survey omitted the importance ratings. 1978 figures are available for some items from the *Psychology Today* survey, which is weighted in favor of professional, executive, and managerial occupations, full-time employees, women, those aged 25–34, the well-paid, and the well-educated.
42. Michael R. Cooper, Brian S. Morgan, Patricia M. Foley, and Leon B. Kaplan, "Changing Employee Values: Deepening Discontent?" *Harvard Business Review,* Jan.-Feb. 1979, pp. 117–125.
43. "I am given a lot of chances to make friends": 51.5 percent, 1973; 56.6 percent, 1977; Robert P. Quinn and Graham L. Staines, *The 1977 Survey,* p. 217.
44. This item is hard to interpret. Perhaps the decrease in jobs where one can forget personal problems is due to the growth of "human relations"—types training; perhaps due to pressure to increase productivity; perhaps due to an increase in friendships and personal relationships at work.

45. For an analysis of the meaning of job satisfaction, see Edwin A. Locke, "The Nature and Causes of Job Satisfaction," in *Handbook of Industrial and Organizational Psychology*, Marvin D. Dunnette, (ed.), pp. 1297–1349. Chicago: Rand McNally, 1976.
46. For example, see Michael Maccoby, "Changing Work: The Bolivar Project," *Working Papers*, Summer 1975, which reports on a study of different satisfactions at work of different social character types.
47. Robert P. Quinn and Graham L. Staines, *The 1977 Survey,* p. 309.
48. It is interesting to note the University of Michigan (1977) reports that workers under 21 showed no increase in dissatisfaction between 1973 and 1977. Their dissatisfaction was already among the highest in the labor force. It would be interesting to trace the satisfaction of a cohort of workers through several years, especially if such a study included social character and type of work.
49. Considered as under $5,000 or between $5,000 and $10,000, depending on the survey used. Patricia A. Renwick and Edward E. Lawler, "What You Really Want from Your Job," *Psychology Today*, May 1978. Sar A. Levitan and William B. Johnston, *Work Is Here To Stay Alas*, Salt Lake City, Ut.: Olympus Publishing Company, 1973.
50. Levitan and Johnston, *op. cit.* It is interesting to note that although their dissatisfaction is lower than blacks, white workers' dissatisfaction is increasing at about the same *rate* as that of black workers.
51. Daniel Yankelovich, "The New Psychological Contracts at Work," *Psychology Today*, May 1978, p. 47.
52. Renwick and Lawler, "What You Really Want from Your Job." Granted readers of *Psychology Today* are a very specialized sample, this finding is also supported by Gallup poll and other reports, indicating that general life satisfaction and job satisfaction go hand-in-hand.
53. Blue-collar craft workers are also reported as becoming more dissatisfied, although still basically satisfied.
54. Robert P. Quinn and Graham L. Staines, The 1977 Survey, p. 306. *The Harvard Business Review* article cited below, however, finds that managerial discontent is not increasing.
55. Michael R. Cooper, *et.al.*, "Changing Employee Values: Deepening Discontent?" p. 118.
56. Robert P. Quinn and Graham L. Staines, The 1977 Survey, p. 306.
57. George Strauss, "Workers: Attitudes and Adjustments", in Jerome Rosow, ed., *The Worker and the Job* (Englewood Cliffs, N.J.: Prentice-Hall, Inc., 1974). Bill Cunningham, "Bringing Productivity Into Focus," *The AFL-CIO American Federationist*, May 1979, vol. 86, no. 5, p. 6.
58. Daniel Yankelovich, in Rosow, "The Workplace," p. 41.
59. Renwick and Lawler, "What You Really Want from Your Job," p. 55.
60. Why is open to speculation in the absence of studies on the question. Daniel Yankelovich foresees an erosion of male job satisfaction as a consequence of the increased female labor force participation rate as the male role as family provider undergoes change. "If . . . the man's role as he-who-makes-sacrifices-for-his-kid's-education-and-his-family's-material-well-being grows less vital, the whole fragile bargain threatens to break down. . . . One unanticipated and unwanted by-product of the women's movement may be to intensify men's disaffection with their work . . . (and) puts at risk a fragile psychosocial balance which has supported men's job satisfaction for many years." Daniel Yankelovich, in Rosow, "The Workplace: A Changing Scene," p. 45.
61. Robert P. Quinn and Graham L. Staines, The 1977 Survey, p. 48.

62. Rosabeth Moss Kantor, "A Good Job Is Hard To Find," *Working Papers*, May-June 1979, p. 45.
63. Carolyn J. Jacobson, "Women Workers: Profile of a Growing Force,"*AFL-CIO American Federationist*, July 1974.
    Also, Eli Ginzberg, "The Changing American Economy and Labor Force," in Rosow, *op. cit.*
64. Robert P. Quinn, Graham L. Staines, and Margaret R. McCullough, *op. cit.*, pp. 10–11.
65. There is some evidence to suggest that many women still prefer to stay home rather than work for pay: as family incomes rise above $7,000, the percentage of wives who work outside the home declines, as family income rises, from nearly half whose husbands earn $3,000-$7,000, to less than 20% whose husbands earn $25,000. Levitan and Johnston, *Work Is Here To Stay Alas,* p. 78.
66. Levitan and Johnston, op. cit., p. 73.
67. Charles F. Sabel, "Marginal Workers in Industrial Society," *Challenge*, March-April 1979, is an exception.
68. There are two theories concerning the effects of the quality of working life on the quality of leisure. One is called "the tradeoff hypothesis" and the other, "the spillover argument." The spillover argument maintains that the way people feel about their jobs will "spillover" into their life outside work. People with uninteresting, dissatisfying jobs can't be expected to lead productive, active lives after they punch out. Preliminary studies seem to confirm this view. But caution (and further study) is needed on this point. It could also be that dissatisfying homelife and leisure "spillover" into work.
    According to the tradeoff or compensatory hypothesis, people dissatisfied at work turn to their life outside for their satisfaction and development. Of course this happens. What is at issue is the quality of nonwork activities. Is it possible to sustain an active challenging, leisure time when work is dull and boring? The limited evidence available suggests it's not likely. However, research on this topic is not conclusive, and much more study is needed to understand the ways in which different people adapt to unsatisfying work life, home life, free time and the changes in work and culture needed to stimulate human development. Robert R. Quinn, Graham L. Staines, and Margaret R. McCullough, *Job Satisfaction: Is There a Trend?* Manpower Research Monograph no. 30, document no. 2900-00195 (Washington, D.C.: U.S. Government Printing Office, 1974). George Strauss, "Workers: Attitudes and Adjustments" in Jerome Rosow, (ed.), *The Worker and the Job* (Englewood Cliffs, N.J.: Prentice-Hall, Inc., 1974).
69. See the work of Richard Walton on the office of the future.
70. The work of Abraham Maslow, so often quoted by managers has contributed to this confusion, with an amoral concept of "self-actualization" as the highest level of human development. Maslow implies that when "lower needs" for survival, security, belongingness, status, and self-esteem are met, individuals automatically seek self-actualization. He fails to distinguish between self-actualization as an expression of self-indulgence and that which expresses an ethically based striving to overcome greed and egocentrism through the development of both head and heart. For a critique of Maslow's concept, see Michael Maccoby, *The Gamesman*, chapter 8.

BIBLIOGRAPHY

Alber, Antone F. "Job Enrichment Programs Seen Improving Employee Performance, But Benefits Not Without Cost." *World of Work Report*, 3(1) (January 1978):8–9, 11.

Cameron, Juan. "I Don't Trust Any Economists Today." *Fortune*, September 11, 1978:30–32.

Chinoy, Eli. *Automobile Workers and the American Dream*. Boston: Beacon Press, 1955.

Cooper, Michael R.; Morgan, Brian S.; Foley, Patricia M.; and Kaplan, Leon B. "Changing Employee Values: Deepening Discontent?" *Harvard Business Review*, January-February 1979: 117–125.

Cunningham, Bill. "Bringing Productivity Into Focus," *The AFL-CIO American Federationist* 86 (5) (May 1979):1–8.

Fields, Suzanne. "For Richer, For Poorer." *Washington Post, Book World*, April 29, 1979.

Gallup Opinion Index. *Job Satisfaction and Productivity*. Report no. 94. Princeton, N.J.: Gallup Opinion Index, April 1973.

Ginzberg, Eli. "The Job Problem." *Scientific-American*, November 1977, 237(5):43–51.

Ginzberg, Eli. "Work Structuring and Manpower Realities." Paper delivered to the International Conference on the Quality of Working Life, Arden House, Harriman, New York, September 24–29, 1972.

Graham, Bradley. "Service Economy's Output Is Questioned." *Washington Post*, March 4, 1979.

Hamilton, Martha M. "Are Jobs Going Begging? Go Ahead, Check the Ads." *Washington Post*, April 8, 1979.

Harris, Louis and Associates. "The Public's General View of Productivity." Louis Harris and Associates, Inc. October 1972.

Hearings before the Committee on Government Operations, U.S. Senate on S.4130-National Productivity Act of 1974 and S.4212-National Center for Productivity and Work Quality Act. Washington, D.C.: U.S. Government Printing Office, December 16 and 17, 1974.

Hearings before the Subcommittee on Employment, Poverty and Migratory Labor of the Committee on Labor and Public Welfare, U.S. Senate, *Changing Patterns of Work in America, 1976*. Washington, D.C.: U.S. Government Printing Office, April 7–8, 1976.

Hearings before the Subcommittee on Equal Opportunities of the Committee on Education and Labor, House of Representatives, on H.R.50. Washington, D.C.: U.S. Government Printing Office, March 24 and 26, and April 4, 1975.

Henle, Peter. "Economic Effects: Reviewing the Evidence." In Rosow, Jerome M., ed., *The Worker and the Job*. Englewood Cliffs, N.J.: Prentice-Hall, Inc., 1974.

Jacobson, Carolyn J. "Women Workers: Profile of a Growing Force." *AFL-CIO American Federationist*, July 1974.

Kantor, Rosabeth Moss. "A Good Job Is Hard To Find." *Working Papers*, May-June 1974:44–50.

———. "Ungluing the Stuck." *New York Times*, January 28, 1979.

Lefebvre, Robert. "Young People Want to Work, but . . ." *Quality of Working Life: The Canadian Scene*. Winter 1979:9–10.

Lemisch, L. Jesse, ed. *Benjamin Franklin: "The Autobiography" and Other Writings*. New York: New American Library, 1961.

Levitan, Sar A. and Johnston, William B. *Work Is Here To Stay Alas*. Salt Lake City, Ut.: Olympus Publishing Company, 1973.

Lindheim, James B. "The New Worker: Motivating Today's Employees." Unpublished paper.

Maccoby, Michael. "Changing Work: The Bolivar Project." *Working Papers*, Summer 1975:43–55.

———.*The Gamesman: The New Corporate Leaders*. New York: Simon & Schuster, 1976.

McConnell, Campbell R. "Why is U.S. Productivity Slowing Down?" *Harvard Business Review*, March-April 1979:36–38, 42, 44, 48, 50, 54, 56, 60.

Meyer, Herbert E. "Jobs and Want Ads: A Look Behind the Words." *Fortune*, November 20, 1978:88–90, 94, 96.

National Commission on Productivity. *Productivity: Second Annual Report*. Washington, D.C.: U.S. Government Printing Office, March 1973.

Office of the Chief Economist, U.S. Department of Commerce. "The Decline in Productivity Growth: Its Causes and Approaches to Remedial Actions." Unpublished paper submitted to the National Productivity Council. Washington, D.C., April 1979.

Quinn, R.; Seashore, S.; Kahn, R.; Mangione, T.; Campbell, D.; Staines G.; and McCullough, M. *Survey of Working Conditions*. Document no. 2916–0001, U.S. Government Printing Office, 1971.

Quinn, R.P. and Shepard, L. *The 1972–73 Quality of Employment Survey*. Ann Arbor, Mich.: Survey Research Center, Institute for Social Research, University of Michigan, 1974.

Quinn, Robert P.; Staines, Graham L.; and McCullough, Margaret R. *Job Satisfaction: Is There a Trend?* Manpower Research Monograph no. 30, document no. 2900-00195, Washington, D.C.: U.S. Government Printing Office, 1974.

Quinn, Robert P. and Staines, Graham L. *The 1977 Quality of Employment Survey*. Ann Arbor, Michigan: Survey Research Center, Institute For Social Research, The University of Michigan, 1977.

Renwick, Patricia A. and Lawler, Edward E. "What You Really Want from Your Job." *Psychology Today,* May 1978:53–66.

Rosow, Jerome, ed. *The Worker and the Job*. Englewood Cliffs, N.J.: Prentice-Hall, Inc., 1974.

Rosow, Jerome M. "The Workplace: A Changing Scene." *VocEd*, February 1979.

Sabel, Charles F. "Marginal Workers in Industrial Society." Challenge, March-April 1979:22–32.

U.S. Census of Population, "Occupational Characteristics." 1970 in table 38, p. 582.

Walfish, Beatrice. "Job Satisfaction Declines in Major Aspects of Work Says Michigan Study: All Occupational Groups Included." *The World of Work Report*, 4(2)(February 1979):1, 14–15.

Weber, Max. *The Protestant Ethic and the Spirit of Capitalism*. New York: Charles Scribner & Sons, 1930.

Weiss, Robert S. and Riesman, David. "Social Problems and Disorganization in the World of Work." In *Contemporary Social Problems*,Merton, Robert K. and Nisbet, Robert A. (eds.) New York: Harcourt, Brace & World, Inc., 1961.

Yankelovich, Daniel. *The New Morality: A Profile of American Youth in the 70's*. New York: McGraw-Hill Book Company, 1974.

_____. "The New Psychological Contracts at Work." *Psychology Today*, May 1978:46–50.

_____. "The Public Agenda Foundation." Unpublished address, March 1979.

_____. *Productivity in the Changing World of the 1980's: The Final Report of the National Center for Productivity and Quality of Working Life, 1978*. Washington, D.C.: U.S. Government Printing Office, 1978.

_____. "Sagging Productivity Contributes to Inflation." *Notes From the Joint Economic Committee*, March 2, 1979, V(7).

_____. *TAP 17 — The Changing Nature of Work, Trend Analysis Report*. Washington, D.C.: American Council of Life Insurance, undated.

Discussion

Question: I see in the banking industry around the country a sort of layering of your work ethics. The nineteenth century paternalism seems still to infect the board of directors. A lot of women who work in the banks have adopted the career ethic, and what I'm seeing even among relatives who are caught in the situation is the paternalistic bank president pushing a self-development ethic so he doesn't have to pay women a living wage.

Maccoby: I said that self-fulfillment should be looked at in two senses. One is the negative search for fulfillment through escapism and self-indulgence. The other involves a deeper human philosophical sense. That is an issue which is so brilliantly dealt with by Ibsen in *Peer Gynt,* a play about a person who thinks he is fulfilling himself and all he is doing is acting out of greed and self-indulgence; and, in the end, his real self, his capacity to love and to reason, loyalty and compassion have disappeared. There is nothing left. There is no self even though he thought he was being himself.

People say as long as you like yourself everything is fine, which is nonsense. We must really understand what self-development is all about. I'm sorry that universities rarely teach that and pay so little attention to it.

We have almost lost the tradition of understanding character and ethical development that started with Aristotle, Thomas Aquinas, Spinoza, William James, authors now hardly taught by philosophers. I believe it would be very important for developing leadership if we teach understanding of ethics and character starting with the great religious and philosophical traditions on these subjects.

But to go directly to your point, in one of the government agencies that we're working in, a union-management project in ACTION, there is a group in an office that combines a positive self-development ethic, a service ethic, and an ethic of equity. They want to redesign all their work so that they can all share the clerical work. They don't believe it is right to have some people do clerical work while other people do higher level work. Well, that is fine for them, but there are a lot of people with a career ethic coming in, who want their jobs to allow movement up through positions and who find this wonderful idealistic idea a threat to them. They don't like it. I think we must have the kind of leadership which allows a structure in which some people can try new ways of doing things and isn't totally uniform. That is going to be a real task. To do it, of course, we are going to have to have the knowledge to say to the head of the bank, "Look, your view of self-fulfillment is all very well to talk about, but these people have a different sense of self-development than you do."

Question: You used a phrase near the end of your discussion of leadership when you said "cooperation necessary to increase productivity." You introduced a notion of productivity when you talked about the entrepreneurial ethic that came out of craft or Puritan individual competence. If the idea of productivity, as you suggest, originated with entrepreneurial and individual competition, then is it still an idea that fits the ethics that you are suggesting have developed since the career version of entrepreneurial ethics, career form of advancement. Can you still use the term productivity?

Maccoby: That's a good question. I think that the concept of productivity needs to be critically evaluated. Productivity has different meanings and can be used differently. The economist talks about productivity as some measurable form of output per man-hour. But of course, you can have an increase in such productivity which causes all kinds of pollution or health hazards, which somebody then has to pay for. So one person gains at a cost to others, or to society as a whole. We might increase output per man-hour using up all our natural resources and energy in certain ways that are wasteful to the national purpose, and so that is why I mentioned productivity in a larger social sense.

If you look in the dictionary, the definition of "productivity" is "the most effective use of resources." Those include raw materials, energy, and people. If we take a look at productivity in that larger sense, what do we mean by that? I think that comes closer to something that would appeal to the new ethic. The entrepreneur felt in the nineteenth century, the Huntingtons Hills, the people who built the railroads felt, "We are making America. If people get hurt on the side, that is a necessary evil. That is the way we build a country."

Today we don't have many tough guys like that around. Some people like to talk that way, but I think most people want to be liked today more than they did in the past. I recall Carnegie who built the steel industry, but who betrayed everybody who ever helped him in his life, including his closest collaborator, Henry Clay Frick. When Carnegie and Frick were old men living on Fifth Avenue, Carnegie, who was unique among these empire builders because he was the only one who had a conscience and felt bad and gave his money to libraries, as an old man sent a letter to Frick and it said, "Can't we meet once more before we die?" Frick sent him back a letter which said, "You and I will meet in Hell."

I think leaders today are not so hard-hearted. They are most willing to develop productivity in socially positive ways. We will see more developments like one in the Bell System, where the kind of leadership that I'm talking about is occurring in one part of the country—with installers and repair people, by involving them, by developing trust, by listening to them, and also by bringing the union into the issues of the business and the problems.

In one year there were savings of $12 million in one city just with people doing their work more effectively. That's the kind of productivity I think everyone would agree is positive. I'll give an example of a factory in Scotland. Once the union-management project developed on principles of fairness, and involvement got going, the union became just as concerned with the business as management did. It wanted to maintain jobs and cut waste.

Question: When you say we have no tough people, when the representative of Exxon goes on national television and says we are not going to make heating oil because there is more money in jet fuel. You don't think he's tough?

Maccoby: No, I think he's tough only in a certain way. I had a conversation yesterday with somebody from *Fortune* who's writing an article, "Who are the Toughest Businessmen in America?" He asked me who I thought was the toughest businessman in America. He was inspired by the thought that tough managers will be needed in a recession. I said you know these people are tough, but not in the sense of a Carnegie or Frick, of going out with troops against the workers. They are rather like football players who will do whatever they can within the rules, but if you change the rules and prohibit certain things, they are going to go along with your changes. They are gamesmen. As one of these chief executives said to me at the end of our debate on what was right for the country, "Listen, we know how to win at business. Society must make the rules. Make any rules you want, as long as they are fair for everyone. We will win at any game society can invent." The point is we've got to invent better games.

Question: It seems to me that there is a dimension of the problem of leadership that you haven't dealt with that I'd like to ask you about. It seems to me that the self-fulfillment ethic is to a large extent not a work ethic but a consumer ethic that is representing a shift from a producer to a consumer orientation, and that industry has to take some responsibility for this in that in its need to sell its goods and its advertising promotion, it has to try to get people to buy more goods. So the problem of leadership that I'd like to ask you about is, how does this leadership reconcile the need to promote a self-fulfillment, a consumer ethic with the need to get people to work hard enough to produce the goods that are needed for consumption.

Maccoby: I think what you said is important. It really is another way of saying some of the things that I was trying to get across. The self-fulfillment ethic can go either way. We have the data from Gallup and others that people do want work that develops their abilities, and where they have a say in how things are done. They do want to work hard, given that their situation is fair and their work is something which leads to self-development. On the other hand, we do know that there is another definition of self-fulfillment, e.g., consumerism, escapism, sitting around watching TV all day.

Some people see a relationship between the two. Research has shown that the more work is not fulfilling, in the sense of self-development, the more people tend to escape, to become passive consumers. Leadership is either going to develop the positive side or the negative side.

Question: Two problems with the concept of productivity. We use it with relation to the corporation. How much sense does it make in regard to society at large? For instance, these two points. One is, we reach our maximum of productivity when one man with his finger on a push button can produce our total GNP. Now if we don't use our iron ore today it is available for our children. If we don't use human labor it is lost forever. And how about the linkage between getting to eat and working. Why do we have to have that linkage?

Maccoby: You raise a number of issues which I think I would like to separate into an analytic issue of the definition of productivity and the use of that concept and the political issue which has to do with the distribution of wealth. You might say there are two issues. One is, how are we going to create it, and the other is, how are we going to distribute it? A lot of people, particularly in government, only talk about distributing it, and wrongly think we have solved the problem of creating it. I think that's by no means solved. I think there is still a problem about how to create wealth and I think it's not just going to be done through mechanization and automation. It has a great deal to do with service and the quality of service, which is the hardest thing to measure. Particularly as we move into service jobs, how do we measure productivity?

What does that mean, to increase productivity in the government? Let me give you an example of the problem. One of the groups that we have been working with has been auditors in the Department of Commerce. How do auditors measure their productivity? One way is the number of criminals they catch. That way of measuring productivity may, in fact, contradict the goals of government. For example, one of the goals of government is support of minority businesses. The Commerce Department has a whole office dedicated to developing minority businesses. You talk to the auditors. They know that many of these minority business people don't know how to keep books and they are going to make a lot of errors and they are going to be caught. However, the auditor could go in and help them set up their books. The problem not usually a matter of fraud; but of technical errors. They could go in at the beginning and help them so they wouldn't get into trouble, but how would they measure that service? That might look like less productivity because there would be fewer errors later and the auditors might be penalized for it, and would be told that they needed fewer people. We have no measurement for productivity as quality of service, as human help. How do we measure the productivity of medicine? We certainly don't measure it by the number of technological instruments used. We don't even have the concepts for it. I'm not ready to throw out the concept of productivity. I think we just need to disaggregate it. We just have to get away from a narrow measurement and include both productivity in the social sense and in the sense of developing administrative creativity in the quality of service.

Question: I just wondered if you saw any relationship between the entry of women into the work place and the fast demise of the career ethic and the rise of the self-fulfillment ethic?

Maccoby: Yes I do. I think certainly that the entrance of women into the work place has been the most important recent change. It has had a big effect in a number of ways. One, of course, is the two-career family, the freeing up of a lot of people from a simple-minded focus on career to be able to think of self-fulfillment in a larger sense. We've also seen that many women who come to work feel that their real work is still at home as homemakers or as mothers, and that they do not want a career. But this does not mean, of course, they are not concerned with conditions at work. They want to be treated with dignity, to have a say about work methods. They are not willing to sacrifice these things for the promise of moving up and pleasing the higher up people. Flexible time, staggered work hours are important to them. Women have been the major supporters for these new practices. In the federal government, where there are many women in managerial positions, they tend to support innovation to improve work. Also, there is the question of moving and not moving. A two-career family is less likely to move for the sake of promotions. All of these things have made a big difference in the critique of the career ethic and the development of a self-fulfillment ethic.

CHAPTER 3

Various Corporate Approaches to the Quality of Work Life

Becoming the Organization of the Future

*Stephen H. Fuller**

Becoming an organization of the future is the number one challenge facing every organization. It is more important than a major technological breakthrough, more important than developing a new product or implementing a successful new marketing strategy. Building an organization for the future is not a side issue. It's not something to be considered when we have some spare time on our hands. It's not something that can be limited to a monthly meeting in the board room.

Assuring the viability of our organizations requires that we examine their very nature, that we carefully look at not only what we do, but how we do it. It requires that we consider not only conditions outside our organizations, but also the human qualities that give our organizations their vitality and their potential. The quality of our organizations ten, twenty, or thirty years from now cannot be left to chance. The kind of organizations we want for the future must be planned now and a process established to see that it happens. In General Motors, we are devoting considerable effort to such a process. I would like to describe what is being done to establish it as a continu-

*Vice President, Personnel Administration and Development Staff, General Motors Corporation

ing effort, an effort which has gained wide acceptance in our organization as the quality of work life process.

When we began to use the term "quality of work life," we had some people who misinterpreted, what it was all about. There were some who:

> thought it was a happiness program. That's not what quality of work life is all about, although happy employees may certainly be a by-product.
>
> felt that it was a personnel department program, and of course, it's not.
>
> felt that QWL was a subtle employee incentive program. It is not, although employees motivated to achieving the goals of the organization certainly ought to be one of the outcomes.
>
> perceived it as another productivity program. Our quality of work life effort isn't that either, although better productivity is certainly one of the important by-products.

Its objective isn't to make working fun, easy, or undisciplined. Rather, its objective is to make working *effective, challenging, involving,* and to put some quality into human work, from top to bottom in a work organization.

What then does quality of work life mean to us?

> More employee involvement at the factory floor and in the office
> Improving relationships, especially between supervisors and the people reporting to them
> Better cooperation between union and management
> Innovative and more effective design of jobs and organizations
> Improved integration of people and technology

All of these are important aspects, and each can help contribute to a better work environment. But there are other, more basic considerations in a successful, total-organization approach to quality of work life.

> The first of these is that quality of work life is a *process*. It's not something you can turn on today and turn off tomorrow—or package in a neat little presentation.
>
> It is utilizing all of our resources, especially our human resources, better today than we did yesterday, and even better tomorrow.
>
> It is developing among all the members of an organization an awareness and understanding of the concerns and needs of others and a willingness to be more responsive to their concerns and needs.

Finally, quality of work life is improving the way things get done to assure the long-term effectiveness and success of the organization.

These are the key elements of our quality of work life philosophy. We purposefully encourage a broad understanding of the concept so that within our divisions, plants, and departments the opportunities for innovation are not limited. Most important, we want our managers and other employees to be free to develop innovations that best meet the unique circumstances of their organizations.

Our current view of quality of work life was not developed overnight. It has evolved from a philosophy of management and has been shaped by events and experiences occurring over a considerable period of time. I would like to discuss some of those major developments of the last decade and highlight some of the activities in progress today.

Our planned and organized approach began in 1969. We had just experienced a series of sporadic strikes in several of our car and truck assembly plants across the country. They were crippling. It was decided the adversary environment had to change—and if it was to change, management must find the way.

We started out with the direct involvement of our late president, Ed Cole, who got us involved in a project with the Institute for Social Research at the University of Michigan.

Initially, four GM plants were involved in research and organization development activities. Major emphasis was placed on employee involvement, information sharing, and training.

What we learned is that there is a close relationship between an organization's performance and how employees feel about the organization—how they feel about the work climate, the quality of management, and employee-management relationships. The project showed us that we could improve performance and human satisfaction by creating conditions in which people can become more involved, work together, and experience personal growth and development. Since then, a number of developments have helped shape our philosophy and the various approaches that were taken.

A key development occurred in 1973. In conjunction with labor contract negotiations that year, GM and the UAW established a National Committee to Improve the Quality of Work Life. Representing the UAW on the committee are two high-level officials of the International Union. The corporation is represented by the officer responsible for personnel matters and the vice president in charge of industrial relations.

The committee meets periodically to discuss joint activities under way in the corporation. For us, it is a focal point for management-union cooperation on quality of work life. One of its chief functions has been to educate executives of the union and the corporation about quality of work life and its applications. Twice in the past four years, the committee has sponsored one-day seminars for union and management executives.

The first meeting took place in 1975 and a follow-up session last year. About forty people attended that first meeting—twenty from the corporation and twenty from the union. It was a good learning experience for both sides. We talked about things important to all of us, and a lot of managers and union people were surprised to see just how much we do have in common. Some operating managers and local union people also attended and told us how they are applying quality of work life principles. All of this reinforced the idea that this is the way to go.

I mentioned that the committee is a focal point for collaborative action. I'd like to share an example of the kind of cooperation the committee is promoting at the local level. We have an automobile assembly plant that's located on the Hudson River in Tarrytown, New York. A decade ago, it could have been characterized as a problem plant. The environment was adversarial. There was an air of hostility between management and the union. And as you would guess, costs were high and performance poor. Something had to be done. Fortunately, we had a local management and local union who were willing to take some initiatives. As both sides explored and discussed their mutual problems and concerns, an atmosphere of understanding and mutual respect began to grow.

In 1972, the plant underwent a major rearrangement. Now we had a good manager. So it was an opportunity for management to involve employees in planning the change, something that hadn't been done before. As it worked out, the rearrangement went well—due in part to suggestions of hourly-rated employees. Then, following the lead set by the GM-UAW National QWL Committee, Tarrytown management and the union established their own committee.

In 1977, management and the union jointly initiated a three-day training program for all employees at Tarrytown. The program provided employees skills in team problem solving. Also it was an opportunity for management and the union together to tell employees about their plant so that people could begin to see how their jobs related to other jobs in the plant. The program was completely voluntary, but nearly all of the 3,600 employees participated over a period of about a year and a half. The investment in the program: well over $1 million.

Now, what about the bottom line—for people and for the organization? Employee morale at Tarrytown is high, absenteeism has dropped, and grievances are only a fraction of what they were eight or ten years ago. All the signs point to a much improved quality of work life in the plant. And, finally, the bottom line for the business—Tarrytown is one of the best performing assembly plants in General Motors.

Another area where we've had some major breakthroughs is in the design of the human organization of our new plants. In recent years, we've built a number of new plants that have introduced significant innovations. Each new plant is a unique opportunity to design from a blank sheet of paper an organization that's more responsive to people and their needs and more responsive to the objectives of the business. The key to our new plant accomplishments is planning. What we've tried to do—and by "we" I really mean the local management team—is to begin a planning process based on the idea that this plant does not have to look like any other plant in General Motors, and that the only real consideration is how the plant can be designed to make it the most effective organization in the corporation. Let me mention a few examples of the innovations that have been developed by our new plants.

A team concept is being used at several new plants. Production teams of hourly employees function without direct supervision. Team members have far more responsibility than do employees in traditional plants. For example, they help select new team members, they're responsible for training new team members, they forecast efficiency, scrap, and manpower requirements, and they are responsible for evaluating their operating performance and the performance of other team members.

Many of our new plants are using assessment centers for hiring new employees, hourly and salaried. In these evaluation sessions applicants are asked to respond to a variety of situations simulating real plant conditions, and teams of assessors then rate the applicants. Hourly employees also are included on the assessment teams.

These are just some of the kinds of things we're doing in our new plants—and trying to spread to other plants. Granted, there's a world of difference between the green field of a new plant and the tradition-bound environment of an existing plant. But while it may take longer, the principles being applied in new plants can also be applied elsewhere. We're convinced of that.

My remarks have focused mainly on our efforts with hourly employees. We are equally committed to improving the quality of work life of our salaried employees. Here are a few examples.

Our Fisher body trim plant in Grand Rapids, Michigan, abandoned the traditional organization structure under the management group a few years ago and adopted a business team organization. The plant is organized into six business teams, each consisting of the necessary production activities and support elements, such as engineering, scheduling, material handling, quality control, maintenance, and accounting. The system has made support people an integral part of the plant's business operations. And support and manufacturing people together can now better function as a team.

A similar approach is being used at our Inland Division in Dayton, Ohio. The division's product lines are diverse. They include engine mounts, brake linings, ball joints, and foam seats to name a few. To compete better with smaller companies that may have only a single product line, the division decided to organize each of its eleven product lines into a separate team. Each team now acts as an independent business with all of Inland's financial data and results reported to the teams, but on a product line basis. Staff area representatives are assigned to each team.

A final area I'd like to mention is measurement. Several years ago we instituted a survey to measure the quality of work life. The survey provides an assessment of a number of different areas of work life, including the physical work environment, economic well-being, the development and utilization of employee skills and abilities, employee involvement and influence, and supervisory and work-group relationships. We feel that the survey can help us evaluate our progress in improving the quality of work life and assess the effectiveness of specific projects.

To sum up, ours is not a packaged nor a single program. We firmly believe improvements have to be initiated at the local level. As I see it, my responsibility in this area—and the responsibility of other GM executives—is to help create a climate that supports and encourages improvement and innovation. We have to be willing to let others in the organization take some risks and try new approaches.

We think we're on the right track and making progress. We also know that we don't have all the answers. But today in General Motors, perhaps more than ever before, there is greater appreciation of organizations as entities—greater appreciation of the need to respond creatively to a changing work force and to a changing business environment.

The task is not easy, but our experience indicates that systems can be developed and managed in such a way that people can contribute more significantly to organizational objectives, that our human resources can be utilized better and that the working lives of men and women can be enriched. This is what our quality of work life process is all about. This is what becoming an organization of the future is all about. And, finally, this is what good management is all about.

The Quality of Work Life—
the Volvo Experience

*Berth Jönsson**

The Swedish labor market has been described as one of the most flexible which ever existed. This is characterized by a variety of work patterns in terms of working hours which are mainly a function of three changing variables:

1. the structure of the work force;
2. the legal structure and labor contracts; and
3. work ethics.

VARIABLES IN WORK PATTERNS

Changing Structure of Work Force

The Swedish work force has increased in heterogeneity very rapidly in the last ten to fifteen years. The pace of change probably has few parallels in the western world. The structure of human resources in industry has also changed greatly. The potential labor force, from which industry once hired the main bulk of its manual workers, primarily

*Corporate Development, Volvo

consisted of Swedish men in their most active years. This category of people diminished continuously in importance during the 1960s. During the economic boom in 1968–69 the situation became acute. During the latter years of the decade, foreign workers became the primary group to be hired into industry. In Volvo today, for instance, about one third of blue-collar workers are non-Swedes.

During the 1970s, however, the largest group entering the labor market has been women. Almost the total net increase in working population is due to women. To a great extent, women demand part-time jobs. About 90 percent of part-time workers are women. Part-time work in Sweden (1–34 hours per week) is characterized by:

1 out of 5 are working part-time—in industry 1 out of 10
9 out of 10 are women
4 out of 5 are part-time workers in the annual increase in labor force (1974–1977)
Part-time less than 20 hours/week is decreasing

A third category of people that continues to enter the labor market is young Swedes with a more basic education than the earlier generation. Compulsory schooling in Sweden today is nine years. Very few young people end their education with compulsory school. Most of them continue studies at the level of secondary education or higher. The increased heterogeneity of the work force has caused some severe problems for industry. For example,

a shortage in the Swedish work force and certain resistance from young Swedes particularly to go into industry. This tendency dominated in the late 1960s and early 70s;

increasing absenteeism and the changing nature of absenteeism on the whole labor market. From 1970 to 1976 the total number of people employed in the Swedish labor market increased by 234,000. In the same period absenteeism increased from 12.6 percent to 15.1 percent. This means that the increase of people who were actually working is 132,000. Almost every second person who is entering the labor market has, in effect, only compensated for the increase of absenteeism. Increasing absenteeism consequently means a greater demand for labor. Causes of absenteeism vary with different categories of people;

a labor force turnover rate on a fluctuating but high level between 1967 and 1974. Personnel turnover has decreased considerably over the last three years and is today around 10 percent or lower on an annual basis. During the late 60s it was as high as 80 percent for large scale plants in certain regions.

New Laws and Labor Agreements

Over the last few years a number of new labor market laws and agreements have been introduced. Many of these have had a restraining impact on the supply of working hours. Although the total number of employees has increased steadily, the total number of effective working hours is hardly increasing. The options for different patterns of working life have become numerous.

The most important laws and agreements which have a *direct* effect on working hours include the following:

parental leave (maternity/paternity)
child care leave
study leave
language training for foreign employees
restrictions on overtime
restrictions on shift-work
five weeks of vacation
part-time pension
work environment law
time for union work
flexible working hours—local agreements for white-collar employees
part-time work—local agreements (four hours; six hours including shift-work)

Certain social benefits have had an *indirect* effect on the availability of working hours. The greatest impact has come from the reforms in the sickness-insurance system.

Changing Ethics in Regard to Work

The evolution of an affluent society like Sweden's has, naturally, also had an impact on ethics concerning work. On the surface, it seems paradoxical that more people are working than ever while opinion research shows that fewer people find their job as attractive as it once was.

Professor Hans Zetterberg at the Swedish Opinion Research Institute has shown that fewer people today express the view that work gives the greatest meaning to their lives compared to two decades ago. Work has been traditionally a "life-style" for many people. Today there are many other "life-styles" competing with work. Work gives the necessary monetary base for people to undertake other life-styles. The most important general tendency is different leisure time activities. One would assume that some kind of optimization of time and money would be the goal. These changes are fairly dramatic and will undoubtedly lead to different job expectations and a call for reforms in life at work.

DIFFERENT PHASES OF DEVELOPMENT AT VOLVO

Development of job design at Volvo has gone through two major phases. Although each phase can be identified with one particular plant at a time, there have been overlaps between plants. One plant may have started redesigning jobs later than another, or one particular plant may have reached a certain stage in its development earlier than another plant. Regardless of these overlaps and different paces of development, there are some common characteristics of each phase.

In the mid-1960s a number of initiatives was taken on a voluntary basis. Programs came out spontaneously with little notice being taken. We call this first phase of redesign the *Spontaneous Trial Period*. Work was going on in different places disconnected from each other and top management's purview.

The motives for change varied from one department to the other. High personnel turnover (sometimes amounting to 50 percent or more), an increasing absenteeism rate, medical and economic problems, production losses and quality problems were some of the forces of change. One can identify a number of personal initiatives behind these first redesign efforts. They came from the shopfloor, supervision, manufacturing managers, industrial engineers, the union, doctors, etc. All the personalities involved had some deep concern for people and the problem of alienation.

At the time of the Kalmar project (1971), there was a demand from top management to take a more holistic approach. In this project a whole new concept was about to be implemented. The only way to do this was to put together all the accumulated experience from the different plants. The effect was not only that the Kalmar plant was built but also that it opened up communication between plants and projects in an interdisciplinary way.

A new strategy started to emerge. We call this phase the *Sociotechnical Strategy Period*. Since 1971–72, a number of projects have started and Volvo definitely has left the disconnected trial period. We built on all the experience gained in the different plants and on active and explicit support from top management. No company can afford experimenting on this broad scale. It must create a strategy and decide how to go about implementing it in the most efficient manner. Hence the term experiment cannot apply to projects during the second phase.

We are right now in an advanced stage of the second phase which includes new creative solutions to flexible hardware technology and the diffusion of ideas to Volvo subsidiaries outside Sweden. By now, change has become institutionalized, with a variety of patterns but with a common ground. Learning and diffusion of ideas are occurring continuously.

FORMULATION OF A STRATEGY

Pehr G. Gyllenhammar, president of Volvo, has stated:

> The modern working man needs a sense of purpose and satisfaction in his daily work. He feels the need of belonging to a team, of being able to feel at home in his surroundings, of being able to identify himself with the goods he produces and—not least—of feeling that he is appreciated for the work he performs.
>
> Factory work must be adapted to people, and not people to machines. This calls for innovation both in the field of human relations and as regards technical aspects.
>
> I believe that humanization of work and efficiency can be compatible. Indeed, I believe that, in today's society, they are inseparable.

It has often been pointed out that to promote a change process requires the backing of top management. Most often it takes more than just verbal commitment. In the case of Volvo's Kalmar Plant, three basic necessary steps were taken by Mr. Gyllenhammar:

1. He wrote an internal memo to explain his vision of how to design work in an automobile assembly plant both in terms of hardware technology and work organization;
2. he gained support from both managers and workers on the final alternative (several sketches had been discussed before the final alternative was decided upon); and
3. he submitted the issue of investment to the board of directors and won acceptance.

The basic shape of the factory emerged from the idea of production teams. Each assembly team has its own area of the factory where it carries out its part of the assembly operation. The autonomy of the teams has been emphasized through the shape of the building and the supplying of each team with its own personnel facilities. The components inventory that supplies materials to all the teams is located in the center of the building. The teams are spread out along the outer walls of the building. Production began in February 1974. The factory is designed for the assembly of 30,000 cars per year, with one shift of assembly workers.

An important innovation in the new production system is the battery-powered assembly carrier that functions both as a transport device and assembly platform. A central computer keeps track of all the carriers and checks their movement along the production process between work areas. They are powered through magnetic tracks embedded in the floor and can be maneuvered manually with operating levers. Thanks to this carrier, assembly can be carried out on stationary cars, which is an extremely important difference from conventional moving-line-fixed-pace assembly. Moreover, the carrier is designed so that it can be easily tilted by 90 degrees when components are being assembled on the underside of the car.

Before and after each work team's area, there are places for incoming and outgoing assembly carriers. These buffers make it possible for the team, within certain limits, to work ahead and accumulate time for extra work breaks. The work is arranged so that it takes the same amount of time to carry out the tasks at one work station as at another. The basis for this balance of task cycles is worked out with the help of method-time-measurement studies, and the task packages at the various stations are normally known as "balances."

After interviewing many employees, the Rationalization Council's investigators reached a number of conclusions. Since this investigation was made in 1976 the Kalmar plant has gained more experience and has reached the level of full capacity utilization. The main results up to now can be summarized in the following points:

The total assembly times in the Kalmar plant are less than in a conventional plant. Particularly, indirect time (planning, quality control etc.) is less at Kalmar. In addition, the Kalmar plant has some advantages that the conventional factory lacks, though it is somewhat more costly. The extra investment is to some extent offset by production advantages, such as a smaller number of supervisors, ease of altering production arrangements, and low absenteeism and turnover.

The total effect of these advantages has now become even more marked at full capacity production, and the extra investment cost is completely offset.

> The team organization and the technological production apparatus permit a higher degree of influence by employees on their own work than in a conventional assembly system.
>
> The design of the factory has provided a good basis for team organization.
>
> Most workers are very positive toward the team organization and have a strong feeling of belonging to their team.
>
> The company has delegated responsibility to the teams to design their own organizations within a certain framework. In a traditional organization, all division of the work is planned at a superior hierarchical level in the line organization. At Kalmar, considerable leeway has been left to the teams to decide the distribution of the work. What happens between the time the incoming materials are received and when completed assembly is dispatched is largely up to the teams to decide. In order to fulfill their assignments, the team members must organize their own work. This includes, among other things, setting rules for job switching and working ahead of extra breaks.

Though Kalmar may be considered a qualified success since it costs around 10 percent more than a conventional plant of equal capacity, seven new plants (one in Holland, six in Sweden) have been built recently based on the Kalmar experience. These installations cost no more than conventional plants. Recent statistics from Volvo show that their total blue collar turnover, which ran 25-30 percent annually prior to Kalmar, now runs at only 6.5 percent at Kalmar. Likewise, sickness typically ran 20 percent annually, while Kalmar boasts only 9 percent. In both cases, the Kalmar figures are well below Sweden's national averages. The "Kalmar concept" has diffused to a great number of projects. The entrepreneurial spirit that Kalmar created is the driving force behind changes of production technology and organizational design in new and old plants. A couple of the most innovative projects will briefly be described.

The personal involvement of the chief executive officer throughout the design process has had a major impact on the thinking and organizational climate. For example, he insisted on moving away from conveyor lines toward a more flexible carrier system not only because it would increase the degrees of freedom of the worker but also because it would have a visual, symbolic effect. This has resulted in a number of creative solutions and organizational models in the different plants.

It should be stated from the beginning that "*the vision*" of an automobile assembly plant did not become a reality at Kalmar. Originally the idea was to have the car completed in a small workshop with a few work stations and with some twenty-five people being responsible for producing a certain quantity. The vision turned the traditional concept upside-down in the sense that it demanded that material flow be directed to one spot (the workshop) rather than distributed along the line. The final solution of Kalmar was not to have one group of twenty-five members assembling the whole car but to have a number of groups each assembling a certain function of the car (for instance, the electrical function). The visionary idea was not dropped despite the fact that it was not adopted at Kalmar. We will see how newer approaches in other plants have come closer to solving the problems involved. The closest so far is a small workshop for truck assembly and a plant for tractor assembly.

TOWARD CRAFTSMANSHIP IN ASSEMBLY OPERATIONS

The Truck Division in the fall of 1974 planned an expansion of the production volume. An initiative was then taken to apply some new ideas of job design in a small workshop. The vision of Kalmar had been assimilated by the people in charge of truck operations even though they had not been engaged in the Kalmar project.

Some managers and engineers met to see if they could apply a system with just one group of people taking full responsibility for the final assembly of trucks. At the same time a parallel project was underway to construct a plant for assembling tractors, construction and forestry machines. The two different project groups each developed an air cushion platform. Two platforms—one in the front and one in the rear—can easily take a truck or any other heavy product. By using compressed air the truck becomes mobile because of the air pads which keep the platform just above the floor. Any person can easily move the truck from one "assembly bay" to the other. Thus the system is extraordinarily flexible and the layout within the plant can easily be adapted to new products and different needs. The total truck assembly process includes:

material handling
preassembly of engines and gear-boxes
preassembly of cabs
preassembly of other components
two stations ("bays") for final assembly
painting and undercoating

All in all eighteen operators produce about 500 trucks annually. The work cycle for preassemblies and final assembly is around four hours each. At the very least people know how to perform within one work area. A few people have gained experience amounting to eight hours or more. Meetings are held whenever needed with the total group of eighteen members. In the start-up phase, meetings were quite frequent but lately a meeting every two weeks has been the pattern. In order to test the new concept, 50 percent of the people were recruited externally; these had no experience with truck manufacturing. Almost all training has been on-the-job. For the four hour work cycle the learning takes an average of about sixty hours. The results from the truck workshop have been most encouraging in regard to such objectives as productivity, quality, rejects, absenteeism, personnel turnover, and attitudes.

The tractor assembly (plus assembly of construction and forestry machines) is based on the same idea as the truck workshop. Tractors are assembled in two areas with two teams in each area—each team consisting of eight members. In the first area the chassis are assembled including engine, clutch housing, gearbox, and rear axle housing. The chassis are painted and then in the second area the final assembly takes place. Certain preassembly takes place in the same area as the assembly. Work cycles vary between thirty minutes and four hours and can be extended beyond this when a person has learned the job of the next team.

In the two cases briefly described, we can witness a logical loop from the first ideas of Kalmar. The likely future development will be a dynamic one using a set of learning and organizational models. Changes will continue not least in the division of responsibilities between manufacturing personnel, supervision and industrial engineers.

TOWARD A STRATEGY OF JOB DESIGN AND LEARNING

Over the last ten to twenty years the trend in mass production industry has been to develop more sophisticated engineering methods and highly advanced hardware technology. The degree of mechanization has increased as a consequence and man has become a cog in a big machine. A highly mechanized assembly line allows a minimum of personal initiatives and thought. People are taught how to use pre-assigned tools and given a pre-planned amount of work to perform, which leaves the degree of freedom of action utterly limited.

In Volvo today the great majority of jobs are mechanized. At the same time the new corporate strategy is to develop production technology and work organization toward two ends: craftsmanship and automation. During a transition period a number of people will naturally remain in highly mechanized jobs.Figure 1 illustrates the pattern of development at different workshops. So far very little of traditional assembly work has been automated.

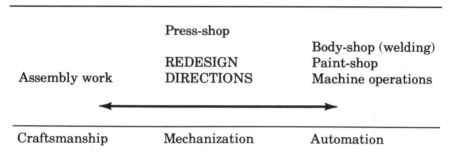

Figure 1. Development at Volvo workshops.

Since the days of the first volunteer redesign efforts in the 1960s, and particularly since the Kalmar Plant (car assembly) and Skövde Plant (petrol engine manufacturing) projects were conducted, the pace of diffusion has steadily increased. Through internal seminars and documents an exchange of experience is achieved to the benefit of participating groups. Over the last two years the exchange of experience seminars have involved Volvo subsidiaries in Holland and Belgium. The mere fact that two non-Swedish operations participated gives a stimulating dimension to the development of new work structures. Each plant has found its own feasible pattern of change. Similar to the development in Sweden, changes in both Holland and Belgium comprise the creation of more flexible hardware as well as new ways of organizing work, including group work.

In industrial engineering the concept of "work cycles" is quite basic. The time it takes to perform one well-defined task is the work cycle. The work cycle may vary from a few seconds in certain drilling and cutting operations to several minutes in traditional assembly operation. Work cycles in car assembly have been reduced over the last ten year period to somewhere around three minutes. The well-known Lordstown plant of GM became famous partly because of the short work cycles of approximately thirty seconds. One of the directions at Volvo to reorganize the job has been to extend the work cycles. However, one set of tasks has not been added to another set of tasks randomly. There has to be some logic behind the way to organize the tasks so as to achieve a more meaningful content of work.

One idea which has been implemented at Volvo has been that of combining tasks so that they either lead to the completion of a product, component, or subproduct (a complete system or subsystem). To combine a set of tasks to achieve some kind of wholeness has appeared to be a key to improving the work concept. By finalizing the product or a subsystem, it is possible for a worker to learn how it functions and consequently the possibility is created to make quality checks at the spot where the assembly takes place. Any corrective actions can likewise be made at the source of error.

This model has been extended both in a horizontal way (longer work cycles combined in a logical way leading to a sense of completeness) and in a vertical way (i.e., integrating other types of jobs with the original one). Such jobs may include:

inspection of incoming material
material handling
quality inspection of the product
rectifying of errors
tooling and retooling
maintenance work on tools and machinery

In several cases at Volvo the logical development of a project has included these two steps: (1) extended work cycles; and (2) vertical integration adding one or more of the tasks mentioned. A strategy of training has been the natural support system to a successful implementation of projects. In some cases the learning has gone beyond what has been described so far. In one upholstery department, in some areas of the press-shop, in one truck assembly, and in one machine operation (to mention a few), additional responsibilities have been taken over by the operators. This could be labeled step three. Such responsibilities include:

participation in production planning;
participation in rationalization projects;
participation in hiring procedures;
participation in evaluating output;
participating in technical development (tools etc.).

By using the three step model we will see how learning develops within a work group.

In Volvo there are two more programs which on occasion serve as support systems to the stop-floor work. The first one deals with lectures and discussions about the product as such, its functioning and its characteristics. The second type of program goes into interpersonal relations, group behavior, and problem-solving.

It should be noted that the total model as just outlined has seldom been completely implemented. However, it shows the possible alternatives available. Based on Volvo experience it could be said that each plant and each department has found a procedure of development which fits its own needs. A general observation can be drawn from recent development work. The less complex work is in itself (i.e., a minimum of possible horizontal integration), the more willing and demanding are people to adopt new tasks and responsibilities (vertical job integration). This is, for instance, true in group work on some of the press lines and in a machine workshop (engine block department).

On the other hand, assembly work in itself can be extended to a large extent (e.g., in Kalmar to around thirty minutes and in the truck workshop to four to eight hours). The possibility of a large horizontal integration seems to lead to a division of tasks. In most assembly groups, for instance, material handling is designated to one particular group member who the group selects. Sometimes this special task is rotated among group members each half day or a person may keep it a full week.

WHAT ARE THE DRIVING AND RESTRAINING FORCES TO SUCCESSFUL IMPLEMENTATION?

As previously mentioned, external and internal forces influence new ways of organizing work. In a recent study at Volvo it has been shown that redesign strategies within the company vary with such factors as management style, social relations, demographic structure, and technology. Consequently, there is no standardized model of change which can be used as a normative tool within a company or between companies.

Some general conclusions can, however, be drawn from the study:

1. that we will fail if we try uncritically to copy solutions from one country to another, from one plant to another within the same country, or even from one production line to another within the same plant.
2. that when management has a deeply rooted understanding of the local characteristics, our chances of success increase.
3. that an active and positive management attitude toward change is a prerequisite for positive results. However, when this atti-

tude turns into an endeavor to impose programs, projects and plans "from above" will tend to fail.

4. that management has to be sensitive to the fact that the change process will sooner or later affect several organizational levels, independent of where the change is initiated.
5. that a process-oriented view should be adopted; the important thing is to learn, to study consequences, to understand, to communicate, and to take risks in new trials. Change requires freedom of action and time.
6. that management development with the focus on change and on the dynamics of both the internal and external social system, will increase the capacity for change.
7. that to ensure lasting effects, initiatives for change must come from the "line" and not from white-collar specialists.
8. that the role of the behavioral scientists should be that of the catalyst.
9. that foremen and industrial engineers have an increasingly crucial role to play. Through training, organizational changes, or participation in joint consultation groups, they have been brought closer to the problems of the shop floor and have acquired a broader awareness of the social requirements related to technical problems.
10. that changes in the work situation must include a "package" of activities introduced over a period of time. The "package" would include delegation of responsibilities, integration of jobs where other skills are required, job rotation, participation in decision making concerning the job situation, and changes in physical working conditions. Isolated trials with the introduction, for instance, of simple job rotation, are doomed to failure. To be effective, changes in the work organization must be fully integrated with a system of joint consultation.
11. that many changes are undertaken spontaneously without the aid of projects, without scientific sophistication, without their being reported to anybody. These changes occur simply on the initiative of keen and interested individuals.

The process by which job design has developed at Volvo is a pragmatic approach to problem solving and an appreciation of the potential energy which only man can mobilize. The solutions are different in different contexts, but by combining inputs from different fields of interest, experience, and knowledge, the system keeps developing.

Chapter 3C

Work Itself and Its Aftermath at AT&T

*Rex R. Reed**

As part of our own corporate search for "a better way," I've had the opportunity to probe into the pioneering work of General Motors and Volvo. Actually, if you have any serious interest in the personnel relations area, you must probe into the work of these two companies, for they are at the tip of the leading edge. Fortunately for the rest of us, they are generous with their time and insights. I'm going to tell you about an opportunity where we dropped the ball and about a hopeful new beginning. However, philosophers are always assuring us that we learn just as much from our failures as we do from our successes. We'll try to take some comfort in that thought.

In the 1960s we made a promising start on something we called "Work Itself." You may recognize, this is the name of a job enrichment concept created by Dr. Robert Ford, out of research he originated with Fred Herzberg. Bob worked for us for almost thirty years, and developed his theory and approach in field trials conducted in various Bell System companies.

It was Bob's idea that workers should be motivated through the work itself—not through economic rewards alone, and certainly not through control systems and disciplinary mechanisms. It was essen-

*Vice President, Labor Relations, American Telephone and Telegraph Company

tially a job enrichment concept—reversing the fragmentary approach to work and putting satisfying, whole jobs back together out of pieces. It was based on the notion that a huge majority of workers could get satisfaction from their jobs and do them better—if management would give them real work to do, and not get in their way with bureaucratic nonsense.

At the peak, we had a few districts and divisions and even an entire operating area working daily under this concept. The operating results were often very impressive indeed. Quality and productivity indices would show improvement. Union grievances would be down. Morale would be reported to be very much improved. Attendance and turnover would be trending favorably. All of these impressive results would be sustained through a management generation. But, unfortunately, in our company a management generation is just two to three years long. After that, the management team disperses up and out. And with the old management team went the Work Itself trial. Nobody would officially kill it. It would simply wither away. And, curiously enough, we noticed that the old team would rarely plug the method into their new jobs.

This led a colleague of mine to remark, "nothing fails like success." For these Work Itself trials *were* successes, virtually always. But they didn't put down permanent roots, nor did they spread through the rest of the organization. This is *not* an uncommon phenomenon. If I had an absolute answer to it, as well as a cure, I could be a very busy and very expensive consultant. I don't know why personnel relations successes don't root and spread. But I do have some observations about our failed opportunity with Work Itself that might be instructive.

First, Work Itself *did* have top level support from the chief executive officer (CEO) and the chief operating officer. In fact they urged the program onto the presidents and operating officers of the system companies. But this support came from an appreciation of the results of the program—not from any deep understanding of the human principles involved.

Second, Work Itself was always an AT&T *headquarters* program—not an operating company program, and certainly not an operating department program. A few individual operating managers became disciples and made the program theirs. But, psychologically, it was always an AT&T headquarters program.

Third, my business is thoroughly unionized. Work Itself was discussed with the union leadership. And local union leaders were always informed when a design was to be introduced. But the unions were never a *part* of the program, the way the full participation of the UAW at General Motors is described. I'm convinced that our unions never fought Work Itself programs anywhere. But I also know they never pushed for them, either. And many of the local union people were highly suspicious of management's true intentions with the program.

Fourth, Work Itself deeply involved the local management team. In fact, it did a very good job of what organizational development people would call management team building—surely a first step in most programs. But it didn't involve craft workers in any ongoing, systematic way. For craft people, Work Itself was something done *to* them, rather than done *with* them. They most often were very pleased with the redesigned work. But they weren't involved in the decisions about it even initially—let alone continuously, as in the GM and Volvo models.

Fifth, we never gave Work Itself *time*. Mike Maccoby often tells the story about Land and his comment about the difference between the way a business thinks of physical research and personnel research. If we approached semi-conductors the way we did Work Itself, there still wouldn't be a transistor—unless maybe the Japanese had invented it by this time. The fact of the matter is that we never gave Work Itself a fair trial and a chance to strengthen and grow through learning. Some of Bob Ford's disciples are still active. Individual managers learned from using it—and some of them have had success with involving craft people with the methodology. But corporately, we dropped the ball. We learned very little in an organizational sense and no longer identify any of our programs with the name.

Now to the hopeful beginning. For the past couple of years many of our people have been telling us in attitude surveys and in conferences and in interview sessions that our management style has become too focused on numerical results and not enough on human customers and human employees. We don't have any turnover problems or any special labor unrest, as it is usually manifested in grievances and walk-outs. But more and more of our people are telling us that the way we're managing the business doesn't adequately match their needs and the service needs of our customers. In short, we're getting what we take to be an early warning.

We're responding to this early warning with new analytical and monitoring methods. We're tracking down any promising new approaches in our own company, with an eye to spreading the word. As I mentioned earlier, some of the disciples of Work Itself have carried the program down to craft levels. One manager, Larry Lemasters out in Ohio, has been especially successful in doing this, as Mike Maccoby knows. In addition, there are a few other managers with success stories. But a few isn't very many in a universe of one million employees.

Too, we are reinforcing the efforts of our job design people under Mal Gillett with emphasis on how the work place is organized. We're sharing with our top managers the successful experiences of companies like GM and Volvo. In just a few weeks, Steve Fuller is going to tell the GM story—with a UAW officer—to our top personnel officers and some of our top operating people. We're not trying to sell a specific approach, but rather a different way of looking at the way we use human resources.

We're encouraging experimentation and sharing of what works. We have over a million people and some twenty-three companies. We know no highly refined approach will work everywhere. But we also believe that the experience of companies like GM and Volvo indicate there are *principles* that will work just about everywhere—principles such as involvement and participation in work decisions, for example.

We're looking hard at the control systems and policies that have grown up in the past few years. Never mind the intent of these systems and policies. How are they being interpreted and used, down there where boss and worker come together on the job?

We're exploring with our union people new forms of joint job effort. Their members are demanding of them some response to what they call "job pressures." This is an area, perhaps, where they need us, and we need them.

The past year of exploring what's going on in the leading edge companies has taught us some rather depressing yet encouraging things. Perhaps depression is the beginning of wisdom. For one thing, there's no quick transition. GM, Eaton, Xerox, Cummins Engine—all the leading edge companies are quick to point out that "a better way" takes a few years to develop and spread, is fraught with peril, suffers setbacks from internal resistance and external factors in the economy, and is generally an act of incredible faith on the part of people and corporations. For another thing, "a better way of managing" is far tougher on the manager than relying on status and authority and the rule book. Perhaps as high as 25 percent of existing managers simply can't manage in a less authoritarian mode. That's a pretty high casualty rate, when you're asking your managers to get on the landing boats.

But I'm personally convinced there's no other way for American business—including my own—to go. We need the productivity of our people, if we're going to be competitive. Workers themselves have changed along with our society, and demand to be well used and useful. Our society itself is demanding improvement in the quality of life—prominently including those important hours we spend on the job. Our own Work Itself people used to call this "the quiet revolution." I think the issues of that revolution are becoming much more sharply defined. It's up to us to help channel the tremendous energy of this revolution into human progress and work-place efficiencies.

Discussion

Question: I'd like to direct my first question to Mr. Fuller and my second to Mr. Jönsson. We recently heard, first of all, that the agreement reached in the recent bargaining session undercut the number of meetings you had with the union about the quality of work life; and secondly, about Volvo, we hear that some of the work teams in the plant have stopped. Could both of you comment on these issues? What is the status of the upper level with the union and the viability of your agreement at General Motors and what is happening right now in terms of work teams at Volvo?

Fuller: I'd almost like to have Mr. Ephlin help me respond to the first question. Mr. Ephlin is the regional director of the UAW in New England, but he has also been one of the leaders of the international union in its efforts to move forward the quality of work life for union members in General Motors. I know of nothing in the recently negotiated agreement that has set back quality of work life. I simply don't know to what you refer. As a matter of fact, I would say that there are several things in the new agreement that further it. For example, we now have a joint General Motors–UAW Committee on Attendance to study absenteeism. I can't believe that you can study absenteeism and not discover a number of symptoms of bad quality of work life. In addition, to the extent to which the new agreement accords almost automatic recognition of the union as the bargaining representative of our employees, I hope to put to bed for all time anyone's apprehension that quality of work life is an effort to develop a nonunion environment. It is far from that, and the union and its recognition is a necessary ingredient without which quality of work life can not begin to operate, at least not in our company.

Ephlin: I'd like to say that in the negotiations absolutely nothing was done to undercut the quality of work life program we have together with General Motors and, in fact, a number of things were done to enhance it. I think that the lady might have gotten her information from an article in the *New York Times* that was full of inaccuracies and which happened to be written by a man who wrote a book that said that the 1970 strike we had with General Motors was done in collaboration with GM. Actually I went bankrupt myself during that strike and I don't think it was much fun. As Steve mentioned, a number of things that were done during the negotiations were a result of better attitudes and better relationships which have developed because of quality of work life; and some of them, as he mentioned, such as the recognition of new plants, will allow us now to do things together in the new plants before we make mistakes, much as is done with Volvo. I think you will see an ever-increasing number of quality of work life programs developing between the UAW and General Motors.

Jönsson: There are many different rumors concerning the status of team work at Volvo today. I can assure you that, in the case of the Kalmar Plant, it is still based on work teams, and I cannot foresee any reason for change in the basic approach. Furthermore, the plant is more effective today than ever before. There are about thirty teams in the plant and they are integrating many different tasks in their total work cycle. However, what is equally important is that our new concept has spread to many other Volvo plants.

Question: I have one question for Mr. Fuller and other general question. I seem to sense some contradictions between the things that Mr. Fuller said and an article in the *Harvard Business Review* concerning Tarrytown. If my memory is correct, the article in *HBR* suggested that the Tarrytown effort was not supported by upper management and has virtually died several times and only through the courage of the local people was brought back. At one point, it was almost killed by a rather mass layoff of several hundred people, which came at a most critical time. The general question has to do with profit sharing.

I am wondering if there is not an issue here about profit sharing. For example, some of the enemies of organizational development, industrial democracy, etc., suggest that it would not go on to the last stage, which is to share the benefits of the increase in productivity, of the decrease in absenteeism, etc. We don't go to that. Are we simply not dealing with a rather ideological and very sophisticated social science speed-up program, often with the heads of people who do not have PhDs and who have not had the benefits that many of us have had, although some of us have worked in factories?

Fuller: I lack the benefit of having read the *HBR* article but let me answer in general. Because of the nature of our quality of work life programs in General Motors, because of their local origin and local initiative, top management in Detroit has almost no involvement in the specific program details in Tarrytown at all. Now quality of work life programs are not going to stand in the way of a very substantial reduction in force in a time of substantial economic downtake. As I said, I don't know about the article and I am not aware that top management hardly knows what goes on at Tarrytown, because this is going on in 170 plants and there are 170 different projects underway. All top management is saying is that quality of work life in General Motors is not optional—you do it, but what you do is up to yourself—it is not a program packaged and structured in Detroit and sent to the field.

*O'Connell:** On the larger issue, the three dimensions of what has been called, in Europe, industrial democracy, i.e., financial sharing rather than the narrow expression "profit sharing," work on the quality of work life, and codetermination, are seen as interdependent. We have focused here on the work ethic, rather clinically separating something that is related. Maybe the companies represented here would have something to say about how financial sharing is related to quality of work life efforts.

Reed: We have nothing going there in that area. It would seem to me that if the work ethic, as it has been described at this conference, is one in which people with full-time jobs want more responsibility, I am not sure you need to go to profit sharing as an incentive. I hope you do not need to go that far because I think it would be very difficult, particularly in major industries as large as ours.

*Dr. Jeremiah J. O'Connell, Dean of the Bentley College Graduate School

Fuller: I think in many ways General Motors has already gotten itself in a position of substantial profit sharing. Since the early 1950s, as you know, the wages of the employees at General Motors have gone up automatically 3 percent each year as a productivity increase, and they have had cost of living protection at the same time; so that for twenty-five years the union has recognized the appropriateness of our workers sharing in productivity increases. Now I do believe that if through new collaboration there are still further increases, then we should always be prepared for sharing new ways of reward. In addition, I believe that we ought to start to examine substantial new ways of increasing job security. When General Motors pays for unemployment compensation when an employee is laid off 95 percent of what it costs to keep him in the plant, it might be an appropriate time to wonder if the employee can't be more beneficially used, whether there is production to be done or not, by looking at alternatives to layoff and all of its tremendous psychological costs. So I think that as quality of work life advances, we need to be highly innovative, especially about all those things that we've done for ten years along. If we did it that way ten years ago, it is probably wrong today.

Jönsson: Profit sharing is not an issue at Volvo, nor in Sweden, and for several very simple reasons. First of all, most of it would go to taxes anyway; and secondly, because of our very particular bargaining pattern in Sweden starting on a national level. Some of the larger private banks have designed a profit sharing system. This has had no impact on industry. We have had major public debates on so-called economic democracy in Sweden and other European countries, but that would take a full conference of its own to explore.

O'Connell: We should just point out that, in the European context, the things that we have said here about profit sharing understate European perceptions of the United States. Otto Sik, the Czech economist, said at a conference not too long ago, "We envy the Americans. We've lost our opportunity to make our workers into minicapitalists." And it was that great professor, Peter Drucker, who in a book on pension funds and other forms of ownership, indicated that we are more socialist than Sweden, since about one-third of the labor force has direct participation in equities and gets profit sharing because the payoff ratio in corporations is about 50 percent. Profit sharing goes on in very interesting ways in the United States system. Europeans, as Berth has indicated, still look at us with enormous envy over the instruments we've had in place for financial sharing for more than a quarter of a century.

Question: My question is directed to Mr. Jönsson. I wonder, even with all these regulations which have been passed by Swedish government, how do you explain the high rate of absenteeism and also the general apathy that is so apparent among workers today?

Jönsson: That is a very complicated question. I think one point I made was that in the kind of society which we have developed since the Second World War there are other parts of life that are competing with work, and these definitely make a great demand on flexible working hours. Part of the answer is that the labor market industry does not supply all the variety of working hours that people need, considering their life-styles and their needs, and so you get a high rate of absenteeism. For instance, if you examine the reason for absenteeism, you will find that more and more leave is for child care and other reasons which are not related to sickness. There is a kind of paradox here that I find striking. You will find that the life expectancy in Sweden is the highest in the world.

Question: I have two questions. At AT&T and General Motors, are their top management people personally devoted to human development and quality of work life as in Volvo? As worker participation increases in decision making, what is happening to middle management and is there any resistance from middle management?

Reed: In terms of the top management commitment, our new chairman's top priority in his new role is that to the extent there has been any erosion in the confidence of our people he wishes to restore that confidence. Over the last year, we have devoted in our discussions with the operating company, who really are the leaders of the Bell system, more time to this subject than we have in the last ten years, and we will continue to do so. I think there is a very genuine commitment at the top level. As I move through the Bell system with the top management, the encouraging thing is that throughout there is a growing recognition that we need to find a better way than what we used over the last ten years.

Fuller: I mentioned in my remarks that quality of work life at General Motors is not a personnel program. In any formal organization, there are functions and individuals who have more influence than other functions or other individuals. In very few companies is the personnel function the one that is the most influential.

Question: Who is personally devoted to this?

Fuller: It used to be Richard Terrell who was our vice-chairman and our immediate boss. When we started in 1971, shortly after the results of the University of Michigan study came in and they showed us what could be done if a little incentive were given the men, he called together in Atlanta all the general managers in all divisions and their manufacturing managers, their chief engineers and their personnel managers and said, "I'd like to hear from each of you. Let's spend three days here and we can listen to what each division is doing to get people involved." The reports were brief. Mr. Terrell didn't scold anybody. He complimented them for their contribution in bringing him up-to-date and said, "We'll meet again in ninety days. This time it will be in Montreal, and we'll do the same thing," and when Montreal was all done he said we'd do it in ninety days again and we'll meet in Boston, and that went on, so that every year we had a two-day conference in which every division reported on what it had done. F. James McDonald, executive vice president of Northern American Car and Truck operations and the principal operating officer of the corporation now, has what is called the "McDonald Meetings." Nobody from personnel staff is on the program at these meetings. I get to sit in the back of the room, if I get in at all. So in quick response to your impact on middle management, I must tell you that some of our managers have said to us that if this is the way it is going to be done, thank you, I'll take early retirement. I thought that you had given it all away before, now you are really giving it all away, you'll never get it back and you're soft-headed. One of the team enlightening the chairman on my background has described the speaker as "the academic socialist run-of-the-muck from the East without the benefit of supervision."

Question: My question relates to a previous one. If I can quote Mr. Fuller, he talked about quality of working life as a process improving how things are done for long-term organizational effectiveness and success. It seems to me that introduces a notion that where the family goes the organization might survive. If survival is the name of the game, then do the members of the panel see themselves as gamesmen?

Fuller: I think that survival is the name of the game. It is certainly true in the automobile industry. We are not competing in a United States market; we are competing in a world market and if you will look back for twenty-five years you will see what has already happened to United States contenders in this market. Or if you don't choose to look back, look at this morning's newspaper or tomorrow's newspaper. I think that it was very recently that I read something about a number of shares of a United States company being purchased, or the principled ownership now vesting in a non-United States company, and no one is going to escape. We are on a world-wide shake-down cruise. Let me say this: There are some industries preceding the automobile industry, and perhaps the United States steel industry is a good example. There are other industries which have already preceded that, such as our ability to manufacture radios or televisions in this country. There are a number of industries immediately behind. In short, it is not the survival of General Motors, Ford, or Chrysler, it is the ability of the United States industrial economy to survive as an industrial economy and we had better get our act together, and fast, including our act with Washington. If we are going to relate effectively with our employees, Washington had better start effectively relating to us, and industry had better have a better solution or we'll go out of business. We'd better get our act together—the Japanese have theirs.

O'Connell: With just about as much passion, I heard an industrialist in Spain, a country that does not have the benefits that we would all admit that our country has, talk about survival issues. He quoted Oscar Wilde and said that the basis for optimism is sheer terror. If you think we have a survival issue in the United States you ought to sit in some of the places where plants from these various companies exist. It really is an issue of survival.

Question: Perhaps in the kind of situation that you were just indicating, about each country having to get its act together for survival, maybe we ought to stop and ask why any individual country ought to survive. Maybe this is an opportunity to begin building toward what some people have been calling the "spaceship earth" concept for planning international exploitation and distribution of the earth's resources. The other question that I want to ask is for all of you. It has been touched upon by one or two of the others. I am brand new to the field of work ethics and I am sure this is a question that many people have already explored and come up with satisfactory responses to. To what extent are the various changes, i.e., work quality and quality of life operations that various corporations are now undertaking similar to the old Taylorism? I gather there were studies made of Taylorism that suggested that it was not what was done for workers that improved productivity, morale, etc., over a short period of time, rather it was the fact that somebody was doing something for the workers. In a sense, is not this long-range planning that you all are talking about going to involve a perpetual scramble for new gimmicks to keep the workers entertained so that profits and productivity will remain high?

Jönsson: I think it is conceivably a matter of both. I think it is very important to know what you are doing, but also how you are doing it. It is not a gimmick in our case, it is a matter of a different way of life at the corporate level. You can't cheat people for a long time; they will discover it very soon. The seriousness of the whole issue is for continuous debate all the time, which makes sure that you deal with it in a serious way.

Fuller: To me, at least, the quality of work life at General Motors represents a rejection of economic criteria as the appropriate measure of the human health of the organization, and it means putting people up front. In the Volvo presentation, some of the slides indicated the need to reject as the single purpose of the corporation the desire to make a profit. We have a whole generation and a whole economy that have accepted this idea lock, stock, and barrel. People are ends in themselves and everyday General Motors makes noneconomic decisions not consistent, in the short run, with increasing its profit because it is the right thing to do or because people are very much involved, and, therefore, quality of work life at General Motors is not a productivity program. It's a program to enhance the work of people. Our workers are no longer willing to leave their brains outside at the entrance door and follow the industrial engineered system that is the cycle and inheritance of Taylorism. They vote, they are members of their school boards, they know their congressmen, the bank welcomes them when they deposit or when they take out a loan for a mortgage, and they do not want to be told any longer exactly what to do, how many to do, and when to do it. They are now fully educated and fully adult and the society that is being turned out is more so everyday so we have to scramble to get our views multidimensional. That's not to say that profit no longer continues to be important but if you take care of people, people will take care of the organization. In the last analysis, people is all we have and, therefore, quality of work life is a tremendous commitment, a declaration of faith in people. They cannot be considered the means, but if considered the ends in themselves and informed about the requirements of the situation in which they find themselves, people will act responsibly. That is the charter of quality of work life and if we are wrong about that we are also wrong about democracy itself.

CHAPTER 4

Labor's View of Quality of Working Life Programs

*Jerry Wurf**

Many years ago the American Federation of Labor established an internal committee on ethical practices and a union president who was appointed to serve on that committee ran into John L. Lewis, who was then the leader and the moving spirit of what was the rival CIO. He told John Lewis about the honor that had been conferred upon him and John Lewis' response to this information was "Let me know if you find any ethical practices."

I must confess that I take even a dimmer view of the ethics of the business community than even John L. Lewis took of the ethics of labor. The ethics of the American labor movement leave much to be desired. The ethics of most of the power institutions in our society leave much to be desired. But I must say the real dynamics, the real pressures, the real pacesetters are in the business community.

As a representative of public employees, I marvel at how corporate America has achieved a public relations coup that is so impressive. Big business has convinced a remarkable percentage of the American people that private industry is more productive, more efficient, more

*International President, American Federation of State, County, and Municipal Employees

accountable, more ethical, and more reasonable than is the public sector of the society.

There are signs, however, that a measure of distress with the behavior of private enterprise is beginning to develop among the American people. I might point out that 1979 was hardly a banner year for corporate America. It was a privately owned electric utility whose nuclear reactor almost melted down near Harrisburg, Pennsylvania. It was a privately owned Virginia power company that is giving up its ability to use nuclear energy because it was trying to save and cheat when it developed its nuclear reactors in that place. It was a private airline company's DC-10 airplane, manufactured by a private sector aerospace company, that crashed in Chicago. It was a private automobile company, Chrysler, that has been appealing for a federal bailout because of managerial ineptness. That, incidentally, was identified by Douglas Frazer, then vice president of the Auto Workers Union, years ago, when he said that that company was going down the tubes because they didn't even know how to run a candy store.

I could go on and on about the fact that my wife, driving an automobile with a Firestone tire from Washington to a house we own on the Cape, had a tire blow. Happily it was a back wheel and not a front wheel, and my family survived the accident. I could tell you about the hazardous products, carcinogenic drugs, carcinogenic foods, the total irresponsibility that permeates the product sectors in pursuit of a fast buck. There's a company named Allied Chemical that, knowing it was producing something so hazardous that it set up a dummy corporation to produce it, has poisoned the James River into our children's children's lifetime. It has caused damage that physicians, hospitals, and the National Institute of Health have yet to measure reasonably. During the crisis of Three Mile Island, the people of Harrisburg were desperately eager for honest, accurate information about what was happening there. It was very clear from our membership, who are residents of that area, that they totally ignored the words that they heard and the information that they got from the experts representing the utility company. The only responsible voice that they listened to and depended upon was the government and the government experts.

I know that you've asked me here to address myself to quality of work life programs and not to discuss the sorry state of business morality, but, unfortunately, they are inseparable. Michael Maccoby and I sometimes agree, but I sometimes think he's a little bit too optimistic even when he's being a little bit sharp and criticizing.

Work life doesn't exist in a vacuum. It's impossible to discuss the quality of work life in a vacuum. You have to mention priorities, and the priority of business is profit. Unfortunately, that's what dictates most of the behavior of private industry. The tragedy is that they operate that way even when it's counterproductive to their own self-interest. As workers, as consumers and as taxpayers, we are well aware that the activities of private industry are determined by concerns other than ethical or altruistic principles.

Workers organize unions in this country to have the collective strength to challenge their employers and to resist the imposition of substandard wages and working conditions. We have going in this American society something that exists in no other free society. The labor movement is not an extension of a political party, of a social philosophy, or an economic philosophy that's hostile to the free enterprise system. American trade unions are probably the strongest advocates of capitalism in this society. Yet, we have had a labor relations history in the United States—in spite of the fact that we don't have the kind of class warfare that often predominates in other Western societies—that's been as bloody and cruel as if we had been a social democratic labor movement struggling with a Christian democratic, capitalist, communist, or neofascist organization. And this often violent history has taken place not only on the picket line, but also in the halls of Congress and in state legislatures throughout the land. It's interesting that in this society where the labor unions say that they'll work with the system, they'll accept the system, even admire it, that the bosses kick so hard and resistance is so fierce.

What the academicians call the quality of working life, we in the labor movement are very likely to call wages, hours, and working conditions. We may not be speaking exactly the same language, but I suspect we're talking about the same thing. The fact is that unions have done more than any other institution in our society to improve the quality of working life for everyone.

We have taken important steps towards eliminating some of the worst indecencies of industrial life by winning such basic guarantees as the forty-hour work week, minimum wage laws, and safe conditions in the workplace. We have never been totally successful. We've never made it as it ought to be. Need I remind you that corporate America has fought us every inch of the way? Nevertheless, business as well as labor has benefited from economic reasonableness and the social amenities that provide working people with adequate purchasing power, leisure time, and the feeling that they have a stake in the system. Through the collective bargaining process, which is essentially an adversary system, working people and their unions have improved the quality of work life in the workplace and throughout society.

We have won other gains in the political arena, but there, too, we have usually faced bitter opposition of the business community. So far

I have been referring to labor relations in the private sector, but as an officer of a union of public employees, I tell you that labor relations in state and local government are also adversary relationships. It's a hard, cold fact that public sector labor relations are meaner, more irresponsible, tougher, and less accountable than those in the private sector.

The bosses our union faces at the bargaining table—state and local government officials—are not for the most part motivated by a concern with simple profit. These public officials are caught up in an equally brutal imperative—their search for political advantage. They impose this concern upon the governments they administer and upon the employees they supervise. I must tell you that public sector workers are as exploited, misused, abused, and are as blatantly mistreated as their private sector counterparts, contrary to all those editorials you read in the *Boston Globe*.

Indeed, public employees have one major disadvantage when compared to workers in private industry. Public employees are not covered by the national legislation (referred to as the National Labor Relations Act) that gives a small measure of reasonableness to the employer/employee relationship. Public employees are generally excluded from federal protections that give them the right to bargain collectively, to be paid at least a minimum wage, and time-and-a-half for overtime, and to occupational health and safety, for example.

I am speaking against the myth that public employees occupy a special station. Almost everything that our union has achieved we have achieved in spite of the inadequacy and the hostility of the legal mechanisms that workers in every democratic society should have access to. In truth, our union exists to protect the public employee from exploitation and from politics and politicians, just as unions in private industry exist to protect their members from abuse in the pursuit of profit.

I must keep stressing the adversary nature of labor relations. We grapple with employers not only for bread and butter, but also for that very crucial ingredient that every human being is entitled to—dignity. With the collective strength of a union, workers are freed from the indignity of being subject to the whims of a boss and often find it possible to speak up to those who have an access to power that they would use to deprive our people of that very essential quality that I talked about.

Let me summarize my views on quality of work life programs. I'm skeptical of any employer, in government or private industry, who states that he's motivated entirely or in part by the quality of his employees' work life. I don't mean that all employers are bad people, but

I do believe, and I have experienced in the long years that I've represented workers, that essentially employers are caught up—both in the private and public sectors—in the harsh imperatives of profit or politics. I doubt that there can be any permanent, meaningful, or dignifying improvements in the quality of work life in an industrial or governmental environment where workers do not enjoy the protections of unions to represent them in the collective bargaining process and to give them a mechanism for dealing with their day-to-day grievances.

Further, I want to make it absolutely clear that a particular employer who is humane does not necessarily mean we're dealing with humaneness. If a particular employer, like J.P. Stevens, defies the law and embodies unreasonableness, that, too, is atypical. But talking about the broad level of what pervades this American system, we're dealing with a measure of meanness, pragmatism and rationalization of that pragmatism that makes life very uncomfortable for American workers. I must emphasize that joint labor management efforts to improve the quality of work life can only be beneficial if these programs respect the workings of the collective bargaining process. They must provide workers with ample opportunities to voice their concerns, make proposals, and deal with their employers with a measure of equality.

American labor unions have been labeled, unfairly or fairly, as uninterested in the quality of work life programs. But the labor movement is aware that there is much room for improving the quality of workers' lives on the job—from the assembly line to the typing pool.

Leaders of AFSCME, at every level, are sensitive to the aspirations of public service employees, from hospital workers to social workers, from laborers to city planners, and from correctional officers to day care workers. We want to make it possible that the eight hours spent on the job are fulfilling and fruitful. But unionists are justifiably skeptical of quality of work life programs that management attempts to impose unilaterally or to hustle workers into accepting. Very often these programs are nothing more than speed-up or union-busting masquerading in the disguise of trendy social science.

Maybe it's because most public officials are not regular readers of the *Harvard Business Review,* but our union has not had extensive experience with management offering to institute quality of work life programs that will actually benefit workers. More often we deal with more ballyhooed management initiative to increase workers' productivity. (Productivity is becoming a kind of religion in America. Some day we'll have to deal with it rationally.) Sometimes also under the guise of boosting workers' job satisfaction as well, the directives in the economy are distorted. How much indignation can be worked up by the abuse of coffee time in a plant or in an office. Measure that against how little indignation takes place while some guys in Texas or Iran are holding back energy from this society so that they can double, triple, or quadruple their profits. One is considered good business; the other is considered a lack of work ethic, or not enough concern for the well-being of the society.

In the city of Detroit a plan has evolved into a controversial failure that is being discarded by a joint agreement between the union and management, although under the terms of the contract management could go on if it so desired. The city government initiated a "one-man packer" system under which sanitation workers would supposedly receive greater financial incentives for increased productivity. The only problem was that the system didn't work. Piece-work pay systems proved as unworkable, abhorrent, and counterproductive to workers who were vulnerable to management manipulation in the Detroit Sanitation Department as incentive pay was abhorrent to auto workers in Detroit generations ago.

In some state and local governments, AFSCME is willing to work with management to devise quality of work life programs, but we're not holding our breath waiting for management to take the initiative. Meanwhile, our union's entire effort to represent our members equitably in collective bargaining could be considered a program to impose the quality of working life. Our contracts provide more than just bread and butter—for example, when we negotiate controls upon social workers' caseload sizes and safer and more secure conditions for prison guards—not only for the correctional officers, but for the inmates as well. We have staffing standards that we find very difficult to get agreement on except for the professionals in the field of public hospitals and facilities for the mentally ill. We want to impose the quality of work life for those people whom we serve. In addition, our contracts provide for career ladders for blue-collar, service and maintenance, clerical, and paraprofessional employees to move up into what have been considered more highly skilled occupations.

Our contracts provide educational programs and other special programs for professional employees who also face their own discontents on the job. We want labor-management committees that will deal with problems before they become confrontations and conflicts. As often as not we find that management at the agency or institutional level is willing to listen and to work with the employees to try to solve problems.

When hospital staffing levels improve, when social workers can treat their clients with dignity, or when a correctional facility becomes secure, the taxpaying public benefits, too. We're not only rather proud of that, but we think that it's necessary in this Proposition 13 environment in which we are now functioning. I suspect also that when workers in private industry, just like workers in public service, work under more reasonable and decent conditions, they produce better goods and provide better services. Asked how to enrich workers' lives on the job, a labor leader once replied, "Enrich their paychecks." I must say I disagree because that's only one part of the solution to the real problems of workers' dissatisfaction.

A man I know, Leonard Woodcock, who sort of retired from doing battle with General Motors and Ford to the easier task of representing the United States as its Ambassador to the People's Republic of China, once pointed out with some irritation, although very empathetically, that how in God's name could he change the nature of the production of automobiles in an environment of unreasonableness. He was sick and tired of discussions of this kind; what he had to do, he felt, was to fight for compensation. I think those who know Leonard would say that he is not a simplistic, uncomplicated person. He is one of the most educated men—whatever definition you use for the word education— that I've ever known, and one of the most sensitive men, too. But with the nature of the system of production in manufacturing facilities that we have in the United States as such, the best you can get is a few more bucks.

The problem of dissatisfaction in the workplace cannot be solved by programs imposed by management out of a sense of "noblesse oblige," nor will the problem be solved by intricate and utopian schemes concocted by social scientists or self-styled management experts. The best quality of work life program is still the system of free collective bargaining which offers workers a mechanism for telling the boss that conditions are changing, that the relationship must change, and that working relationships can be made decent only by bilateral discussions and by bilateral agreement. The mission of our union and the mission of all unions remains the task of articulating our members' demands for better working conditions and making sure that these demands are translated into tangible improvements.

Discussion

Question: I'd like you to comment more on this area of the use of force and power. Am I understanding you correctly that there is no hope for social or ethical change or quality of working life improvements except by the process of adversarial relationships and head-to-head power confrontations?

Wurf: There is kind of a subtle philosophical contradiction in your question. Fundamentally, relationships in a democratic society must be adversary relationships. We don't depend upon reasonableness at the workplace or reasonableness from our landlord, or shopkeeper, or tax collector simply out of the purity of his motivation. We don't live in that kind of utopian society. So the way we achieve reasonableness in the kind of society we live in is to have an adversary relationship—adversary meaning that men and women who have differences of opinions have a mechanism that is rational for solving that difference.

It seems to me that that is the essence of much that goes on in a democratic society. If the system works well, then that on which we have disagreed we find solutions to. Sometimes we find these solutions simplistically and uncomplicatedly, although heatedly, at the bargaining table. At other times, we have to resort to a strike as a trade union. Other times in the international community, they sort of play fun and games with treaties and agreements at the United Nations and other times they drop bombs on each other. What I'm really saying is that I like to think that we're all going to solve our problems without confrontations and conflicts, but the only way in which we can solve them justly is by giving both sides equality in the adversary relationship.

Question: Granted, I accept everything you have said about the worker in America and perhaps that which you've been too delicate to say. Granted, I accept that all quality of working life programs will take place in a union and management setting, but we've now come to a position where some of the time, whatever the intent of management is, it becomes possible to develop a program that will in the long run profit the worker in all areas of his life. However, unions seem to have the fear of quality of working life programs such that if I, as the union, give into this you'll want more productivity from me, which I see as being a concern with profit, or I, as the union, will lose my power if this occurs. How do you view this? And do you on the national level do anything to cool that attitude down? You yourself just said that there is a need now for change in the way that we operate, but don't you think that this change has got to come from some of these "old-line unions" as well as from management?

Wurf: Let me start off by saying to you that not too many years ago I was the "boy wonder" of the executive council of the AFL-CIO and now I'm one of its oldest members. So the old men that dominate labor are much younger than they used to be. We old, mired, limited-resource people are not as bad as you think we are. Much has not changed on the attitudes of trade unions for a very simple reason. If you're Murray Finley and you are president of the Textile Workers union, you know that a worker in a textile plant is treated with a measure of meanness that can't be equalled in any other society in this world. He'll get lung disease and die. Even in capitalist Hollywood, they produced a picture about a textile organization. I wonder how many of you know that after the happy ending in which the young woman organized the textile mill, she will spend ten or fifteen years in a frustrated fashion because the J.P. Stevens Company will frustrate what has been the policy of this country for over forty years and the law of this country for over forty years.

If you're a representative of the Oil, Chemical and Atomic Workers of the United States, you know that a third of your membership are subject to carcinogenic substances every day of the week and we have reached the stage, we old-line unionists, that we have a lot of trouble with our rank and file. For example, in Syracuse, New York, General Electric knew that the electric company has been poisoning the Hudson River, poisoning the environment, and poisoning, destroying, and jeopardizing the workers of that plant. A rather left-wing union, a product of the old left in the CIO that still dominates the work force in that plant, refuses government intervention to protect their lives because they are so fearful of the economic dislocation that would come about if General Electric would shut down the plant because it didn't want to be bothered with cleaning up the environment.

There's a company named Hooker Chemical that has plants all over the United States. You don't go to Niagara Falls for a honeymoon; you go for cancer. They have literally destroyed everything around them. I won't talk about what happens to the workers. Every once in a while very sensitive TV stations run a story about some workers who don't dare produce children or who can't produce children.

Perhaps to get to the root of your question, what happens is that a union in an effort to protect its constituency becomes a silent partner of an unreasonable employer at the expense of the rest of the community. What I'm saying to you is that us old-line labor leaders may be old-line, but those new-line labor/management consultants are much more effective in destroying the quality of work life for American workers than were the plug-uglies who were hired to kill people by the Republic Steel Corporation forty or fifty years ago. I would also like to end a discussion like this by pointing out that the principle character in *The Godfather* tells one of his sons what a fool he is not to get an education. It's much easier to steal and rob with a leather briefcase than with a loaded .45. That's the bottom line on what's wrong with the American labor movement, what's wrong with America today and the quality of work life programs which deal with esoteric social dynamics that aren't a reality.

Maccoby: I think that by sweeping a huge sword over everything in all activities, you do a disservice to people in your own union who are pioneers in developing new approaches to change which are based on a combination of both strong adversarial relations and the ability to develop cooperative relations along side of them. I'm personally working with an AFSCME local with people who I think have shown real dedication, willingness to learn and to struggle with democracy, and who have themselves tried to develop things that are never going to be developed unilaterally by management or within the government and they need support and help. I think that one must distinguish the nature of management in business just as one must not treat all labor union leaders as though they're the same and have the same viewpoint. I can say also to you in contrast to the AFSCME group that I worked with, I can point to another instance in which I discussed the program with a union in a factory and they said to me, "Look, you are a nice guy, but don't give us any aggravation. We don't want the workers speaking up. We take care of them. If the bosses want something they come to us and if the workers start having a say and start talking up, we're just going to have trouble." That exists too. If you were to say the majority of the world is the way you describe it, I would agree with you. I also think you do a disservice to your own experience and knowledge to lump all of social science in the same box. One of the major difficulties with social science has been that it has perpetrated an attitude as though it were value free when in fact it has often served power. What we need is a social science that's committed to values, that stands up for principles, that does not cooperate with things that are against those principles and we need leaders like you who can support that kind of development of social science and can point out the difference between programs which are honest union/management joint programs, such as are going on with the UAW and AFSCME, and those that are shams amd manipulations. Unless leaders make those distinctions, what's going to happen is you're going to have the same polarization so that the business side which doesn't want to cooperate with unions and people can just say, "Look, even our own leaders say these things are no good so why are you asking us to do things that are cooperative?"

Wurf: I think it is the pervasive, ongoing problem that we face everyday. I talked and explained that we have joint committees. I talked about the fact that we push this into our contracts in addition to wages, hours, and working conditions. I also pointed out that there are social scientists who just really are not worth their salt and there are social scientists who I respect. You happen to be among those I respect who are doing very credible and useful work. We've always encouraged you to come in. We have never imposed any pulls and tugs on you. You have never found any struggle with us over power or input or anything like that. Now, you might find a local leader with enough power that a phone call to management will end a particular problem, but not very often. The truth is that there are phony, self-styled management experts who really are trying to find mechanisms to avoid unions or distort the mission of unions. Secondly, we believe in joint committees to improve the qualtiy of the workplace, and improving the quality of the workplace for AFSCME members generally means we are improving the quality of the workplace for lots of people who perhaps are not even members of AFSCME or any other union.

What I was really getting at is that that can only be achieved when we have been able to develop a collective bargaining agreement with the boss. The bottom line on what I'm saying is not to attack or denigrate your work. I don't always agree with your utopian view of some of the employers we deal with, but, nevertheless, I'm willing to go along so long as we have the protection of collective bargaining agreements.

Fundamentally, I am expressing personal cynicism. I am not attacking bilateral mechanisms to enhance the quality of work, and I don't think you have had any trouble getting cooperation from us, nor will you ever have as long as I'm president of the union.

Question: Even if one were to grant the picture that you paint of the management posture, how do you deal with an equally real concern of many people that unionism does not manifest a genuine concern for the common good, but rather represents another set of its own special interests. (When, for example, unionism can be accused of racism, when it can be accused of energetically supporting the Vietnam War, when it can energetically support the continued use of throw away bottles and cans, and when it can energetically support the continuance of funds for highway construction in the face of attempts to channel some of this money into mass transit.) What I'm suggesting is, is it really a white hat versus black hat kind of situation, or don't you have a very considerable dose of selfishness on both sides of the question?

Wurf: First of all, I was very frequently the single person of the executive council of the AFL-CIO that opposed the Vietnam War. I think the disservice that the American labor movement did was wrong. I think the fact that labor unions have to fight against rational laws dealing with bottles and cans is because we live in a society that would put the workers that produce redundant bottles and cans out of work and on to welfare rolls because we don't provide alternatives for families to live reasonably.

I can't get terribly angry with building construction workers when they push for development of highways so that they can create work for their members so that the fantastic unemployment that existed in this very state among building construction workers can be alleviated. Perhaps, and most importantly of all, this burden that you put upon a labor union to be the deciding mechanism on what is purely a managerial function, except as it affects a worker's input into production, is absurd. I would say to you that much that the American labor movement has done has been counterproductive. I would say to you that I have been appalled, and mentioned in my speech clearly, that we have been guilty of racism. I am saying to you, as one who has been an outspoken critic of the shortcomings of the American labor movement, that conditions there have improved considerably.

But in talking about the quality of the society, you may recall that in my earlier remarks I mentioned that the society is bad, and essentially the institutions in this society are out to satisfy most only the simplistic pragmatic needs. Frequently, the labor union becomes a partner in protecting its constituency which is married to that pragmatic piece of society, or that pragmatic fragment of that piece of society, in countersocial activity.

I remember during the Vietnam War, I marched in every march. I made every speech. I became an enigma to my colleagues, and distressed even our membership. What I'm saying to you is that we in the trade union movement should be, but frequently are not, better than the rest of the population; sometimes we're worse. But the point that I made in my speech was that those who have real power in this society come down on workers who resist them with a fierceness and a meanness unknown in any other industrial society—even though those same workers are willing to support this economic system and a reasonable amount of profit for employers. What I'm saying to you in a very painful way is that we in the labor movement are paying for our sins, and we will continue to pay for our sins, but those sins are the product of those who have the most clout in this society, namely business and industry.

Question: When talking of the quality of working life, why not think in terms of unions and neighborhoods working cooperatively to (1) make the neighborhood a safer place, and (2) also to make the work of the policemen a more pleasant and more fulfilling job?

Wurf: I think that there should be collaboration between neighborhood groups and police. I am afraid of a kind of semivigilanteeism developing in America. We've had some bad experiences in our history with that, but I think fundamentally that there aren't enough cops and there aren't enough civic groups to assist those cops to deal with the kind of street crime that makes neighborhoods unsafe. The thing that makes neighborhoods safe is giving people availability to jobs, giving people alternatives to stealing, giving people the opportunity to work productively.

In Washington, white folks, 25 percent of the population, are firmly convinced that the blacks won't work. Well, last winter we had a lot of snow in Washington and the commuter railway advertised jobs at $5 an hour and all these unwilling-to-work black folks had a riot to get a couple of days work at $5 an hour. Certainly there should be cooperation, certainly we should work with the police force, certainly we should give policemen a more reasonable existence, and give communities a more rational opportunity to function, but again we've got to have a society that says those who are able to work should be able to work. We even passed a law to that effect not too long ago.

Question: I am interested in the issue of power because it seems to me that the weapons of power are always double-edged. In the case of the unions, the growth that is necessary to have some clout and the expertise that is necessary to be able to deal with management inevitably create a distance between the people who bargain and the people who are being bargained for, and that same indifference is part of the problem. It seems to me that the unions are finding ways to overcome the gap between the leadership and the members and that these devices will be useful in management. I am interested in what you have to say about ways of keeping in touch with the workers when you are dealing with hundreds of thousands of people.

Wurf: I would like to say that in a union such as AFSCME, there is a great deal of autonomy for our local and regional units. And, in fact, in the thirty years that I have been a member of the union, there is more and increasing sensitivity to the constituency now than there has ever been before. I would say this is a fact across-the-board for any union. There's an important reason for this fact, which is to a degree premised on a theory developed by a University of Wisconsin labor relations economist. That professor, in his theory of the American labor movement, talked about the power of the American union—meaning for power, the control of work. But, recent developments in trade unions have been such that that kind of power is diminishing. For many unions—certainly those in the public sector where officials never had control over the hiring process—that was never the case. But, by and large, for union leaders to be elected, they must be sensitive to their members' needs and concerns.

There is outrage in the business community. I think there is a lot less outrage in the trade union movement, but any outrage is intolerable. I do think there is better communication, and I think there is more sensitivity. Is it adequate? Is it enough? No!

Last night at a local union in New York City which has 13,000 members and which is in deep difficulty, we had a meeting and only 250 people showed up. We provide all kinds of incentives to bring out people to the meetings and we have great difficulty. We live in a society where only 40 percent of the electorate gets itself involved in electing the Congress and then complains about how irrational Congress is. We live in a society where no more than 50 percent are involved in the election of the president, and then criticize their president, who is elected by 28 percent of the people of the United States; and they wonder why he isn't concerned with the other 72 percent. So, I'm saying to you that what is wrong with many institutions in America is also wrong with the trade union movement.

CHAPTER 5

Affirmative Action and Equal Opportunity Employment

Affirmative Action and the Progress of Women in the American Work Force

*Vivian Buckles**

The Women's Bureau, in case some of you haven't heard of us, is a small organization created by Congress in 1920 and established in the U.S. Department of Labor to help working women. Women from throughout New England call in or drop into my office daily to discuss their problems—many of which have to do with discrimination. And the Women's Bureau in the National Office conducts substantial research on the status of women and on their work related problems.

What we see is not encouraging. Eighty percent of all women workers are still clustered in the low paying, traditional women's jobs averaging no more than $8600 a year (compared with men's $14,600). There is still a 59 percent earnings gap between men's and women's pay and women account for only 2.3 percent of those earning $25,000 a year or more. So it's obvious women have not yet arrived at equal employment opportunity in this country.

The Women's Bureau is heavily involved with low income and disadvantaged women and this perhaps colors my viewpoint. We are trying to improve their labor market skills so that they can compete successfully for jobs that will pay them enough to support their fami-

*Regional Administrator, Women's Bureau, U.S. Department of Labor, Region I

lies and allow them to go off welfare. They cannot do this on a minimum wage job.

These women have no equality. They represent, more than any other group of women in this country, the effects of society's thinking about "woman's place." They have been conditioned to rely on a man for their economic support, and when they are left alone for whatever reason, most of them have no choice but to go on welfare—especially if they have small children or if they are past forty years of age and have not worked outside the home in many years.

The facts about poor women are startling. I don't think people in our country are fully aware of them. More than *75 percent* of the population who live below the federal poverty line are women and children. More than 90 percent of the current AFDC recipients are women and children. More than three million women receive AFDC payments compared to only 70,000 men.

A recent Labor Department study shows that there are more than 2.8 million displaced homemakers in the United States (there are more than 189,000 in New England.) These are older women, left alone, who have never worked outside the home and, therefore, have few, if any, labor market skills. They are too old to receive AFDC benefits and too young for Social Security. A large number of them have no means of support. For these women to get a job and become productive citizens instead of a tax burden they must first receive special counseling and pretraining to build up their self-confidence and basic skills.

One of the reasons for the wide earnings gap between men's and women's pay is the type of jobs women hold. Two-fifths of all women are employed in only ten occupations. Primarily women work in the low-paying traditional "women's labor market" as secretaries, typists, clerks, waitresses, bookkeepers, registered nurses, elementary school teachers, retail sales clerks, sewers, and stitchers. All are relatively low-paying jobs. We hear a lot about the enormous increase of women in the workforce. It's true. Women represent two-thirds of the labor market growth since World War II but this is not necessarily progress. It is doing little more than increasing the size of those traditional occupations; we just have more women clerks now than ever before.

Bare bones stereotyping keeps women out of good jobs. We learn early on that women are supposed to do "this" and men are supposed to do "that," and what men are supposed to do pays better, provides more challenge, and greater upper mobility. I asked my dentist last week if he had ever hired a male dental assistant. He looked at me in surprise and answered, "There aren't any." Well, women make up only 3 percent of the dentists. Dentists earn on an average $40,000 a year while a dental assistant earns only $9,100. This is an example of the economics of sex stereotyping in action.

Women are socialized rigorously in our society to accept these lesser roles regardless of their traits, and to be content with lesser jobs with lesser pay in the workplace. It's difficult for women to break out of this mold. I'm sure everyone is aware of the controversy, and sometimes almost hysteria, surrounding women's entrance into traditional male dominated fields such as construction work, mining, and upper level management.

What's the role of equal employment opportunity (EEO) laws and affirmative action in all this? Are *they* improving women's position in the workforce? I think they are, a little, for some women.

There's no question that women are making more progress today than ever before and are moving ahead slowly into better positions, but not to the extent that meaningful changes can be measured. For example, in 1962 women were less than 3 percent of the lawyers and judges; today they are 9 percent. They moved from 1 percent of the engineers to 3 percent; from 12 percent of the economists to 23 percent; and from 4/5ths of 1 percent of the carpenters to a full 1 percent. It's in these blue collar jobs that women are making the least progress. In 1962, women made up such a small percentage of the skilled trades work force that they didn't even show up on the statistical tables. Today we are beginning to see figures, although most still average around 1 percent.

Women are probably making the most progress in mid management positions—where they make up about 5 percent of this work force. Some firms are aggressively recruiting female business managers and women are being hired in the financial departments of many large corporations, banks, and insurance companies. However, women are still too far down the pipeline to be reached for top management posts. In 1975, women comprised only 15 of the 2,500 presidents of large companies.

I can tell from the many calls we receive that individual women are becoming more aware of their rights and are more willing to fight for them. We also receive a number of calls from irate husbands about their wives being discriminated against and seeking information on ways they can help them fight. Currently pregnancy rights are a big issue. The Women's Bureau has prepared a handy little booklet called, "A Working Woman's Guide to Her Job Rights," which we disseminate widely.

Women in the past have made the most progress under these laws when they have come together as a group and filed a class action suit with an advocacy group to sponsor them, such as in the American Telephone and Telegraph (AT&T) $60 million case.

Today AT&T is in the forefront in placing women and men in all job categories throughout the organization; 10,000 women are in craft jobs and one-third of their managers are women. But they still have no women in the four higher levels of management.

I think cases like this have made other companies aware of the seriousness of these laws and have prompted them to improve their EEO posture—which is great because once talented women are promoted they will be able to show how capable and efficient they are and will pave the way for other women.

Women make up 20–25 percent of the business graduates today so they are seeing themselves more and more in business roles. But there are still many societal problems to overcome: men have trouble perceiving women as peers and bosses and the majority of officials reject the notion they should hire a woman, however competent, if a competent male is available.

The federal government has recently taken some important steps to strengthen EEO. The Labor Department issued two new regulations last year to help move more women into apprenticeship and construction work, areas that have been traditionally closed to women. And we established specific goals and timetables to bring this about.

There has been a consolidation of some of the scattered programs which enforce EEO laws. The Office of Federal Contract Compliance, which enforces EEO and affirmative action for women and minorities on federal contract work, has been reorganized to bring all compliance under the Labor Department. It was scattered among all the many contracting agencies. OFCC is establishing a network of local offices across the country to receive complaints on discrimination and also to provide assistance to Federal contractors.

The new CETA legislation passed last year is especially favorable to women, as well as it should be, since women represent 68 percent of the poor and 40 percent of the unemployed. It refers to the elimination of jobs and the need for upward mobility. It also speaks about supportive services, such as day care, part-time arrangements, and flexihours, all programs which women vitally need to be successful in the workforce.

Another important action favorable to women is the recent Presidential Executive Order that created a national women's business enterprise policy to aid women-owned businesses.

All of this is encouraging. But I don't want to end on a positive note—not as long as the earnings gap is so wide between women's and men's pay, and not as long as three-fourths of the female labor force remains in the lower segments of the labor market. I realize, however, that solving the equality problems also involves unsocializing and debrainwashing women, making us more aware of our options.

But more important, I think, is getting word to young girls about the realities of life. They must be made to realize that even though they may become wives and mothers, nine out of every ten of them will still work outside the home for most of their lives. This is the time of the dual income family. The "Dick and Jane" family model with Mom at home in her apron with Spot and the white picket fence is a thing of the past.

Young girls must be encouraged to study proper subjects, such as math, so that when they reach college they do not have to opt for liberal arts. We have a lot of college educated clerks today. The Equal Employment Opportunity Commission estimates that one in every five women college graduates is working in a clerical position because she has a liberal arts education and no marketable skills.

I think for women to reach equal employment opportunity that affirmative action's laws have to be enforced and attitudes have to change. Job segregation has to go, so that there are no "men's jobs" and "women's jobs," and sex is not an occupational liability.

Affirmative Action in a Declining Economy

Marlene Gerber Fried*

As Vivian Buckles has argued—and her claims are supported by virtually every statistic imaginable—women and minorities continue to suffer from discrimination. Despite the facts, however, it is now popularly believed that women and minorities are being recruited to positions from which they have traditionally been excluded. Indeed, it is believed that this recruitment is at the expense of the white male population. It is common to hear that "reverse discrimination" has become perhaps as serious a social problem as discrimination against women and minorities was in the past. This belief, and the feelings of resentment that accompany it, crystalized in the public debate around the Bakke case. It is evident to anyone who discusses the issues of affirmative action with any group: especially with those who are about to enter the job market.

While there is no doubt about genuine cases of reverse discrimination—hiring an unqualified person solely on the basis of sex or race—and while I also know that there is great personal pain involved in such cases, all the statistics tell us that reverse discrimination is not a problem. Instead every indication points to the existence of tokenism: a few women and/or minorities being placed in highly visible positions

*Associate Professor of Philosophy, Bentley College

in industry, education, or government while the position of the vast majority of women and minorities remains the same or worsens.

Given all of this, I take there to be two basic questions: 1) Why does the belief in reverse discrimination exist and why is it so pervasive? and, 2) Why hasn't affirmative action produced more significant improvements?

On question number one: the demands of women and minorities for equal access to jobs and education has coincided with economic hard times—recession, runaway inflation, rising unemployment, shortages of basic necessities, and large-scale layoffs. These economic conditions have affected different groups in different ways: for many people it has meant increasing difficulty just surviving each month—difficulty in paying the bills for basic necessities like food, shelter, and health.

For others of us, the issue is one of thwarted expectations: sectors of the population not previously affected by downturns in the economy have been so affected. Professionals find themselves in the position of having invested a great deal of resources and efforts in their training only to discover the no jobs comparable to that training await them (academics is a good example of this).

We are all in competition for an ever shrinking pie and Affirmative Action has been one of the scapegoats of this situation. White males are told that they are not getting jobs because women and minorities are taking them away while women and minorities are told that this is not a good time to press their demands. Increased opportunities for women and minorities are not responsible for the current economic conditions: in fact, they (women and minorities) are the first people to suffer the consequences and the least able to afford it.

The problem is one of economic scarcity, not the promotion of un-qualified over qualified people. There are simply too many qualified people for available positions. (In the recent Weber case, only six slots had been set aside for blacks to be trainees in the skilled trades while 46 percent of the surrounding community is black. Obviously this situation produces fierce competition and it is clear from the outset that many qualified people will not be given a chance.)

What I have been describing is a situation of diminished opportunity. This situation is at variance with the picture of America that we all grew up with as the land of opportunity where opportunities were there for the taking. Money, connections, noble birth, and social standing were all to be irrelevant factors—rather, individual effort and ability were to be the determinants. It was up to the individual.

But now this sort of opportunity does not exist in America—whether it ever did will be left aside here. A career in law, accounting, medicine, or teaching is not available to someone simply because he or she has the desire, capabilities, and willingness to exert the necessary effort. What is available is the opportunity to compete with others who also have the desire, capabilities, and willingness to exert the effort for a limited number of jobs and places in professional schools. And this number is substantially smaller than the number of people who want and have the ability for them.

The point is not just that there are many people who would want to be lawyers or accountants and are unable to do so because of the limited number of places. But rather, that many of these people would actually be competent lawyers and teachers if they were given the real opportunity to acquire the qualifications. Their hopes are vain not because they lack ability but because our society does not provide a sufficient number of these jobs. So, in a real sense, our society is not providing opportunities. Into this already diminished sense of opportunity women and minorities are at a competitive disadvantage in many areas. While the law may not legitimize this unequal treatment, the practices of businesses, unions, and professional schools still favor white males.

Our beliefs in genuine equality of opportunity (which, I have argued, does not exist) blinds us to these realities and makes affirmative action an easy scapegoat. And those who benefit push this idea. We need to give more thought to who is benefiting from our attention being diverted from the real problem and we also need to avoid the trap of allowing ourselves to be divided by the competition.

On question number 2, all of this suggests some answers to my second question: why hasn't affirmative action been more successful? It implies that economic conditions seriously constrain what can be accomplished through Affirmative Action. In the absence of expanding economic opportunities Affirmative Action is doomed—it will only exacerbate the divisions that already exist in the society between races and sexes, and worse, it provides employers with new legitimacy for discriminating. Affirmative action programs are primarily procedural, that is, they aim at securing good procedures on the assumption that discrimination is only possible if we have methods of selection in hiring decisions which enable prejudiced individuals to have power to implement their biases. So the solution is to create better methods: watchdog agencies are set up to insure fairness. This excessively bureaucratic notion of equality is one which the facts show does not work. But it enables many people to believe that we have achieved justice and all that remains is to allow the passage of time to correct the evils of the past. It blinds us to the continuation of discrimination at both the institutional and individual level and makes plausible the claim that present inequalities are only hangovers from past denial of opportunity: we only have to wait for women and minorities to become qualified. Notice, too, how this leads to a view of reverse discrimination: once fair procedures are operating, giving preference through Affirmative Action to those who have been discriminated against in the past, goals or quotas seem at best unnecessary, and at worst as unjustified reverse discrimination.

The procedures are inadequate for two basic reasons. The first is that they are not being administered in a situation of good will. The underlying biases against women and minorities have not been eradicated they have only taken new form. The mere fact that the popular understanding of affirmative action is hiring the unqualified is ample evidence of this.

Most often those institutions which are pursuing affirmative action plans do not believe that they have ever discriminated—they point the finger elsewhere: at the schools. And within businesses and educational institutions those offices which are charged with administering affirmative action are part of the administration against which claims of discrimination are being made.

The fact that those who have been discriminated against have recourse to the courts is in most cases irrelevant since court cases are costly burdens: ones which most individuals cannot afford to bear while most institutions have the resources to deal with it. The second reason is, more fundamentally, the approach itself is too limited. The demand for equality of opportunity must be linked to an analysis of the inadequacies of the opportunities which currently exist. And sexual and racial inequality must be challenged on all fronts so that the deep causes of inequality at the workplace can be changed.

Chapter 5C

_____

Affirmative Action as a Human Resource Tool

As a representative of the National Association for the Advancement of Colored People, and as an engineer and businessman, I would like to approach this entire issue of affirmative action from the point of view of a businessman and an optimist; one who has an understanding of the real world issue that we are facing, and who wants to try to design a system to meet those issues as they really exist. Because I am a member of a minority community, I have had an opportunity to spend many years looking at the system and seeing how the system has been designed to protect those who control it. Once you learn how the system works to protect those who are in control, you realize either how to penetrate the system or how to modify it so that it truly will serve the people it is supposed to serve.

We look at the many problems in this nation. People who are running the system, and think they are really moving along and are looking forward to retirement, don't realize that you have a new breed of young people coming along who want their place in the sun.

Let's look at some of the real problems that are facing this nation and facing the world. Once we look at the problem and then look at the resources which we have and say, "how do we use these resources

*President, KGA Associates; Board of Directors, Boston Branch, NAACP

to deal with the problem," then we can start to tie affirmative action into it as one of the tools available to deal with our problems, one which will be accepted by people who recognize what we have to face today.

In the newspaper *the Wall Street Journal,* it was reported that the United States Navy is having great difficulty in recruiting nuclear engineering officers to man the nuclear submarines which are currently on patrol or under construction. They are short by approximately 772 officers. They are trying to use methods short of drafting officers to have them reenlist. This is a problem that doesn't concern black people or white people or men or women. It concerns the defense of this nation. People are going to use whatever resources are available or necessary to see that this need is filled.

Secondly, let's look at the energy situation facing the world and the nation today. We now know that the energy producing system, as well as the energy distribution system, must be changed. How has the old system operated? It has operated as a forum for those who are on the inside to protect themselves, whether it is the telelphone company, the electric utility of which I am a director, or the gas company. They have a policy of developing employees from within, and minorities have traditionally been kept out of the input pool so that they couldn't grow and rise to the heights. When you hear some of the utopian executives speak before you, they like to talk about "how I spent thirty years with this company and how I became president." They had an opportunity thirty years ago to start with that company, but those who were not in the structure of the system did not have that opportunity of starting with the company. The supply that they deliver has now changed from what it was thirty years ago when the company received the franchise to provide the communications system for the nation, or to provide electricity for the nation. Therefore, they need new ideas and new thinking to deliver on the needs of the people of our community.

Let's go to the third issue, the international situation. As you well know, it's not just fuel oil that we are short of in the world. We can list forty-three different elements and minerals that this nation is short of and which we must obtain from other parts of the world. How, for example, will the West avail itself of the natural resources of the non-white Third World? How will the West obtain coal from Rhodesia? No authority in Rhodesia will give us the coal they have there. We will have to go to Rhodesia and negotiate. That's why the British are having conferences now with the rebels and nonrebels, and the whites and the blacks. They are going to reach a compromise and then we will go there to try to obtain our share of it. And I certainly have a greater opportunity of sitting down in Salisbury and negotiating for the United States than someone who has gone to the Harvard Business School, come out of private schools, and has white skin.

We have to look at that from the point of view of reality. We are part of a global system. We have resources within this nation, resources which have been underutilized in the past. And we must now develop these resources and use them. Not because the law says we have to do it, but because our survival depends on it. In 1973, the leaders of this country, in the industrial sector, took a hard look at the pool of technical people of this nation, particularly in this region. Look in the want ads and you'll see. Go out there to Prime Computer on Route 9. They will hire an Eskimo if he can design that system. There is a need to use our human resources well and the excuse of white, black, female, young, or old, that's out the window. There is profit involvement in it. There are changes in our society, so, therefore, I did not look at America or the world as being in isolation, because those that look upon it in that way are going to go down the drain.

Now let me go into the educational institution. We had the recent court cases with regard to whether or not minorities should have special goals. The hard facts of life are that we do have a shortage of competent trained people; besides that, we have a shortage of educational institutions which can provide the trained people who we need to run this world.

Let me be very specific about it. I currently have a business consulting firm. We were asked to bid on a contract dealing with institutions of higher education in the system here in Massachusetts. They wanted us to develop a program for recruiting more minority students for two reasons: (1) so that they can meet their affirmative action goal; and (2) because there is a shortage of candidates to fill the spaces within the institutions of higher education, be they white, black, or any other race. We sat down and discussed what the scope of work and the situation were. And if we discussed what they said we'd have a multitude of candidates to get into our technology courses and our computer courses, but we have a scarcity of candidates for our liberal arts courses. As a businessman I would certainly say, well why don't we have more engineering and science courses and fewer of the liberal arts courses. Let's shift our resources. No, I can't do that because they don't have the staff. The faculty cannot transfer from one sector to another readily. In the business world we realize that the market place is dynamic and ever changing. If we don't meet those changes, we will be out of business. Yes, I believe in the old capitalistic system. I'm not going to try to change the American system, I'm going to try to make it work for me. I believe in it. I think it is a great system.

I'll try in a different way to let you know that this world is a very competitive world. It's a competitive world and the people who run it are the people who survive and understand it. General Motors understands that they must change from the big car to the small car or else they are out of business. Chrysler didn't understand that and is now coming back asking for welfare. That's the hard reality of life. We may give welfare to Chrysler. So, therefore, the position of NAACP confirms that we do need affirmative action, because, as you all know, affirmative action really means not reverse discrimination, but equal opportunity to start the race of life; don't tie one leg and say now you can go out and compete against the fellow that has two legs and a full stack of steam. Therefore, the NAACP does look forward and has pushed in the past to have laws passed to get the job done that has to be done in America, because we realize that that is the American system, and we're fully prepared, have, and will continue to challenge it.

Discussion

Question: I think that there really is a moral dilemma here. That is to say, if one is going to defend a principle of equality, then there are serious questions to be asked about it. If you are going to identify past injustice because an irrelevant difference was treated as relevant, and now you are going to say that an irrelevant difference is relevant, that is certainly a problem. You are as well aware as I am certain philosophers have pointed out that if you decide to bend and break constitutional safeguards for certain purposes, then you could do the same thing with torture, censorship, and invasion of privacy as means to an end. I wonder why you doubt that question.

Fried: I am happy to answer that question. First, let me begin by making the point that everything is not the same. I am trying to understand what you think the moral dilemma is. There are some people who think that the moral dilemma is passing over qualified people for unqualified ones. I don't know if that is what you are saying. I would say phrasing the dilemma in that way is actually itself an expression of bias based on nothing because it is assuming that women and minorities will be unqualified. It is assuming that if we suddenly changed the data and see a world in which women and minorities get promoted and hired in ways that they didn't before, then it must be that they weren't qualified in the first place. That doesn't seem to be a reasonable way to pose the moral dilemma. So then I think that maybe there's a second thing you are saying, which is, "Since we wanted equality and equal opportunity employment, isn't it contradictory to use color and sex as conditions when using color and sex has gotten us where we are today?"

The second thing about that, as far as I can tell, is that there is no other way to achieve equality in the areas we are talking about. If what was involved is discrimination that only needed to be pointed out and people would say, "Oh, we didn't know that we were doing that; ok, we are going to shape up and we won't do that anymore," then it might be theoretically possible to have color-blind and sex-blind procedures, but, in fact, in every area equality has been fought by institutions; not just fighting against laws but fighting against any improvements. So it seems as if there is no way to achieve what seems to be the goal unless you alter the procedures that you use. We are nowhere near having a problem. What is wrong with sex and race as criteria? The problem in the past has been that discrimination disqualified large sectors of the population. Now you say that there is going to be a comparable problem with using sex and race. Women and minorities never get special treatment. You need affirmative action even to get equal treatment and that is what you were saying as well. What is going to be wrong with that? What is wrong with saying that your sex and race are relevant because society has made it relevant. Well, if what you said is wrong with it is that it is going to put white males in the position that women and minorities have been placed in, there is just no evidence of that. Discrimination against white males qua their sex and race is simply not one of our social problems. The problem is that even with affirmative action, even with goals, we have not altered the position of women and minorities. So it seems really like a concern that really doesn't emerge when you look at the social world.

Question: I don't know if you want any rebuttal on that. I think, first of all, that it is an extremely empirical plan to substantiate if you want to contend that the only way to achieve that "in" is by a color and sex consciousness which earlier is defined as discrimination when it is working in another direction.

Fried: Let me say two things. The alternative is to wait around for women and minorities to become qualified. That assumes that discrimination is based on a lack in women and minorities. That is false. It may be that some of what goes on is based on the fact that women and minorities don't have qualifications, but that doesn't address the overwhelming problem of discrimination against those who are qualified. Secondly, if we are going to maintain a scarcity, then moving up one group is going to be at the expense of another group. Now it does seem to be that that's a rational procedure. It's a rational way. It meets certain ends, but it certainly doesn't meet the needs of most of the people of the society. And so all those people who have a common interest in genuine social equality (not in getting ahead while somebody else goes down) need to get together and make demands for more, rather than fighting over the little bit there is. If you are going to take inequality as a given then there is no question that somebody is going to lose. And that doesn't seem to me to be right. What is unjust here is the scarcity of opportunities like jobs. The injustice lies in the denial to any of that which is a basic need and which ought to be a right.

Question: Do you expect political pressure to build up in the 1980s for a four-day work week to expand the work employment line?

Guscott: I don't think that that is an issue to be taken up in an affirmative action workshop, but I will answer it. From a practical point of view I do think that we are going to reduce the work week because there are not enough jobs for the masses of people we have in the world today. We can run the world with fewer people, so I think that sooner or later, not for the reason of affirmative action, but for a better utilization of people, we are going to go less than a forty-hour work week. In regard to qualifications, our organization does not accept that because qualifications are a relative type of thing, not dependent upon sex or color. Qualification, to put it bluntly, is who you know to see whether or not you get the job. Take a police department like that of the city of Boston, which years ago had less than one hundred minority police officers while 20 percent of the city was minority. You had only four women in the police department as patrol people and they were doing probationary work with wayward girls, yet 50 percent of the population are women. So that just didn't make sense. We had a system, in existence, which as soon as you passed the blue book and knew somebody you got on the Boston City Police Force, regardless of the needs of the police force. There was also a need to have Spanish-speaking people in there. It is a political issue. We have to put it down front. That is how this nation was built. Fellows who went out and pushed their way west didn't get involved in any debates. They just went out, took the land from the Indians, and put something on it. I love the American system!

Question: Professor Fried, when you said that that problem wasn't whether or not the people were qualified in going up for the jobs, if you meant that they were equally qualified people, wouldn't that suggest that there was no discrimination in education?

Fried: I think it is different for women and minorities because they have different experiences. I actually think that if qualifications were translated into training, then minorities have been barred from training in areas where women have been allowed in. For a long time men have wanted educated wives so wives have had certain educational opportunities that people with color have been denied. I think that there is that imbalance. I think that there is obviously discrimination in education and there still is, but it has not worked out the same for women and minorities. But there is an imbalance, so you have more women who are qualified in the sense that they could take on their training if they ever got training.

But I actually think that the deepest issue in the first place is that in a world of sex and race, which is primarily what determined qualification, it is really impossible to know who is qualified and who isn't. You know what certain biased standards lead to. But to assume from the onset, which is what the critics of affirmative action do, that the people who were out of jobs, out of education, weren't qualified, you assume that there is something inferior about them.

Question: I think that the purpose of bringing up something like treating an irrelevant difference as being relevant is to bring it to the floor for a popular opinion and circulation. It allows that issue to be worked out and in doing so you bring it to a conclusion where everybody settles up and is happy and it becomes irrelevant again. That is the only way that it can become irrelevant like it was supposed to be in the first place.

Buckles: I would like to say something about education because I don't think women have received equal education. I think women have been shifted into the wrong courses, guided into the wrong subjects, and now we are not as well qualified for some of the better jobs as the white males.

Question: You don't elaborate on that point. Is it necessarily the wrong courses or should there be some efforts made by the government or someone to upgrade those traditional women's jobs?

Buckles: There is that of course, too, and studies are underway on how to upgrade these jobs. Right now if you don't have some math, you cannot obtain even a good blue-collar job—a machinist job, for example, or a carpenter.

Comment: There is no reason why teaching, nursing, etc., are branded so low that they are women's jobs.

Question: On this matter of qualification, often there is a lot of hypocrisy involved in setting certain qualifications for jobs. They automatically screen out people. But often beyond hypocrisy, people who hire want automatic screening devices just to cut down on the number of people they have to deal with, and so there are often qualifications that really have no bearing on what you need in a job. Now I want to relate this to a specific point, to your statistics about women with liberal arts degrees. I mean, I don't know the legal technicalities about this, but clearly there are many jobs where people with liberal arts degrees are automatically screened off. That really doesn't bear on what you need in jobs. But there doesn't seem to be any enforcement, at least systematically, if that is illegal, so if you are talking about all these women with liberal arts degrees who are clerks and things like that, there is a stereotype about a liberal arts degree such that maybe we need new regulations or more vigorous enforcement.

Buckles: I think women with liberal arts degrees have troubles initially in the job market because we are a technical society and for many of the jobs that are open you need a technical education. You need mathematics and science and this is what women are not studying, although I'm happy to say that more women are studying these subjects now. For women to get ahead in the business world they need business management and accounting, or employers feel they do.

Question: What I am saying is that in a lot of those cases where a management degree or a management course is required, I'll bet you can empirically verify a difference in performance given a different background. So it becomes a screening device that works against everybody in liberal arts, especially against women who have traditionally gone into that area.

Buckles: I agree with you about a liberal arts degree. I think it sets you up to be a better human being and a better citizen and worker. Nevertheless, employees will turn you down. Liberal arts majors should add some practical subjects to their liberal arts and they can have the best of both worlds.

Comment: I think women are their own worst enemies, though. When the employment managers ask you if you can type, they say yes. So, therefore, they go into a clerical job. If they said no then they'd get put in a low-management job.

Question: I'd like to get back to the point that was raised earlier about women protecting themselves in the job market. We know, for example, that there are shortages of secretaries, of nurses, etc., traditionally women's fields. We know there is a tremendous resistance to paying secretaries a decent wage. So women aren't going into those fields any more. You wonder, for example, if accounting would have become popular with women if the wage rates were down. Does the Department of Labor have some way of addressing that?

Buckles: Yes. You are talking about what we call "equal pay for work of comparable value" or "comparable worth"—and the Department of Labor as well as other federal and state agencies and private organizations have studies underway to devise methods of equalizing pay. Jobs traditionally held by women—even when they demand more skills effort and responsibility—pay less than jobs traditionally held by men. For example, cross-city bus drivers are paid more than registered nurses.

Wholesale change in pay equity will not happen overnight but it's gaining momentum. In 1978, twelve countries met at Wellesley College for four days to discuss this subject on a global basis and to develop strategies for implementing change. Last October, a large national conference was held in Washington, D.C. on comparable worth that brought together experts in job evaluation, unions, research associations, civil rights groups, and federal and state government organizations. As a result, small conferences are being held throughout the United States on this subject.

The most action on this subject right now is being taken by federal and state governments. This concept was included as a merit principle in the 1978 Federal Civil Service Reform Act. The Equal Employment Opportunity Commission (EEOC) and Department of Labor (DOL) have commissioned a major study on job evaluation from the National Academy of Science to determine whether or not a system can be developed for evaluating the comparability of jobs according to the skills, responsibility, and effort required.

State governments are active. In 1974, the governor of the state of Washington commissioned a study to examine and identify salary differences that pertain to job classes predominantly filled by men compared to job classes predominantly filled by women. The study covered 121 Washington State job classifications and revealed that women received about 20 percent lower pay than men for jobs of comparable worth. The state of Michigan is now in the process of conducting a comparable worth study and the state of Connecticut recently passed a law authorizing a pilot study to assess state positions on the basis of objective job criteria.

In addition, unions and groups of women are filing discrimination complaints and lawsuits on pay equity. But I don't believe any cases have been won as yet. The International Union of Electrical Workers has been in the forefront in this effort. I know of two cases they have filed against Westinghouse—one in New Jersey and one in West Virginia. The West Virginia case was settled out of court, with the result that thirteen formally all female job classifications were raised in pay and the incumbents received retroactive payment.

Queston: I'd like to address a question to Mr. Guscott. From your special vantage point do you see the world changing in any way that is going to open up comparable options for women?

Guscott: Absolutely. I truly do feel that the world is changing and it is changing much more rapidly than people think. For our supplies, as human beings, we are going to have to look at what resources we have and reorient them and reuse them in a different way. When you bring about change it means that men, women, blacks, and whites should position themselves so they have an opportunity not to be discriminated against when these changes come about because there would not have been any seniority line established. Let me be very specific without talking about the international situation alone. I mentioned electric light. There is no question about it, whether you go nuclear, solar, wind-power, etc., there will be change in how we produce that electricity in the next twenty years. Having to bring about change means that the delivery system will be changed, the distribution system will be changed, the production system will be changed, and bringing the change about means we have to train more people to do it. Young girls who are in school right now should be counseled so that they can have an idea of what those changes are going to bring about, what type of training they need, so that they are in a position to help bring about those changes. You are then a critical and active participant. Women and minorities are going to benefit from that change, not enough, but it is going to be a step in the door.

Question: I have an abstract question whose friendliness or unfriendliness I won't characterize for Professor Fried. You spoke in your presentation about the scarcity of resources and, therefore, active competition and you seemed to have an unfriendliness towards that situation; unfriendly to the point of seeing some injustice, and then in this latter comment about people deserving jobs in a similar spirit. Let's suppose that you, personally, have an immense set of resources with which you make purchases, buy services, etc. In making your purchases and buying services you are going to be selective. By the very fact that you are selective, you're giving over your benefits to some people but not to others. Do you consider that fundamentally unjust?

Fried: It would be unjust but I think it is the wrong assumption. First, the hostility to the scarcity: if I thought that scarcity was a natural, inevitable factor in the world then it might be unjust, but futile to rail against the universe. But I don't think that these are natural, inevitable scarcities, so that's why I think we ought to be hostile to them and not trust them. When people tell us that there isn't enough money to help people who can't afford to heat their homes, but dump it into nuclear power plants instead, that's not natural scarcity. That is a certain decision about where to put social resources and where not to put them.

Now on this issue of how, if I could be queen for a day, would I do it. I think that what you need is to figure out what principles you would use. At the moment, as we talked about in the last session, the dominant principle determining where resources go and where they don't has to do with profit and then human needs. While decent quality of work life and equality for women and minorities may not be hostile to that goal, it is clearly secondary and often is hostile to it. I would turn it exactly upside down and as a criteria for selection I would say meeting human needs would transcend profit.

Question: Let me see if I understand the point. Inequality of distribution may come about through justice. If you make your decisions based on just and rational and reasonable considerations and inequality results—this storekeeper has more and this one less—then that's still an unjust situation.

Fried: No, I don't think so. Why imagine that that needs to be true?

Question: Unless you are going to take all your resources and divide them up equally among all the potential shopkeepers. . . .

Fried: That's a possibility, isn't it?

Question: That doesn't strike me as a reasonable possibility, even given a larger number of resources.

Fried: Why not?

Question: That eliminates the whole function of your making a selection.

Fried: No. I think what you are assuming is that people do things because they are motivated by the fact that they will get a greater reward than somebody else.

Question: I am trying to transpose the issue from the producer's and the preparer's of goods and services to the side of the consumer. In a society that would approach something that you would consider more just, consumers are still going to make selections, and that is going to lead to inequality of goods on the part of the people from whom they buy.

Fried: I think that it is not necessarily the case that it will lead to inequality. Inequality doesn't just mean difference. I am not unequal to you just because we are different. Inequality is something that has to do with power.

Question: Then if nobody buys from me I'll soon lose whatever power I had.

Guscott: Maybe you are a bad salesman.

Fried: It may be that you'll want to think about a different system of distribution.

Guscott: I have been to so many of these discussions for years and I hear people innocently take it away from what the real topic is supposed to be and start talking about some philosophical thing about which you cannot come to a yes or no answer, so it means that the audience has to determine whether or not you have achieved something or whether we've merely had a nice debate. In this world, it happens that you buy according to how the product is merchandised. It all depends on advertising. I want to speak on the issue of liberal arts. Black young people with brain power have been misdirected into taking anthropology or liberal arts subjects like sociology, which they cannot use unless they get a PhD. They get their undergraduate degree and they have no resources to go on to schools of higher education. If they try to get into schools of higher education they are told that they are not qualified. So, I am not going to have my young people misdirected into something to support an establishment that needs students to fill those seats. I am being very practical about it. I am not against liberal arts; Bob Henderson, who is the president of Itek, has a degree in history, but he is also a good salesman.

Question: I have a follow-up comment concerning a question on the liberal arts issue. I think how people are talking about this particular example is analogous to the kind of problems that go on when people talk about issues in affirmative action. If you think about people's lives, some people work sixteen hours a day but a lot of people work eight. That means a lot of other hours are left in the day. When you talk about the purpose of an education you would think that education would prepare people for the whole of their lives, and not simply for the eight hours in which they have to work. I am not going to say what kind of education I think would do that. I would suspect that it would be a combination of different kinds of education that would allow people to enjoy their leisure as well as to find their jobs and their work enjoyable. The reason that nobody is talking about it in these terms is the same reason Professor Fried raised in connection with affirmative action. There are scarce resources. People are fighting for jobs, and in such a situation, of course, it is going to be that you don't want people to go into anthropology and not have marketable vocational skills. But what you really want is a society in which people wouldn't have to fight for jobs and be educated in ways that would also fit into their leisure. I would try to connect affirmative action to some of the issues that we raised about education.

Guscott: I agree with you, but on the issue of affirmative action, what really comes about I can cite an example of by comparing the Brookline schools with the Boston schools. There are some Boston schools that could compete with Brookline schools any day of the week, but they are selective. They are very selective. The method of getting into those schools, in my judgment, and in the judgment of my organization, happens to be discriminatory because the selection process is made during the time when you are a young kid. By the time you are old enough to get into those schools you have had it. You can't get into those schools. Regarding the other issue of how do you use your life, one of the things that we have to do is learn how to survive. Then after we survive we'll talk about enjoying the niceties of life, not the other way around.

CHAPTER 6

Government Regulation and Intervention in the Workplace

Chapter 6A

Ethics and the Workplace

Eula Bingham*

For a moment, try to identify with the following, all too common, reality: Tom Brown leaves the plant, as he does many days, slightly dizzy, nauseous, and exhausted from the heat and humidity. His ears are still ringing from the din of the day's production. He is concerned and increasingly anxious about the dangers of his trade. Not only are his coworkers continually discussing the accidents and injuries that seem inherent to their work, but they have been noticing an increasing number of people suffering from breathing problems, and the fifth person in their crew this year has been diagnosed with the same type of cancer. They've asked their foreman, and even the company doctor, about these illnesses, but they have received no specific information. No one will tell them the specific substances they work with except that one is ×100. No one will tell them about the specific hazards they face, even if they are carcinogenic. No one will let them see the information in their own medical records.

Should Tom Brown and his fellow workers accept these conditions as their fate? Should Tom Brown's employer be held accountable for some, or all, of these conditions? What should be the role of government? The issues have important ethical dimensions.

*Assistant Secretary of Labor for Occupational Safety and Health, U.S. Department of Labor

Society's view of ethics in business is changing. It is no longer a sufficient justification for action simply to meet marketplace demands or participate in a public meeting. It is very important that the needs of the public and of the company's employees be an important part of corporate decision making. Accountability for one's actions is becoming the name of the game. If it is being demanded of lawyers, physicians, teachers, and government officials, then why shouldn't it be demanded of the president of the company?

I could pick any one of a number of specific topics which are of concern to the Occupational Safety and Health Administration (OSHA). What responsibility does management have to disclose to workers the nature of hazards they face, the types of substances they are handling and the contents of their health records? Who is ultimately responsible for injuries and illnesses in the workplace, and to what extent is this responsibility recognized in the system of civil and criminal liability? And, under what circumstances should those managing and working in industry be relied upon to supervise their own compliance with government regulations? These specific subjects merit careful consideration. If we limit ourselves to specific issues alone, we miss the important point, because the real issue is: What should the ethical framework for industry be, and what is government's most appropriate role in influencing that framework?

I have chosen to view ethics using what I think are very well-established values. This means that basic human rights in the workplace must be protected and that really is the basis for the Occupational Safety and Health Act. Unfortunately, there are basic human rights violations in the workplace everyday. We and the Congress are aware of them and that's how we came to have the Occupational Safety and Health Act. When a worker dies in an industrial accident, explosion, or fire; or when a worker develops occupational cancer, chronic lung disease, sterility, or suffers some other material impairment, nearly everyone would agree that the basic human rights of that worker have been violated. Yet, hundreds of thousands of workers every year in the United States lose their health, and sometimes their lives, to workplace hazards. Our awareness of this serious problem, and of the fact that every working man and woman in America has the basic human right to a safe and healthful workplace, led to the passage of the Occupational Safety and Health Act of 1970.

In addition, most would agree that basic human rights are violated when corporate officials know the hazards and refuse to make the existence and extent of those dangers known. I have lots of examples. I can tell you about a company that knew workers were becoming paralyzed and psychotic, yet went to great efforts to prevent the workers from obtaining information about the correlation between the pesticides in the workplace and the conditions.

Certainly I can go on and on about 2'3 dibromochloropropane causing sterility, and about cave-ins of trenches, etc. I think that we need to talk about accountability, and when we do, we need to talk about information—especially the information that is absolutely necessary for workers and for the public to view to hold the company accountable. I want to make a couple of general comments about economists and their techniques.

1. Workers, for the purposes of analysis, are viewed as capital. This view of workers as human capital implies several things. First, it implies that a worker's life and a worker's health can be assigned a value in dollars and cents, just as is done for a machine in need of repair or replacement. Pain and suffering, anxiety and hardships on family members become unimportant, and only incidental, and are not included in any industry oriented analysis. The quality of life which results from feeling healthy and well is likewise not included in the analysis even though such variables are as important as they are to us precisely because it is very difficult to assign them a dollar value.

I think the view of workers as objects rather than as human beings may well be behind many issues relating to disclosure. Workers as human beings, not as inputs to a production process, have a right to know the health risks they face, the contents of their medical records, and the chemicals and other materials with which they are working. The participation of workers in protecting their own safety and health requires such disclosure or they cannot respond appropriately on safety and health committees.

2. Data for so-called analyses, in the war against regulation, are consistently used by industry in what I think are biased ways. Usually we overestimate the costs of regulations and underestimate the benefits. Perhaps this is because we cannot put those intangibles in terms of dollars and cents. All comprehensive data sources emanate from industry files, but the data are rarely, if ever, available for other responsible experts to analyze and corroborate. Emphasis in analyses has been placed on estimating the costs of regulation while mentioning potential benefits, if at all, almost in passing. Such information, however, does not provide a useful analytic tool to help decision-makers. There are other assumptions which also skew the information in analysis. When, for example, one measures costs—especially given today's economy of rapidly growing and improving technology—and uses only data based on current technology, one allows neither for cost saving improvements or for the acknowledged "learning curves" which flow from industry's regulatory experience. When one draws a

distinction between innovative R&D and compliance R&D, an unrealistic division is made in a process that may simultaneously achieve goals of both compliance and innovation. Vinyl chloride is one noted example.

3. I have found those economic analyses that have been used by the antiregulation forces to be unrealistically segmented. The cost impact of each standard is counted separately, even though, for example, technological improvements developed to meet the vinyl chloride standard could also be used to control acrylonitrile; even though a company may choose, based on what is about to happen, to get ahead with some anticipatory regulatory actions as a result of building new plants.

4. Much information is simply "left out" when industry reports on economic impacts. As stated above, new and improved technologies may increase productivity as well as comply with standards. There are some companies which have actually developed substitute products. Some of these are highly profitable. There are some companies who are now putting in their annual report the fact that they are getting into the business of developing new antipollution systems.

5. One of the most important issues, I think, that has an ethical aspect to it, has to do with reasons given for plant closings. When we read the arguments against regulations, particularly safety and health regulations, we often see them incorporated in full-page ads that give these regulations as a reason for plant layoffs or closings. I suggest to you that few industrial decisions are a result of any single variable and that there is an ethical question in this whole area.

6. I would like to raise the issue of the ethics of a company doctor in objectively diagnosing and evaluating worker illness.

7. I have pointed out already the use of the media which plays upon the fears of the public in terms of loss of jobs and sending business overseas.

ROLE OF GOVERNMENT

Now what should the role of government be in all of this? I view the Occupational Safety and Health Act as a labor law that must guard against violations of basic human rights and must at the same time encourage and demand corporate accountability. I would like to see the government in some way be able to encourage and reenforce those few individuals in the business community who are courageous and I can name one for you: Maurice Johnson, who worked for B. F. Goodrich, is a physician who blew the whistle on the angiosarcoma among B. F. Goodrich's workers. I can tell you that that company, along with that physician, fell into disrepute among the rest of the industry and that comes from a personal discussion with the individuals. The rest of the industry felt that they should have held off and kept the hazard to themselves. I'd like to find a way to encourage such appropriate behavior.

I think that the government has a responsibility to see that workers are trained. Certainly the act says we should train workers and employers. At OSHA, we have been concentrating on small employers. It is fair to say that workers must be trained and educated before they can even begin to take some responsibility for themselves in the workplace, before they can even begin to be a member of, let's say, a labor/management committee dealing with safety and health issues. Certainly a set of interactions must be developed among the federal government, business, and labor to come up with solutions to these problems.

One of the things that we are attempting to do is to localize the enforcement. We are starting a series of experimental projects. One of them is underway and we are about ready to begin another one with a university evaluating the project that will look at the potential of labor/management, health, and safety committees to provide some self-policing. We will have to see that there are appropriate measures taken to guarantee that worker rights are maintained. In the particular experiment that I am referring to that is occurring now in California, while we ask that complaints go through this labor-management committee, we do retain the right of workers to complain if they are not satisfied that this labor-management committee is acting appropriately. Certainly we all know that there are situations throughout the United States where corporations and unions are in bed with each other when it comes to safety and health issues.

The last thing I want to mention is that there must be a way for the government to encourage that the public demand accountability for all those people concerned at the workplace. I think that very frequently we in the Occupational Safety and Health Association have been remiss in carrying out our mandate under the Occupational Safety and Health Act and we must be held accountable also.

What Should We Do about Government Regulation?

Dennis Laurie*

GROWING CONCERN TO ALL CORPORATE MANAGEMENT

A decade ago it would have been unusual for a major oil company executive to participate in a conference dealing with government regulation and intervention in the workplace. No longer. To an ever increasing degree, we have been caught up in government-related issues.

Atlantic Richfield Company holds a 20 percent interest in the Trans Alaska Pipeline System (TAPS). As chairman of the TAPS construction committee, I viewed first hand the role of EPA, OSHA, and a dozen other federal and state agencies in the design and construction of this critically important crude oil transportation system. As much as $3 billion of the total completion cost of $8 billion has been estimated as due directly or indirectly to government regulation and intervention.[1] The actual figure is still under review. The project will provide an excellent case study for the impact of government regulation when all of the facts are in.

*Director, Community Relations, ARCO Transportation Company, Atlantic Richfield

On a day-to-day basis my staff is involved with DOE, MARAD, BIA, EEO, ERISA, and the Departments of Justice, Interior, and Transportation. Current pipeline divestiture actions by the FTC are also demanding much attention.

Atlantic Richfield recently participated in a nationwide study commissioned by the Business Roundtable to measure the cost of government regulations. That study, completed early this year, substantiated our belief that corporate costs due to government regulation are large and growing.[2] My company's situation is not unique. Professor Leone, of Harvard, has pointed out that throughout U.S. industry, government regulation demands more management time than ever before.[3]

In the remarks that follow, I will review the significant expansion of government over the last decade, comment on the regulatory record, discuss the influence of regulation in the workplace, consider existing free market alternatives to regulation, and close with some recommendations for legislative and regulatory reform.

THE EXPLOSION OF GOVERNMENT IN THE 1970s

While the taproot of big government traces back to FDR's new deal of the 1930s, it was not until this decade that a veritable explosion of government involvement occurred. 1970 was the watershed year. Consider this. The thirty largest regulatory agencies now employ an army of a quarter of a million. Twenty new agencies have been established including EPA, OSHA, NHTSA, CPSC, ERISA, and DOE. While the budgets of these agencies are significant (e.g., the DOE with its staff of 20,000 has an annual budget of $10 billion, which is greater than the total profits of the eight largest oil companies)—it is the cost of government regulation produced by these agencies that is of the greatest concern. Professor Weidenbaum of George Washington University has estimated the annual cost of regulation to be in excess of $120 billion a year.[4] These agencies with their direct involvement in planning, pricing, operations, marketing, and transportation have added a new dimension to government and to the U.S. economy.

Another element of government, relatively unimportant ten years ago, has come into great power and influence. *Fortune* refers to this element as "the shadow Congress the public doesn't know."[5] It is comprised of some 17,000 professionals, assistants, and clerical personnel who act in a staff capacity to the senators and representatives in Congress. These staffs have the responsibility for drafting and evaluating new legislation and for orchestrating pro or con lobbying.

Many of the current rules and regulations which constrain the U.S. economy originated with these staffs. A thumbnail sketch shows a typical staff member to be under forty, trained as a lawyer, ambitious, lacking business experience—a number having come out of "public interest" groups. Members of this "shadow Congress" are well positioned for future job opportunities in the administration, as a member of Congress—one hundred current congressmen got their start as staffers—or as highly compensated lawyers or lobbyists working on the regulations they helped create.

Add to the above the expanded budgets and influence of the old line agencies, a Congress always jealous of its prerogatives and demanding participation, and a far more activist judicial system, and then multiply all of that by an appropriate factor to account for state and local counterparts of the federal structure and my message begins to become clear.

MACROECONOMIC IMPLICATIONS

The bill for all of this government comes to about 35 percent of the nation's GNP. Recent work of Professor Laffer, of the University of Southern California, and introduced on the floor of the House by Congressman Kemp, argues that tax revenues required to support this size government is having dramatic impact on the economy.

Newsweek recently published productivity data for the major western nations and Japan.[6] The United States is dead last except for the United Kingdom and Margaret Thatcher may change that. Barry Bosworth, the director of the Council on Wage and Price Stability, has estimated that at least two percentage points of our inflation is due to the cost of government regulation. Both of these factors contribute to our national balance of trade deficit.

Government regulation creates paralyzing uncertainty in key industries. Planning has become even more difficult in an environment of new, changing and retroactive government rules and regulations. Chrysler has argued that the almost $700/car cost of meeting government imposed regulations is a major reason for its difficulty. Calls for divestiture and antimerger legislation are heard. For example, IBM is a fine company with decades of technical achievements to their credit and should be a source of great pride to the country. Apparently it isn't. Following the recent announcement of the system 4300 by IBM, *Newsweek* indicated it was as if Ford had just introduced a family car selling for $3,000 and getting 40MPG. IBM's reward—a Justice Department official was quoted as saying this now opens the door for a renewal of the decade long antitrust attack against IBM. Forget the economic benefits to the consumer, forget the IBM sales that contribute to U.S. balance of trade. The Justice Department lawyers have spoken. The Japanese who have been encouraging their computer companies to consolidate must be shaking their heads in amazement.

THE RECORD

Ask Milton Friedman what has the country received for its massive expenditures for government regulations, and his response would likely be, "not only has there been little benefit but the regulations have been counterproductive." Ask Ralph Nader, and you will find him in total disagreement. The truth lies somewhere in between. Fortunately, the issue is not totally subjective. It does lend itself to objective evaluation. The question of the value and efficacy of government regulation must be addressed in a national debating arena.

Regulation over the last decade has probably achieved cleaner air and water, a safer working place, and better opportunity for all people in the workplace. Perhaps those same results could have been achieved more efficiently with better regulation. Government regulation is marked by examples of incomprehensible language, oversimplification, misdirection, and contradiction.

For example, the EEO has a regulation dealing with job testing which reads as follows:

> A selection procedure has criterion related validity for the purpose of these guidelines when the relationship between the performance on the procedure and performance on at least one relevant criterion measure is statistically significant at the .05 level of significance. If the relationship between a selection procedure and a criterion measure is significant but nonlinear the score distribution should be studied to determine if there are sections of the regression curve with zero or non-zero slope where scores do not reliably predict levels of performance.

What that will do for minority unemployment is doubtful, but it should be a boon for statisticians, sociologists, and psychologists.

The HEW's alcohol, drug abuse, and mental health administration (ADAMHA) is responsible for funding alcoholic rehabilitation centers throughout the states. To determine the extent of need by each state, ADAMHA has invented supposedly scientific indices called the frequency of heavy drinking (FHD) and current tangible consequences (CTC). The validity of these indices, taken to five decimal places, determine the flow of millions of dollars to the states. Gross flaws inherent in the FHD and CTC measures however, will not cause Congress to dump the program, but rather to fund new commissions and studies to "improve" the indexes.[7] Incidentally, at least in California, Alcoholic Rehabilitation Centers are thriving as a result of the outpouring of federal funds. Maybe Californians have a high FHD or CTC. We probably also drink a lot.

Before you head for the exit, here is OSHA's definition of an exit:

> That portion of a means of egress which is separated from all other spaces of the building or structure by construction or equipment to provide a protected way of travel to the exit discharge. Exit discharge is that portion of a means of egress between the termination of an exit and a public way. A means of egress is a continuous and unobstructed way of exit travel from any point in a building and structure to a public way and consists of three separate and distinct parts: the way of exit access, the exit and the way of exit discharge. A means of egress comprises the vertical and horizontal ways of travel and shall include intervening room spaces, doorways, hallways, corridors, passageways, ramps, stairs, enclosures, exits, escalators, horizontal exits, courts and yards.

Paradoxically, while much of government regulation is marked by complex language, there are also cases of the other extreme of oversimplification. For example, the Delaney Clause states that any food additive must be removed from the marketplace if it produces cancer in animals or man. This is simple, but in its simplicity there has resulted chaos in regard to the country's use of nitrites and saccharin. Never mind that a withdrawal of nitrites, which are essential for meat curing, could lead to a national outbreak of botulism. Never mind that the human equivalent of saccharin which induced cancer in rats is 1,200 cans of diet soda per day for a year and never mind that saccharin has important therapeutic characteristics in dealing with tooth decay, obesity, and blood sugar problems; never mind all that, Uncle Sam has spoken.[8]

Misdirection is also a characteristic of government regulation. The NHTSA has imposed the seat belt ignition lock system, $500 per car air bags, and forced Detroit to call back 7 to 10 million cars every year for the last seven years. Some benefit may have resulted but most of the effort may be misdirected. Over 90 percent of all traffic fatalities are driver caused due to careless driving, speeding, or drunkenness. Perhaps it might be better to enforce vigorously the 55mph speed limit and throw the book at drunk drivers. The problem here is not regulation but misdirected regulation.

In another example of misdirection, the FTC has leveled an attack against the sugar-coated breakfast food producers who advertise on kiddie cartoon shows. To quote *Fortune:* "proposed FTC rules depict a world in which consumers are idiots, children are sneaks, advertisers are deceivers and all parties are in need of lots of regulation." Listen to the words of the FTC. "Parents will not intervene to protect children from television advertising because of intense feelings of helplessness, and because they are afraid of enforcing rules that they fear might help to make their children social outcasts or social isolates." What world are these regulators living in? Are parents really concerned about making their children social isolates, whatever that is? By the way, while one can support the FTC's presumed objective of reducing per capita sugar consumption, it is necessary to ask why the Department of Agriculture continues to subsidize sugar production.

There are a multitude of other contradictions in government regulations. The Business Roundtable study mentioned earlier supports this. The EPA favors stepped up unleaded gasoline production, but the DOE supports a go slow policy to conserve oil. The HEW (at least under Califano) took a strong stance against cigarette smoking but the Agriculture Department subsidizes tobacco planting. The EPA favors hoods to capture gaseous materials before they escape into the atmosphere, but OSHA bars them because of potential worker health factors.[9]

Then there is the classic "pajama case." Because of an environmental ban on phosphates in New York, mothers are forced to use detergents on children's pajamas that tend to wash out fire-retardant materials demanded by the CPSC. Does a loving mother smuggle detergents with phosphates from New Jersey? Does she commit an act of illegal laundry?[10] It's funny, sort of.

INFLUENCE ON THE WORKPLACE

Government regulation and involvement have a great impact on the workplace. Management and staff attention is diverted from productivity to completing and filing endless forms, fighting antitrust cases, battling interminable permitting processes, and fighting charges of past "law breaking." Consider the permitting problems of the SOHIO pipeline project—wanted by DOE but shut down by the delay of California permitting. Right now there are over half a dozen rate cases before FERC, including TAPS, dealing with major changes in what pipelines will be able to earn. Meanwhile, the FERC staff is rejecting increases and imposing new rate concepts. No one knows what to expect. All of this adds great uncertainty to the planning process, and capital markets abhor uncertainty.

FREE MARKET ALTERNATIVE TO REGULATION

There are significant forces within the private sector that achieve many if not most of the ends sought by the volumes of regulation. Simple good business practice demands that companies maintain low insurance rates by providing a safe and healthy working environment. One of the major findings of the Business Roundtable study was that, in general, big business goes significantly beyond OSHA requirements as part of company standards to assure an efficient workplace.[11] Further, labor negotiations are frequently directed to the question of work rules and safety.

The marketplace of wages tends to adjust for higher risk professions. It is impossible to remove risk from fire and police protection, crop dusting, deep coal mining, etc. Those who make the free choice to enter these professions presumably do so for the higher wages, for the added risk. Finally, in any extreme case, there are adequate laws on the books to deal with criminal liability. It is noteworthy that large corporations, with their brand name investments, tend to have a much better record in areas of equal opportunity, safety, health, pension plans, environmental controls, and so on. Maybe big is not quite so bad.

STEPS FOR THE 1980s

My remarks should not be interpreted nor are they intended as a call for ending government involvement and the birth of a laissez-faire economy. To the contrary, the country is now a mixed economy, and an appropriate role for government is essential for continued progress. Thus, the issue is not should there be government regulation, but rather how much and in what form?

Government itself has been outspoken in regard to excesses of the current regulatory system. The Carter Administration has formed the Regulatory Analysis Review Group led by Charles Schultz.[12] Dr. Bok, of Harvard University, has recognized the need for a new cooperative effort between business and government and has recommended curricula changes directed toward achieving that end.[13] A recent Louis Harris poll indicates that the public demands increased government efficiency.[14] Thus, there is a growing agreement among many in the universities, government, the public sector, and, of course, industry, that the regulatory process should be rendered more efficient. Yet, there are no quick or easy remedies to be proposed. However, important directional and evolutionary changes can be made. Consider the following.

Economic impact statements might accompany any proposed government regulation which influences business activities. This would force a benefit/cost analysis thus providing the nation with the basis for a decision to determine whether program benefits justifies the social and economic cost. And there are indeed costs. For several years, Ralph Nader has misled the country into believing that regulation costs come out of the deep pocket of big industry.[15] He knows better. The man's ideas are dangerous at any speed.

Second, regulators must recognize that we live in a world of trade-off and imperfection. While considerable progress can and has been made in addressing 80 percent to 90 percent of major problems, further advances come only at ever increasing costs. We must seek programs returning the largest social benefits for a given cost.

Third, broad regulatory targets ought to be set rather than detailed targets. This would overcome the problems of inefficiency resulting from overregulation, and would put to work the ingenuity and innovation of the private sector. The bubble concept for example, has been proposed to deal with environmental standards within a refinery complex. A hypothetical bubble is placed over the facility and a minimum level of acceptable water/air pollution set. The refinery can then engineer an overall system to meet the target that is most cost efficient. Another example of regulatory overkill has to do with recent energy conservation measures imposed by the federal government. Twenty pages of detailed regulations were issued dealing with temperature controls in office buildings. Not only are these regulations confusing, but this approach to conservation has been difficult to implement in many buildings because of design problems. It may well have been far better to impose a percentage reduction in power and let each building manager find a way other than thermostat adjustments to achieve the reduction.

Fourth, a broader systems approach should be sought to guard against the contradictory rules and regulations discussed above.

Fifth, sunset type reviews might be helpful to assure that any regulation which has outlived its usefulness is removed from the books. While there are advantages to such periodic reviews, it must be emphasized that any regulation develops an immediate supportive constituency comprised of implementing bureaucrats, consultants, sponsoring congressmen, largess recipients, and businessmen who have adjusted to the status quo. It is no accident that established industries oppose deregulation—witness the airline's opposition to CAB deregulation and the trucking industry's opposition to ICC proposed deregulation. There is nothing corrupt or sinister about this. It is simply a case of economic units adjusting and optimizing their operations to a given environment. Hence, while sunset legislation is a good idea, greater attention should be directed to analyzing a rule *before* it is placed on the books.

Sixth, the "career triangle" should be encouraged. This triangle refers to free movement from industry to government to universities and back. Compare this to the current state of affairs, where because of potential conflict of interest, nobody with significant energy experience can be employed by the Department of Energy.

Seventh, the power of nonelected congressional staffs needs to be dramatically tempered. They never tire of inventing new legislation which tends to slow down the growth of the U.S. economy.

Finally, there is an imperative need for a national change in attitude away from self-interest and toward cooperation. The Japanese have set something of an example. If the United States is to survive economically, socially, and politically with the traumas of energy, international trade competition, the presence of the third world nations, urban challenges, demographic shifts, health, housing and defense— then the internal conflict and special interest pursuits must stop. We are, as a nation, in this together, and have to find ways to work out these problems together. I hope I have suggested a few changes that might help.

NOTES

1. "TAPS: A Synopsis of Engineering and Cost Factors," Owner companies of the Trans Alaska Pipeline System, 1978.
2. "Cost of Government Regulation Study," *Arthur Andersen & Company*, 1979.
3. Robert A. Leone, "The Real Cost of Regulation," *Fortune*, January 1979.
4. Murray L. Weidenbaum, "The Cost of Government Regulation," *Center for the Study of American Business*, February 1977.
5. Juan Cameron, "The Shadow Congress the Public Doesn't Know," *Fortune*, January 15, 1979.
6. "Innovation: Has America Lost Its Edge?" *Newsweek*, June 4, 1979.
7. Daniel Seligman, "Keeping Up," *Fortune*, July 1978.
8. Tom Alexander, "OSHA's Ill-Conceived Crusade Against Cancer," *Fortune*, February 26, 1978.

9. Robert Crandall, "Is Government Regulation Crippling Business?" *Saturday Review,* January 1979.
10. Daniel Seligman, "Keeping Up," *Fortune,* July 1978.
11. "Cost of Government Regulation Study," *Arthur Andersen & Company,* 1979.
12. "What Price Regulation," *Newsweek,* March 19, 1978.
13. Walter Keichel, "Harvard Business School Restudies Itself," *Fortune,* June 18, 1979.
14. Everett Ladd, "What the Voters Really Want," *Fortune,* December 1978.
15. "The Experts Polled," *Saturday Review,* January 1979.

Cost-Benefit Analysis of Government Safety and Health Regulation

*Marvin H. Kosters**

The subject that I will discuss is the role of benefit-cost analysis in analyzing occupational safety and health regulation. Although this particular area of regulation—workplace safety and health—is only one of the ways in which government intervenes in the workplace, I will focus on this area because these goals of regulation are frequently discussed in terms of ethics and values. The reason for choosing this topic is that application of this analytic framework is frequently discussed as if it were seriously at odds with basic and widely shared principles of ethics or morality.

The general intent of the legislation establishing OSHA (1970) is quite straightforward: "to assure so far as possible every working man and woman in the nation safe and healthful working conditions. . . ." But how is this to be accomplished? What is an assistant secretary to do to achieve this ambitious goal? Well, the law provides for establishment of standards to regulate workplace hazards, standards that "most adequately assure, to the extent feasible, on the basis of the best

*Director, Center for the Study of Government Regulation, American Enterprise Institute for Public Policy Research

available evidence, that no employee will suffer material impairment of health or functional capacity . . ."

At this point some ambiguities become apparent: What does it mean to assure "most adequately?" What interpretation should be placed on "to the extent feasible?" When does impairment become "material?" What emphasis should be placed on making the "best available evidence" better, and how do we deal with the uncertainty that will inevitably remain? In actually carrying out a regulatory program, it is necessary to arrive at answers to these questions, at least implicitly. What sort of logic, what kind of analytical framework might be used to help arrive at reasonable answers?

I want to discuss benefit-cost principles as a framework for policy analysis because the issues are relevant when the problem of carrying out regulation is viewed from a number of different perspectives. For example, the view that a major role should be assigned to political factors may be correct, but it leaves open the question of what type of analysis should be applied to inform these political decisions. If regulations to reduce or remove workplace hazards are viewed as a matter of legal right, some framework for analysis is required to define the relevant rights. Similarly, the view that distributional consequences should be taken into account presupposes a framework for analyzing the distributional incidence of regulation.

I want to sketch out two different lines of reasoning in order to explore their implications for the logic of the analysis and for their ethical implications. Consider first the framework of *benefit-cost analysis*. Simply stated, applying the framework involves identifying all of the benefits and all of the costs of alternative policies and expressing them in common units (usually dollars) for comparison. In the context of this framework, the test of whether a policy should be pursued depends on whether benefits exceed costs, to whomever they accrue; and the guide to how far the policy should be pursued is whether marginal benefits are at least equivalent to marginal costs.

Stated in this way, these principles may seem lacking in capacity to excite enthusiasm for vigorously pursuing regulatory goals. Because the general principles are distributionally neutral, they do not suggest that something is to be done to favor the especially deserving, to correct practices, or problems that are most objectionable; or to penalize those responsible for performance that is regarded as unacceptable. Placing emphasis on analysis seems technocratic in spirit. And trying to express incommensurables in common units or attach dollar values to "priceless" benefits (or costs) seems a "green eyeshade" approach at best, ethically questionable or downright immoral at worst.

Consider now a second line of reasoning. On matters relating to safety and health—reducing the risks of accident, disease, and death—there is another principle that can be considered, call it the *benefit principle.* Under this principle we should pursue policies with potential for improving human safety and health to the point where no further benefits are in prospect, essentially without regard to the willingness or ability of individuals to pay or the costs to society. This is a rough approximation to the principle that shapes our thinking about provision of health care services. Most of us would be sympathetic to the idea that health care services should be provided, more or less irrespective of costs and surely without regard to ability of an individual to pay, whenever such services have some promise for improving health or prolonging life, especially when we think about young children. We do not, in general, withhold health services from the indigent, although quality differences undoubtedly are present. Programs and proposals have been developed with the aim of limiting health care costs, but, so far at least, their rationale has been expressed in terms of increasing efficiency of resource usage or preventing unnecessarily high fees—not in terms of actually withholding or reducing provision of health care services.

The main difference between these two lines of reasoning, expressed in terms of benefit and cost comparisons is this: applying the benefit-cost principle means assuring that benefits, both in total and at the margin, exceed costs; applying the benefit principle means assuring only that benefits, again both in total and at the margin, are positive.

There are a number of ways in which following the second principle appears superficially attractive in comparison to the first—in moral or ethical terms. Applying the second principle does not require explicit measurement of benefits; only the fact that benefits are present needs to be confirmed. Moreover, "priceless" benefits (such as reducing the risk of death and disfigurement) need not be measured in units that permit comparisons with costs; there appears to be no need to "exchange dollars for human lives," to choose between "people and profits," if this principle is applied. Finally, there appears to be no need to impose arbitrary limits to the scope and stringency of regulations that are extended to reduce hazards in the workplace.

From a moral and ethical perspective, these features of the benefit principle appear attractive compared to the principles of benefit-cost analysis. But we need to examine more carefully what application of the benefit principle would mean, in practical terms and in ethical terms, in order to judge whether this is a promising principle for application to workplace safety and health regulation and to other areas of regulation.

Pursuing the benefit principle—extending regulation or expanding spending to the point where no further benefits can be realized—may be possible in practice for a single, relatively narrow problem area. Even for an area as broad as health care services, however, increasing concern with rising health care expenditures suggests the possibility of only limited pursuit, or at least partial abandonment of this principle. But consider what would be implied by applying this principle to all of the workplaces in the country for all of the hazards that are known, suspected, or as yet undetected. If regulations to reduce workplace hazards were expanded to the point where no further benefits are achievable, this would be extremely costly. That is, a very large share of our overall output would be absorbed by such an approach.

To get some insight into the potential for very large costs that can result from workplace regulatory standards, consider some cost estimates that have been made for meeting carcinogen standards. Regulatory activity has been completed on only a few substances and cost estimates have been made for even fewer. The estimates available suggest costs of meeting the standards in the range of at least $100 to $150 million per carcinogen, and some 1,500 to 2,000 substances have been identified as "suspect carcinogens." If we take the lower end of both ranges and apply these cost estimates to the number of possible carcinogens involved, we obtain costs that amount to more than 10 percent of current annual personal consumption expenditures for the entire economy. Now questions can be raised about the cost estimates and the validity of applying them across the board to all suspected carcinogens; but, on the other hand, carcinogens are only one class of hazards—we are considering only hazards—in the workplace, and even more stringent standards would presumably contribute something to reducing hazards from exposure (and higher cost standards should presumably be considered if costs are to be ignored).

A number of points become clear when we consider the benefit principle for general application. The first point is that when we consider applying to a major portion of the economy a principle that seems sensible for application to a particular, limited problem area or group of workers, a critical flaw is exposed. Costs then become too large to be ignored. A second point also becomes apparent when general application of the benefit principle is considered: weighing benefits against costs is not essentially a matter of trading off such important goals such as saving lives for dollars. Instead, the dollars serve as a convenient unit for measuring the value of goals, such as reduced exposure to risk of injury or death, for comparison with other human goals, such as, for example, maintaining nutrition levels that might contribute more to improved health.

These two points can be restated in a way that points toward the direction in which the benefit principle needs to be modified. First, an approach that may seem feasible from the point of view of pursuing a single, limited objective can prove to be unfeasible from a broader perspective when everything that could conceivably be done in a particular area to further that goal is considered. Costs can accumulate to the point where it is necessary to reduce what can be spent in other areas that contribute the same goal. Second, an approach that may seem desirable when a single, limited objective is considered can prove to be undesirable when other goals are taken into account. Workplace safety and health is important, but it is not the only goal in the society. How can analysis be structured so that it takes into account not only the many factors that contribute to the same goal but also the multiple, and often conflicting, goals of society? Clearly, costs need to be taken into account. The extent to which they should be taken into account is implied by benefit-cost analysis principles; no single goal or policy that contributes to achieving it should be pursued to the point where benefits are worth less than their costs.

It is appropriate at this point also to reconsider the ethics or morality of benefit-cost principles, the extent to which application of this kind of analysis takes into account widely shared human values. In the first place, it becomes clear that application of the benefit principle to workplace safety and health regulation can give rise to costs that are so large and real incomes that are reduced so much that worker health may be reduced more by poor nutrition than it is improved by workplace health regulations. This would be the predictable outcome if absolutely no consideration were given to costs. This, of course, also leaves all other worthwhile objectives out of consideration. When other activities that contribute to a particular goal and when goals other than health and safety improvement are taken into account, it becomes clear that devoting more of our resources to further any single goal, in any particular way, will generally mean fewer resources available to improve human health in other ways or to further other worthwhile goals. If, for example, workplace health regulation became so costly that human health could be improved more by better nutrition than it would be harmed by less costly health regulation, this would hardly seem an ethically or morally attractive result. Moreover, while most of the goals of regulation are desirable, most do not have the exalted status of ethical or moral absolutes.

What may appear on the surface to be an ethically myopic approach—weighing benefits against costs in each case—appears in a much more favorable light when its general policy application is considered. Pursuing a goal only to the point where benefits equal costs turns out to be desirable from the point of view of insuring that any single policy approach does not have the result of either achieving less safety and health improvement than could be achieved in other ways, or actually detracting from the goal itself by leaving fewer resources available to further it in other ways. It also guards against pursuing any single goal to the point where other goals are seriously compromised.

What I have discussed so far is only the logic of the benefit-cost framework. Applying the framework requires identifying and measuring benefits and costs, to the extent feasible. It is possible in principle that applying the analysis is feasible to only such a limited extent that the results can give little practical guidance for policy decision making. If so, this can be viewed as a legitimate criticism of the analytic framework. It should be noted, however, that it can also be regarded as a commentary on the complexity of the real world in which regulatory policy decisions are made, and the difficulty in making illuminating comparisons to judge whether or not a particular regulatory approach makes sense and is worthwhile.

Benefit-cost analysis is frequently criticized along these lines. The appropriate discount rate to be applied to benefits to be accrued or costs to be incurred in the future is usually not obvious. The full range of indirect effects that impinge on both benefits and costs is not easily determined. How to measure the value of such desirable objectives as a small reduction in the risk of death is a controversial question, to say nothing about the qualms often experienced when "dollar values are placed on human lives," as the expression goes. The fact that we have only limited knowledge of the character and extent of risks to health of exposure to possible hazards, the adverse effects of which may not be apparent in the near future, or the incidence of which may not even accrue to the generation that is exposed, seems to underline the difficulties of quantification and comparison.

These, and many others, are surely formidable difficulties in applying benefit-cost analysis. We should be careful, however, to make the relevant distinctions in evaluating criticisms along these lines. First, it should be recognized that measurement issues and difficulties do not in any way invalidate the principle of weighing benefits in the balance against costs. Second, measurement difficulties should be recognized as the inevitable counterpart of the complexity of the real world. It would be foolish to pretend that these complexities are not present by refusing to recognize them. Third, it is usually possible to go at least a considerable distance in identifying and quantifying costs and benefits, and proceeding to the extent this is feasible can make a valuable contribution. Thus, for example, using a discount rate when future benefits and costs should be considered, even if the appropriateness of the specific rate chosen is subject to question, is likely to be preferable to disregarding the problem entirely.

In view of the complexity of real world regulatory decision making, proceeding to quantify and compare benefits and costs, to the extent this is feasible, can give valuable insight into at least some elements of what is relevant in judging whether a particular policy is worth pursuing. And application of benefit-cost principles is more appropriately viewed as an approach that contributes toward more systematic sensitivity to human values than an approach that fails to take human concerns into account.

Discussion

Question: I'd like to express, as rapidly as I can, my dismay over the people who organized this conference and all three speakers. It seems to me that to give us an apologist for business and a member of an oil company, and then, on the other side, a woman from the administration, is definitely unfair. This is an academic audience and not a corporate one. He says that we have costs and benefits and we have benefits only. Then what does he give us? He talked about cost only. He talked about costs to the company. He didn't talk about costs to the individual. I'm talking to you, Mr. Kosters. You said that we had costs and benefits, but all you talked about were costs.

Kosters: I'd like to make a brief comment before it is necessary for me to leave to catch a plane. I recognize that analysis of almost any sort is very much the enemy of advocacy, in moralistic terms, based on the view that choices among alternatives are choices between good and evil. In my remarks on the benefit-cost analysis frameworks, I noted that both benefits and costs should be listed and quantified to the extent this is possible. Such an analysis usually indicated that issues are more complex than simply a matter of whether workers' safety is being traded for corporate profits. I don't mind being criticized by people with strong views. But what I do mind is any suggestion that I am an apologist for either workers, business, or any other specific sector in my discussion of benefit-cost analysis.

Comment: Let's be reasonable. Dr. Bingham, I think, was quite helpful in saying that what we really ought to be talking about are answers to frameworks. What we were treated to was Jerry Wurf making all sorts of unsupported allegations which he happens to believe in. I am delighted to know that he believes in them, but they are not a basis for a reasonable discussion. Dr. Bingham has been much more helpful to come forward and say, "how do you get at some of these questions?" I would like very much to pursue this question of the responsibilities of a company doctor to employees. If a doctor has certain information and, if a reasonable person, having the information at hand would behave in such a way that he or she would operate more safely, then that information must be given to that person. What I have a problem with, in industry as elsewhere, are people who take a number from one poll and then generalize about a whole case. The J.P. Stevens Company may be the worst case. I don't know what the right number is for occupational health hazards, but I know that there are serious problems. Nobody takes seriously the 20, 30, and 40 percent numbers. We do have hazards and all I am trying to suggest is that some of these things are so polarized that I think we can approach the legislature directly. Regarding some other things we need to get a framework for discussion.

Question: I can't actually recall a particular case where we have some practical terms. As you were speaking, you were talking about people dying. As I was hearing both of you, I remembered working in a General Motors foundry. As I heard Mr. Laurie speaking, I was afraid people would unnecessarily lose eyes or lives, which happens because of a production problem. On the other hand, I hear you [Bingham] suggesting that a factory would have to shut down, since no matter what they do that is practical, that is going to be a dangerous place to work.

Bingham: Standards have to be feasible.

Comment: Even with feasible standards people are still going to get killed. Now it sounds as if you are saying that you are not going to let people do anything where lives are going to be lost.

Bingham: No, I am not saying that. I'm telling you the framework under which we operate is the Occupational Safety and Health Act. That does not require perfection. It requires feasible technology and it speaks of feasibility in terms of economics. What you have heard are those people who have charged us with wanting to reduce risks to zero. We cannot. Too many lives are still being lost because we don't get down to what is achievable in this country.

Question: I'd like to have Mr. Laurie address the question on market failure and market solution and also to comment on why the business community, or defenders of free enterprise in the market system, don't give the same time to the market solution of problems as they give to the cost of government regulation?

Laurie: Let me identify several market solutions to potential workplace health and safety issues. Companies obviously like to keep insurance premiums as low as possible. They abide by rules and regulations that are needed for a healthy and safe environment, not necessarily because OSHA has a specific rule or regulation, but because it is desirable to minimize insurance premiums. That is one important market solution. Further, corporations seek an effective and on-going level of production. They don't want to create a large number of labor absences, or work stoppages and slow downs due to safety or health problems. Note also, that unions have a role in encouraging corporations to provide a safe working environment. Government is setting labor aside. Finally, in any extreme case, if a company is found guilty of abuses there are court actions that can be taken and the last thing a corporation wants is a costly lawsuit. I am not saying that these are sufficient necessarily to remove the rules of OSHA, but I am saying that these market solutions are very effective in most cases.

Bingham: I'd like to comment on that. What he has said I agree with. There are some companies who go further than the government requires. I happen to know what the situation is with oil companies, and I can tell you that your company is one of those that goes further than required. Now let's get back to what I said. You should hold companies and corporations accountable. Let's also separate those who are doing their job and somehow give them recognition. What troubles me is to hear you damn all regulations, even health and safety regulations, when you know your company is doing a good job. Why don't you separate out and be one of the good guys?

Comment: I think we have caught on to problems. But I think it is necessary to show the example. What we are supposed to be talking about is business ethics. I think the whole point is the point of self-regulation. We keep on looking at the worst case scenarios. Now, I think we have to say that in fact there are bad actors. There are companies who are bad actors and there are millions who are also bad actors and the need for trade unions can be debated.

Question: I would like to ask Mr. Laurie why he is tired of hearing about the J.P. Stevens case. Secondly, why did American business organize an all-out campaign against the extension of the National Labor Relations Act if they believe that labor organizations are an alternative to government regulation?

Laurie: In the interest of time, I'll only respond to the first question. The reason I am tired of hearing about J.P. Stevens at this conference is that it is a relatively isolated case with some unusual history and special circumstances. Yet, it is represented as though it somehow typifies all corporate-labor relations. Cease the rhetoric over the issue. If J.P. Stevens is breaking the law, there is a legal system to deal with that. If the public chooses not to buy Stevens' product, let them do so. If Stevens' employees choose to leave, let them do so. Let us all be free to choose.

CHAPTER 7

Extension of the Workplace into the Community

The Work Ethic in the Context of the Community

Sloan K. Childers*

As a member of the petroleum industry, I seem to be best qualified in only one subject this year. And that's: "How to keep smiling when everyone hates the ground you walk on." But as I thought more about the topic of the work ethic, my thoughts put the work ethic in a different light.

There are two major social concerns facing American corporations today in the context of this conference. The first concern is directed outside the corporation and usually goes by the name of corporate social responsibility. It involves businesses taking voluntary actions to improve the environment, to help the underprivileged, to support the arts and education, and to rescue the inner city. This movement began receiving a lot of attention about ten years ago and is still very much alive though the pressures have lessened. The second major social concern facing business today is directed *within* the corporation. That concern is worker alienation and what to do about it.

According to a survey by Daniel Yankelovich, only one person in four today views work as a source of personal fulfillment. And only 13 percent find their work truly meaningful and more important than

*Vice President, Public Affairs, Phillips Petroleum Company

leisure-time pursuits. All across America, workers are taking their noses off the grindstone and asking, "Is this all there is?"

Many businesses are saying "There *is* more." So you are seeing broader benefits, more worker input into decisions that affect them, improvement of working conditions in offices and factories, and corporate involvement in the community. I see a trend toward corporate social action projects beginning to merge with job enrichment, all to the benefit of America's work ethic.

It used to be that "worker environment" was the machine on which textiles or shoes were sewn. It later extended to the entire floor where laborers mingled. We later saw partitions providing some privacy and quiet—then stark, battleship gray cubicles occupied by just a few workers. Then came very private offices for individuals. Status could—and still can be—judged according to the size of your chair and desk, the number and color of your file cabinets, and the value of the paintings on your office wall.

Concern about the worker's environment in recent years has prompted corporations and businesses by the thousands to remodel dreary old buildings. And in the last two decades it has become fashionable to build a new building in a suburban industrial park—with lighted parking lots, fountains, and malls. Our worker's environment is expanding. It's not uncommon to see acres of wooded retreat available to employees—9-hole golf courses, swimming pools, tennis courts, and other refinements.

Now employees are becoming involved in their communities and look to their employers to support schools, capital improvement bond issues, parks, and other social programs. Business in recent times has adopted a policy of giving credit to employees who devote time to public service. Everyone wants a better community. Our worker environment may cover several hundred square miles. That's quite a change from the few square feet around a sewing machine earlier this century.

The principle behind all of this is that if business provides more pleasant working conditions and a better place for employees to live, learn, and play, everyone will benefit. The work ethic will improve; more productivity will be realized; the corporation or business will profit from the investment in its own people—and the community. And the community will profit from a better financial performance by the company. You may wonder to what extent business is making such investments.

According to The Conference Board, the dollars that American corporations allocate to social action have increased every year since 1970. And total corporate giving is now estimated to be approaching

$2 billion annually. Community-related contributions accounted for 11.5 percent of corporations' total cash gifts in 1977—nearly double the percentage in 1967. And more and more of this money is being channeled into areas that will accomplish two purposes: help solve a community problem and help improve the workers' environment.

I'm thinking especially of examples such as Crown Center in Kansas City, where Hallmark, Incorporated, turned a blighted downtown area into a desirable complex of offices, shops, condominiums and a hotel, all near Hallmark's corporate headquarters. Another example is the $350 million Renaissance Center in Detroit, an urban renewal project promoted by the Ford Motor Company and other Detroit businesses. And also in Detroit, General Motors is building a $40 million corporate headquarters, plus an office complex and shopping center. Included in the project is the proposed renovation of a run-down neighborhood. I'm sure there are similar examples here on the East Coast.

Projects like this don't have to be as grandiose as the Crown Center, Renaissance Center, or the GM Complex. My own company, for example, has traditionally operated in small communities. Our headquarters is Bartlesville, Oklahoma, a city of some 30,000. Most of our major facilities are also in smaller communities.

Phillips allocates most of our corporate contributions to traditional social actions such as education, the arts, and general welfare projects. But in recent years we have put an increasing share into projects which combine social action and job enrichment. For example, after Bartlesville's old civic center was condemned, Phillips took the lead in financing a drive for a new combination civic and performing arts center designed by the Frank Lloyd Wright Institute of Architects. It is scheduled for the early 1980s.

We've converted a Bartlesville parking lot into a landscaped plaza for civic and cultural activities, and for just plain employee enjoyment. And we're also involved in a number of other projects, ranging from a housing development near a uranium mine in New Mexico to a new playground and park in a small town near a company refinery.

We don't for a moment maintain that these projects are purely altruistic. But neither is enrichment of our bottom line our motive. They are done because:

they will enrich the lives of employees and their families and friends;
they create good community relations;
private enterprise has an obligation to act on its own and not wait for government to do everything for us;

and, contrary to popular belief, big corporations are composed of people, people who are as concerned about human needs as other citizens are.

Of course, these projects don't enjoy universal approval. Many people are asking legitimate questions about them. One question runs something like this: Does the involvement of a large company in the affairs of a community tend toward corporate domination of that community? Does big business capture city hall? This is a concern not only of the city, but of the company as well. There is no benefit to a corporation taking on duties that rightfully should be assumed by the citizens and elected officials of a community. That creates a drain on the corporation and keeps communities from standing on their own feet.

But, fortunately, if the projects I've been talking about are properly carried out—with joint involvement by the community and the company—I think the town's interest is not in conflict with the corporation's. Instead, the two interests merge into one. An improvement in the company workers' environment is also likely to improve the environment for business owners, property owners, civic organizations, and churches.

A second key question is this: since community improvement actions cost money—often big money—do they actually work to the detriment of employees and stockholders by siphoning off their income? As a stockholder in the business world, I'm not too concerned about the cost. Today, as an average, contributions amount to about one percent of pretax net income.

Certainly, you can't show a direct and immediate economic payout from a civic renewal project, even if it does improve your employees' environment. But I believe that using some company funds on projects that combine social responsibility with job enrichment does have a positive effect, on both worker satisfaction and company performance.

Corporations—particularly those that deal in oil—are frequently blamed for being big. But being big also carries a lot of responsibility. Not only must you serve your customers, your employees, and your stockholders—but you must also serve your communities. Or you can get small pretty quick.

Considering the variety of experience and talent at this conference, I think we can be optimistic that progress on the work ethic will be made. We in the business world are trying. And it's reassuring to know scholars in educational institutions like Bentley College are involved in this effort.

Small Business Involvement in the Community

Frederick G. Frost III*

In the 1920s Calvin Coolidge stated "The chief business of the American people is business." Also in the 1920s, journalist Stewart Chase noted that American businessmen had taken the place of "the statesman, the priest, the philosopher, as the creator of standards of ethics and behavior" in this country.

The respect for business and business leaders up to the late 1920s was nearly unshakable. By way of proof, it could be noted that only a few mild government regulations were imposed on business in general during the period.

Business was prospering and the boom stock market of 1928–29 reflected that fact. Many individual stocks doubled and tripled, and many working Americans invested their hard-earned money (hard-earned because wages never really grew much during the twenties, which contributed to the vastly improved U.S. productivity), in anticipation of great wealth.

Black Tuesday, October 29, 1929, saw the dramatic start of the downfall of business as the unquestioned leaders of all things that were good. That loss of faith in business people has not been reversed. Three generations of Americans: those who as adults in the 1930s had

*President and Chairman of the Board, A.T. Wall Company

to suffer the direct consequences of the loss of savings and foreclosure of their loans; those who were the children of the thirties who would witness firsthand their families' economic deterioration; and those who today are the grandchildren of the thirties, and who are constantly reminded by their parents about the need to display caution towards business and business people so as not to allow a repeat of Black Tuesday—these three generations have shared in that loss of faith.

In a nutshell, business in the last fifty years has not been looked upon as "the creator (or caretaker) of standards and ethics and behavior." Nobody has! What, then, has business done in these last fifty years to contribute to our improving way of life? Certainly business cannot be accused of sitting idly by.

Clearly there are three main sources of support which a community may call upon. Besides business, they include private foundations which primarily supply funds. Public support usually comes in the form of funds from state governments or from the federal government. As has been widely noted in the last few years, private foundations are having to reduce drastically their spending as economic ills have shrunk their assets. On the subject of government support within the community, the following quote from economist Alfred Marshall, many years ago, might best describe the situation. I tend to agree:

> Government is the most precious of human possessions; and no care can
> be too great to be spent on enabling it to do its work in the best way; a
> chief condition to that end is that it should not be set to work for which
> it is not specially qualified, under the conditions of time and place.

The other area, and the area we are talking about in this forum, is that of business relations in the community. Howard Morgens, as chairman of Procter & Gamble, put it best a few years back when he said that, as businessmen, "we bear certain responsibilities and one of them is certainly public service." He then went on to quote Aristotle, "one citizen may differ with another, but the salvation of the community is the common business of us all."

Businessmen are in a fortunate and satisfying position of being able to bring a good many of our society's aspirations into practical realities. An article in the July 11, 1979, *Wall Street Journal,* titled "Return to Boosterism—More Firms Seek to Improve Their Cities Instead of Giving Up and Moving Away," describes how business has provided substantial support in Cleveland, Ohio, which is but one more example of large companies involving themselves in their communities.

Like you, I am very aware of large businesses and their attempts to be responsive to their communities. As a matter of fact, as a director of a large, New England based broadcasting and retailing company, I am proud to have been a part of this corporation's strong stand on the need to revitalize urban America. I would like to talk a little about small businesses and the contributions that they have and can make to their communities—a contribution which clearly should be recognized as important.

As a brief aside, the significant business commitment to the communities of Minneapolis and St. Paul is probably the best example available today of what we all should be trying to accomplish. Using Providence, Rhode Island, as the basis of my experience is more difficult because most of the world thinks of Providence only as a traffic jam on the way to the Cape during the summer.

I should note here that while I am a director of several large, publicly held corporations, as well as chairman of an audit committee, my own business is a small business and it is from that base of operations that I am most able to explore this subject.

Small businessmen's desires may be strong, but our resources and time are limited. Historically, small businessmen have spent too much time in awe of too many things. Therefore, because we don't have the dollars, the clout, or the time, or because we don't think we have the time, we often have been unable to gain the respect of our local political entities. So somewhere along the line, small businessmen gave up on the idea that they, too, can impact their communities; that they, too, can make a worthwhile contribution to the quality of life for their employees, for their neighborhoods, and, in fact, for themselves. I suggest that in response to this small business isolationism, community institutions as well as political institutions have bypassed this very important and actually very available asset.

It is this relationship between small business people and their community institutions which must be changed. Large businesses often assign people to community involvements, but such assignments are transitory in nature and concern for the community among such representatives lasts only as long as they are assigned there. Small business people, on the other hand, often grew up within the community, live, work, and school their children in the community, and ultimately will retire within the community. They are the people who should care most about the quality of life in their area.

Additionally, today it is more evident than ever that the survivorship ability of the small business must include a strong interface with its community—or communities, in the case of multifacility operations. It should be recognized that the primary responsibility of management of a small business is to keep that business going. But, by no small measure, this includes its local tax situation, labor situation, and citizenship situation. The growth of the entrepreneur is closely tied to his or her ability to respond to relations in this area. My personal experiences in community involvement have had three major benefits:

1. I broke the isolationism of myself and my small business.
2. I forced myself to bring my middle management up to a level that could handle the business in my absence.
3. I gained a great deal of self-satisfaction in working in my community.

Finally, I would like to note that today small businesses, while made up of hundreds of thousands of components, are still a mighty force employing more than half of the U.S. work force. It is encumbent upon the owners and managers of these small businesses to stop being in awe of the big businesses and political systems around them, and to stop relying on trade organizations and so forth to represent their interests, and simply to get involved with their communities on a personal basis. The small businessman's meaningful involvement in his community could begin to turn a fifty year tide in community relations, because money alone from private foundations or from the public sector is not sufficient to replace human involvement. What Walt Kelly's Pogo once said can be applied to the small businessman, "I have seen the enemy and he is us."

A Conceptual Framework for Business-Community Relations

*Fred K. Foulkes**

Let me suggest that the extension of the workplace into the community can be viewed from many perspectives. Certainly we can all consider specific cases that are positive. We can also find some cases that are negative. Furthermore, there are situations in which we'd probably have to say a company's impact is neither positive nor negative but neutral.

Let us ask outselves, what does the phrase "extension of the workplace into the community" mean? What is the community: is it 500 yards around the plant? Is it a town? A city? I suppose for Motorola it's the state of Arizona. Motorola is the largest employer in that state, yet Motorola's headquarters is in Chicago. AT&T's community is no doubt the nation. For IBM and ITT, it would have to be the world. The definition of the community, of course, depends on many factors, but certainly the size of the corporation and the locations of its facilities are of great significance.

I would like to begin by talking about some of the negatives and suggest ways to understand what I mean by "extension into the community." Then, we must find ways to understand a company and its extension activities. Finally, what are some of the principles and what

*Professor of Business Administration, Harvard Business School

are some special initiatives which companies have adopted which, to my mind, can be viewed as quite positive?

We can all cite negative instances: environmental damage, damage to the safety and health of the employees, the customers, and the community, traffic problems caused by the way some companies which don't stagger hours locate their plants, and cases where some companies are simply unresponsive to local needs. People in the company simply don't get involved. Their managers don't participate for one reason or another. All of us can cite cases of plant closings that have occurred for economic efficiency which were necessary but which were handled in an unresponsive manner. Senator Williams is currently proposing a bill which will require many changes in the practices of some corporations with respect to plant closedowns. I think we can all say that if there are too many negatives, possibly even if companies are too neutral, something will happen—as a result of action in the nation's capital, the United Nations Multinational Corporation Commission, the state capital, the mayor's office, or simply the various pressure of community groups trying to redress those wrongs or to minimize those negatives.

In terms of understanding the activities of any corporation, it is useful to start with an examination of the top management of that particular company. What are top management's attitudes, values, philosophies? Also, what is the nature of ownership of a particular company? I maintain that you cannot understand Cummins Engine and all that it has done for Columbus, Indiana, without understanding Irwin Miller, the chairman and large stockholder. Similarly, in this area, you cannot understand Polaroid's activities without understanding Dr. Edwin Land, the founder, chairman, and still director of research.

In addition to looking at top management, which, I maintain, is fundamental, we obviously also need to consider the resources of the corporation. Simply stated, we have different expectations for IBM than for Woolworth. We also need to look at the environment, the problems, the needs, and the opportunities. In thinking of ways in which we might understand the activities of any corporation, there are simple principles that our panelists have suggested as well.

First, the corporation should view itself as a guest of the community, whether it is in Bartlesville, Oklahoma or Singapore. Policies should be adopted, as best as possible, to be a good neighbor. In most cases, what is done in the community is also good business. This is certainly so in the long run. But many times, in the short run, it is very costly. I would maintain that if we look at what Continental Bank is doing in Chicago in trying to improve the educational system, in the long run, Continental Bank and many other companies will get more qualified employees. And if you look at what Cummins Engine is doing in Columbus, Indiana, these actions make it easier to attract top-notch people to its employ. In the short run, however, surely there are costs which some companies, for a variety of reasons, choose not to bear.

Next, if a company is committed and if it adopts these principles, it seems to me that after looking at the top management commitment, we should look at the quality of the staff. Are there good people assigned to the community relations function? It can be a broadening and developmental experience or it can be a dead-end job. Some companies view their foundation work as very separate and do not want to involve it with the corporation. Other companies view a short-term assignment in the foundation to be a very good development experience for managers who are going to be future general managers; they will be more effective managers for having had that particular experience.

Finally, all line managers, including supervisors, need to know that community relations is part of their job. They need to know why the company is doing what it's doing and the strategic importance of the particular activities. They need to be assured that the time they devote to designated community activities counts.

On the positive side, there are five initiatives that seem to me very important. First, we can talk about the benefits of employment security in those companies which emphasize security as well as special employment and training programs. Job security is very positive not only for employees but also for those particular communities. On the employment side we can also talk about special efforts that companies make for the disadvantaged, handicapped, ex-convicts, as well as programs for drug abuse and alcoholism, and English as a second language. All of these programs benefit not only the employees and the corporation, but the community as well.

Second, companies can also lend people and facilities for worthy community projects. Merging community affairs and job enrichment, some companies solicit recommendations from employees about how the company contribution dollars should be spent. This can be viewed as a special form of job enrichment and also quite useful to target limited resources in a particular community. Some companies, for example, have a procedure through which any employee can make nominations and recommendations. Such recommendations may be a movie projector for the PTA or a hall for the meeting of some community group. In these companies, employees can take the initiative (and get credit and recognition for it) as opposed to just

184 / The Work Ethic in Business

having the corporate contribution committee review requests from outsiders.

Third, it's been the experience of many companies that their job enrichment efforts also have had very favorable spillover effects in the family and in the community. Many innovative companies have examples of employees who grew and developed because of work teams and autonomous work groups. People were willing and able to take on more responsibility. These companies suddenly noticed that the same employees were now on the school boards, they were mayors, they were active in the community where in the past they hadn't been. Certainly that can be positive.

Fourth, small companies find ways to contribute or join with other companies to help solve community problems. In Wichita there is an employee assistance group that has developed into cooperative efforts by twenty-two business concerns in that city. Twenty-two companies doing what no company can do by itself. The Wichita Group offers counseling to troubled workers. It has been reported that it has been highly effective.

Finally, in the area of health care and cost containment, companies as well as individuals are worrying about the quality of health care as well as its cost. We all know about the soaring cost of health care. Analysis reveals that companies are paying most of the bills. In this area, Raytheon, Polaroid, Digital, and New England Telephone pay a very large percentage of hospital bills. Increasingly, we see companies trying to get managers involved in asking the right questions, particularly if they are trustees or directors of a local hospital. Some companies have formal training programs for their executives who are hospital trustees not only so that they will be better trustees but also in the hope of raising the important question of the quality of health care being improved at the same or possibly a lower cost. More importantly, companies in many areas are cooperating to examine health care delivery from a systems point of view. These efforts can have very positive effects.

In summary, we can say that, first, to be sure, there have been many workplace extensions into the community which we would all now view as negative. Legislation as well as more enlightened management are, however, changing this in significant ways. Second, to understand what can be expected of any corporation, it is essential to take into account the attitudes and values of top management and the resources of the corporation, as well as the nature of the community. Finally, the positive extensions of the workplace into the community on the part of so many corporations give much encouragement for the future.

Discussion

Question: I'd like to address my question to Mr. Frost, if I may. I have spent most of my career since graduation working with several businesses and handling some of their problems. You are what I would consider big business. May I address that issue? You mentioned that you have under you management people who could assume responsibilities in your absence. The businessmen I work with, who would like to get involved in the community, don't have that luxury in that when they leave the shop, they leave a vacancy. They leave hourly-type employees who do not have the same kind of management responsibility. Perhaps they could take on some of the responsibility, but management would not feel confident enough to leave them in charge. How would you recommend that they be able to extend themselves into the community? What can they do?

Frost: That is a good point. The term "small business" does cover a wide spectrum of size. As of yesterday afternoon my company made, if you consider the employees, a major acquisition and, therefore, we now have fifteen or more employees than before, so we now have seventy-five or eighty. Prior to this acquisition we had sixty employees, of which thirteen were salaried workers and the rest hourly. But if that is big business from the angle you're looking at then OK, but I think that through the course of business growth—and one must presume that a business will go through some growth cycle—you'll find that there is a time in the beginning stages of any business when the total business has got to be the business at hand. But at some point, it then emerges and begins to join the flow of the enterprises within its region. I think that that is the point that I'm talking about. My definition of size is not a technical number. It's when an enterprise becomes a business in the stream of our capitalist society that there must be more free time for the owner, and there ought to be good secondary management in place. These steps were self-serving in my case because, as a consequence of my business running on its own, not only do I get involved with my community, through drug programs, functional activities, etc., but I also became a director of several other companies due to the fact that I have time and agitate a lot. All of those activities came about as a consequence of my stepping out of my business, forcing the growth of the business in the reasonable span of time and then moving on, getting out of it, and letting it run on its own. I think you can't sit back and wait and just see what lies ahead.

Question: I'm talking about electricians, small shop keepers, etc., whose dream is never to be more than a business with a son or family, nothing as big as what you are talking about.

Frost: Then they have to continue through their associations, rotaries, and the other functions of which they are already members.

Question: I guess I'll start off with a question to Mr. Foulkes. You talked about identifying what the community is and about what seemed to be geographical divisions. Who is the community that lives in these geographical designations that you suggested? I note that during the high point of urban planning there was often talk about how what was done was to take over an area, and the progressives are taking and rehabilitating areas. Certainly we're not rehabilitating them for the people who lived there, and I am wondering to what extent, when a corporation does become involved in something like the Renaissance Center in Detroit, does the feeling of responsibility and involvement reach toward those who had been living in the area previously. What happens to them? Is that part of the community which is considered as part of the corporation's responsibility, or is the objective to bring the community which is involved up again to a level that nice respectable people would live in and feel safe in?

Foulkes: There are two points to your questions. One is that sometimes community relations and employee relations can merge, because sometimes some employees in the corporation may live in the area. If that is the case, the company which is responsible has to have the employee input or employee involvement in the plan and the implications of those particular plans. Second, part of the plan is to be concerned with relocations or developing systems with respect to relocations. That has begun in some places but where it hasn't begun it will be to the detriment of those corporations.

Childers: We have had similar problems with the area of your concern. We try to work with the community and provide services where a corporation, for example, has some expertise. It is that type of help when our engineering department would go to the city and offer its services. A small town of thirty thousand may need assistance in drafting new street plans. Whatever the technical problem might be, we try to provide the capability. We provide a great deal of manpower to help our community solve some of those types of problems, even to the point of going to a particular real estate firm to work with them to purchase certain lands, which, in turn, can be donated back to the city to get your evacuation problem resolved and at the same time assure that people have some place to go.

In Boulder, Texas we are considering over the long-range an expansion almost 50 percent of the size of that refinery so that we can utilize heavy crude oils, which most of the refineries in this country cannot, because it was always preferable to use the light crudes and not have the sulphur problem. Today, however, we are approaching the end of an era and we are going to have to face the reality of having to burn heavier crudes. We have to expand that refinery right into a community that we built. We built the school, we virtually furnished an existence for the people in the way of housing and local government. Now we are facing the sober reality that we have to move those people for that expansion. So we have carefully planned and developed a new area in a nice part of the community, putting in utilities and streets. We've had town meetings and forums to convince the people that the change is necessary.

They come back to us and say, "Look, you're a big corporation, look at our problem. We are about to lose our church because it is down in that area and you are moving us way over here where the church doesn't exist." We are going to move that church or build a new one and we will rebuild the park and playground for the children. So you can accomplish things as a large corporation but you have to work with the community, you have to work with the people and it takes time, but it is well worth it.

Question: Apparently I did not make myself entirely clear. I am not talking about situations where the corporation has to expand and change the nature of the community from residential to manufacturing, or when the town is going to build a civic center in what would totally be a residential area. I thought I heard some of you talking about improving the quality of housing and some in areas around civic centers. This is the situation that in urban renewal's heyday was often regarded as "Negro removal." We clean up the area not so that the people who lived there before can go back to live again, rather we get them out of the way so that nice respectable people can come in to live. No, what I am talking about is, in this kind of environment, to what extent would the old charge of "Negro removal" be something that you would recognize as a problem within some of the works in community development that corporations today are becoming involved in? This does not necessarily include employees; it may be people who have nothing whatsoever to do with the company or its product, but people who just happen to live in an area where the company has acquired an interest.

Childers: We are in a unique situation. We are in a community where the black population is virtually nonexistent because they don't like our community, because people up here have had so many nice cultural things to offer that we don't have, and we can't convince anyone to come to our community for that very reason. That includes medical doctors, professionals, and research people. In any event, we do have a lot of poor people who have to be moved from time to time. We approach this problem primarily through our own volunteer actions as employees. For example, as president of the Bartlesville Chamber of Commerce I advocated that we not rebuild housing in our core area rather than expand suburbia; that it is better for the community to use existing laterals than to build more pump stations, and to change our building code to allow more family units per square block. It started in 1976, and today we are building townhouses and complexes downtown where people can walk to work, saving energy. You have to do it through motivation and civic pride.

Question: I have two questions, one of which I'd like to address to Ken Childers and one of which I'd like to address to Fred Foulkes. One thing that interests me is, what do the stockholders feel? What are your responsibilities to them as opposed to the community? In other words, don't the stockholders have a right to earn a profit on their investment in Phillips, and if we go out, or if Phillips goes out and spends money in the community, doing all the fine things that you mentioned, is there a conflict of interest regarding the stockholders? Regarding my other question, from talking with you earlier, Fred, I know you are concerned with the issue of company pullout from a community. You even mentioned it in your talk and I'd like you to elaborate a bit more. What is the responsibility of a corporation when and if it feels the need to pull out, let's say Youngstown or another community, and move South or to some other area? Obviously, that has certain repercussions on the community and I'm wondering what kind of responsibility, if any, does the corporation have to the community it leaves behind.

Childers: I don't feel that the average stockholder has a major concern about corporate spending in behalf of the community or any worthwhile endeavor in the area of philanthropy. Truly it only represents about 1 percent of pretax net income, which is not a staggering amount, and yet it does constitute in this country about some $2 billion. So I don't feel that they have an enormous complaint considering that if the corporations are civic minded, if they are good neighbors in their community, then they have to make a certain contribution toward society. We further think that it's good for our business. We think that it's gratifying for our employees. In fact, I have never had employees react negatively to any of our expenditures in the public arena in which we operate. I think they are rather proud of the company that takes the time and makes the effort to improve the quality of life. The shareholder is primarily interested in having the company he has invested his money in remain healthy and viable, and as long as the financial analysts in the community recognize that the corporation is giving about the proper scale of dividend to its earnings, I don't think that the contribution end of that picture really affects it negatively in any sense.

Question: If the law permits you to give up to 5 percent and you are only giving 1 percent, why not give 5 percent and have more impact on the community?

Childers: You are absolutely correct and I believe it was former President Lyndon Johnson who criticized some of big business in this regard. He said, "Well, you boys aren't really utilizing the laws that we gave you." It says you can give away up to 5 percent and truly the average across the board in the United States is only about 1 percent, and truly it is a tough problem because I know that there are smaller companies than Phillips that do attempt to give away 5 percent, but they are in the minority. I think we feel that in the long-term we are going to remain at 1 percent of pretax net income, because based on anticipated increased earnings each year we expect our contributions will go from about $5 million up to about $12 million over the next five years. That is a wholesome increase. I think we just have to walk before we run.

Foulkes: Of the two companies that give 5 percent, Dayton-Hudson and Cummins Engine, one has to look at the top managements of those companies. Both companies are governed by enlightened people. And, although publicly owned, a significant percentage of company stock is held by the founder and other family members. In terms of the pullouts, I think that obviously there are obligations to the employees and to the community. I think they both involve adequate notice, help in relocating, help in finding jobs, maybe attracting another company to their facility or giving training. If you look at the provisions of the bill that Senator Williams has proposed, it is much like the bill that Senator Mondale proposed several years ago with respect to notice and aid to communities when companies pull out.

Question: Two questions. First, in cities that have any major fiscal problems in recent years or inner city problems, are there any correlations between such problems and participation of the business community in the planning or major decision making? Secondly, with the price of imported oil continuing to spiral and the degree to which that impacts industry, are there patterns involving a move of corporate manufacturing activity to the sunbelt of the country? I am just wondering whether that type of pattern has begun to take place.

Foulkes: I don't know of any correlation between such difficulties and business involvement in planning a city. Certainly after the riots in Detroit in 1967 there was much greater business involvement in resolving inner city problems.

As for the second question, rising energy costs are forcing companies to do a number of things differently. They are a factor in helping to explain company migrations to the South. Rising energy costs may also lead some companies to expand night shifts, if utilities adopt peak load pricing. More night workers can be expected to have ramifications for family and community life.

Childers: Many major petroleum companies are transferring employees to the South, particularly to Houston, and there seems to be a reasonable acceptance by employees of that migration. I suppose there are a very few who say, I can't take that hot, humid climate, I'm going back to New York, but most of them adjust rather rapidly to the change in environment. There is a study and there are some gentlemen from Harvard and other institutions who have been given a challenge to make a twenty-year study on the energy problems and its implications through a Ford foundation grant. Some of these studies are very enlightening. John O'Leary of the Department of Energy indicates that those studies are very accurate. O'Leary is something of a pessimist, but he says there is a certain bureaucracy in government today which believes it is doing the proper thing for the human race. What they are doing is retarding nuclear. They've killled it for all practical purposes in this century, and they are not going to advocate the use of coal, our most abundant resource for many esoteric reasons. For example, there are accidents in coal mines, etc., so they have made up their minds. I finally discovered who "they" are. It's a layer of people like Dawson and Schlesinger. Many are unseen bureaucrats who seem to run the country today. Their philosophy is that they are going to do away with the oil and gas industries as far as being an effective producer of energy for this country. If they do away with us, and the coal industry, and nuclear power, what are the alternatives? Frankly, they think it is solar. We have a very mobile society. What are we going to do about transportation? This group believes we'll go to electric. Well, I think most of us know, for at least most of this century, we are going to have to rely on oil and gas to keep this society going. I do think there will be a distribution of energy such that the crude oil and its by-products will be allocated primarily to the northern sectors of the countries of the world and the southern tier will utilize solar. I think there may be a possible solution to distribution, but I don't think you'll see that for a long time, fifty years or so.

O'Connell: I'd just like to contest with Mr. Childers the observation that the shareholders do not object to philanthropic behavior of the corporations. We have forgotten that it was no longer ago than the A.P. Smith vs. Ballow case in 1957 in New Jersey that we had any legal precedent for philanthropic behavior. We've had practice with that precedent. There are shareholders who do object, but there is a change in shareholder patterns so that institutions who tend not to be articulate at this moment do not object to the patterns of corporate behavior, though they could under the law.

The $2 billion you speak of is much larger. It is closer to $26 billion when you include all of philanthropy and much of it from corporate directors. I do think we sometimes wrongly mistake shareholders being inarticulate for shareholders not having objectives. The shareholders could become very articulate, particularly under circumstances in which the company behaves out of line, as in the fishing industry in Gloucester, or when Mobil Oil in its advocacy ads takes a position that all of a sudden becomes unpopular. Jane Fonda and her economic democracy pitch may have something to say about the vehicle through which the shareholders would become vocal. It is not only the Gilberts and those parental visitors to stockholder meetings who object to corporate philanthropy. There are others who are not articulate; some are lying low, but when the issues arise or the corporation changes its pattern, then the shareholders could get up on their hind legs.

Childers: I'll very quickly try to respond to you. This is a country of contributors of wealth into charitable causes and most of the money that is given in the United States is given by individuals and private citizens, not by major corporations. They far outweigh anything we give. Secondly, we monitor very closely any letter that comes in by a stockholder on any subject. We do not have letters of criticism of our giving for charitable purposes. The information on contributions is available. We do not get a negative feedback so we must conclude that we must be doing something that they don't disapprove of, and so we continue to give because we think we should and we think it benefits our company to be cooperative in this arena. I am not concerned until they get concerned, and we are keeping our heads screwed on straight. Fifty percent of the money that we give goes to higher education, and I haven't found anybody in those circles who wants us to quit.

CHAPTER 8

Some Aspects of Worker Dignity in the Corporation

The Moral Contract Between Employer and Employee

*Norman E. Bowie**

Our challenge is to discuss aspects of worker dignity. The phrase itself has many connotations that make a crisp, precise discussion of the concept extremely difficult. I will limit my remarks to a discussion of dignity and individual rights. My central thesis is that if a corporation or business is to treat its employees with dignity, it must recognize that these employees have certain rights that must be respected. In arguing for this thesis, I will contend that the "factors of production view of labor" is ethically unacceptable. Although I support David Ewing's strategy of extending constitutional rights to the workplace, I will argue on moral and conceptual rather than legal grounds. Specifically, I will claim that the very practice of business presupposes a recognition of employee rights on the part of the corporation. Hence I will conclude that the central issue is how to implement employee rights rather than how to defend them.

THE ARGUMENT

The Contractual Context

One of the most useful devices in the practice of business is the notion of a business contract. The contract device is used in the hiring of em-

*Director, Center for the Study of Values, University of Delaware

ployees, in the establishment of credit, in the ordering and supplying
of goods, and in the issuing of a warranty. Now a contract is a kind of
promise and, hence, is a moral device. In other words, since the use of
contracts is central to business, the morality of promise-keeping is
central to business. Persons who are engaged in the making of contracts are essentially engaged in moral activity.

We can use the contract notion to establish the central thesis that
business firms must admit that employees have certain rights which
must be respected. The structure of the argument is as follows:

1. One person can enter a valid business contract only if the parties
   to the contract are responsible, autonomous adults.
2. If a person is a responsible, autonomous adult, then that person
   must view himself and be viewed by others as a moral agent.
3. A person can be a moral agent only if he has rights which he or
   she can press as claims against others.
4. Therefore, a person who enters a valid business contract is a person who has rights.
5. To recognize that a person has rights is to recognize that other
   persons entering the business contract have rights as well.
6. Therefore, a person entering a valid business contract must recognize the rights claims of the other contractees.

Let us examine this argument in some detail. First, the notion that
valid contract-makers must be autonomous, responsible adults is a
settled principle of law and morality. Generally speaking, contracts
with children, mental defectives, and criminals are not valid
contracts.

Premise two asserts that in considering yourself as a responsible,
autonomous being, you must consider yourself to be a moral being—
an agent who can make moral claims against others. After all, what
must a person be like to be capable of being a moral agent? He or she
must be a rational person capable of making his or her own choices
and willing to live by the consequences of the choices. In other words,
a moral being is a rational, autonomous agent—just the kind of being
which is capable of entering into contracts.

Premise three is the key to the argument. It asserts that one can be
a moral agent only if he or she has rights which can be pressed as
claims against others. The essential concepts in a defense of this premise are responsibility, dignity, and rights. A responsible being is one
who can make choices according to his or her own insights. He or she
is not under the control of others. He or she does not live simply for
another. In other words, a responsible person is a person who has dignity and self-respect. But a person has dignity and self-respect when
asserting himself or herself in the world. He can only have dignity and

self-respect if he can say such things as "I may be wrong, but I am entitled to my opinion," "I will not change the research results because such behavior would violate the code of professional ethics which I have voluntarily adopted," or "What I do on my free time is none of the company's business." In uttering these remarks, he is asserting rights claims since rights are moral entitlements. What I have been arguing is that rights must be presupposed to account for our use of moral language and moral concepts. The following quotation captures my point exactly:

> Rights, we are suggesting, are fundamental moral commodities because they enable us to stand up on our own two feet, "to look others in the eye," and to feel in some fundamental way the equal of anyone. To think of oneself as the holder of rights is not to be unduly but properly proud, to have that minimal self-respect that is necessary to be worthy of the love and esteem of others. Conversely, to lack the concept of oneself as a rights bearer is to be bereft of a significant element of human dignity. Without such a concept, we could not view ourselves as beings entitled to be treated as not simply means but ends as well.[1]

Let me review the argument thus far. A person can enter a valid business contract only if he or she is a responsible, autonomous adult. But a responsible autonomous adult is the paradigm case of a moral agent. He can be a moral agent, however, only if he has rights that can be pressed against others. Therefore, a person who enters a valid business contract is a person who has rights.

The remainder of the argument is rather simple. Premise five represents nothing more than the straightforward application of the moral principle of universalizability. What counts as a reason in one case must count as a reason in relevantly similar cases. The argument for our conclusion that persons entering a business contract must recognize the rights claims of others is now established as both valid and sound. Since the relation between an employer and an employee is essentially a contractual one, the thesis of this paper that an employer must recognize that his employees have certain rights has been established. Our analysis has shown that a focal point for any discussion of worker dignity in the corporation must be employee rights.

WHAT RIGHTS DO EMPLOYEES HAVE?

To establish the conclusion that contractees must recognize the rights of other contractees is one thing. To argue what such recognition would amount to is something else. In this section I shall propose one analysis of what would constitute appropriate recognition. Our focus on contracts will continue to serve us well. Contract makers must look upon each other as rights bearers. What human right is closely associated with contract making? Surely it is the right to liberty. One cannot conclude a valid contract unless one is free to do so. That the market economy presupposes at least a negative right to liberty is accepted by almost the entire spectrum of political opinion from libertarians to welfare democrats.

To move from the claim that every human has a right to liberty to a list of specifications as to what the right to liberty entails is a difficult enterprise. On the most general formulation the right to liberty is a right to noninterference. But obviously that right to noninterference is not open-ended. We are not free to do whatever we want. The classic specification of a right to liberty is provided by John Stuart Mill:

> ... the sole end for which mankind are warranted individually or collectively in interfering with the liberty of action of any of their number is self protection. That the only purpose for which power can be rightfully exercised over any member of a civilized community, against his will, is to prevent harm to others. His own good, either physical or mental is not a sufficient warrant.[2]

The concept of harm provides a wide escape clause, however. Corporations could and, indeed, have argued that apparent violations of individual liberty are necessary to prevent harm to the corporation. On the basis of that argument companies have regulated the dress, social life, family life, and political opinions of employees. Any employee action which adversely affects profit "harms" the corporation and could be restricted. The problems are not just theoretical. Let me amplify this analysis with some practical questions raised by the senior vice president of a major life insurance company as we discussed the issue of employee rights. Suppose an employee of a major private health insurance company exercises his or her free speech to lobby actively for the passage of a government health insurance bill which would eliminate private health insurance companies. In effect, this employee seeks the elimination of his job and the jobs of his colleagues. Does the insurance company or his employer have a right to constrain his or her freedom of speech in this case? Consider freedom of religious conscience. Suppose a life insurance company acquires a health insurance company. This health insurance company pays medical bills for abortions. The claims processor from the parent company is a member of a church which holds abortion to be a deadly sin. On grounds of religious conscience, he or she refuses to process claims for medical expense to cover abortion. Does the company have a right to fire this person, and if the company did, would it violate the employee's freedom of religious conscience? Specifically, the company must balance the harm caused if it denies an employee an opportunity to exercise one of his liberties against the harm done if it doesn't deny the employee that opportunity. Such balancing must often be done if the employee's exercise of his or her liberty would not violate Mill's condition. Does this mean that companies have unlimited justification for limiting employee freedom of action whenever profits are adversely affected? I think not.

Business activity takes place within a social framework. Society permits business to seek profits only insofar as business plays by the rules society establishes. Hence, business activity should conform to the laws and basic moral norms of society. Once this background condition is understood, a business cannot restrict the freedom of an employee when that restriction requires the employee to perform some act which violates either the law or a basic moral norm of society. An employee cannot be ordered to falsify experimental data relating to product safety or to discriminate against a fellow employee on the basis of race. The fact that the falsification of the data or the discrimination would improve profits is irrelevant.

But what about restrictions on individual liberty that do not violate fundamental moral norms or statutes of law? Some further specification of the extent of a person's right to liberty is provided by the Constitution. It is here that the work of such writers as David Ewing is so important. Introducing constitutional rights shows how additional constraints can be placed on business. Since business activity takes place within American society, presumably business activity should be conducted consistently with the Bill of Rights which specifies our right to liberty. For example, free speech and freedom of religious conviction are specific examples of the right to liberty embodied in the Constitution. As such, these rights should be honored by business practice.

But what about those difficult cases where the rights of employees clash with the rights of management? After all, the employer is a party to the contract between employer and employee and the contract argument works just as well in establishing employer rights as it does in establishing employee rights. For example, it is already an established point at law that an employer has a legal right to loyalty. This right is captured in the so-called law of agency. For example, Section 387 of the Restatement of Agency expresses the general principle that an agent is subject to a duty to his principle to act solely for the benefit of the principle in all matters connected with his agency.

Specifically, "The agent is also under a duty not to act or speak disloyally" and the agent is to keep confidential any information acquired by him as an employee which might damage the agent or his business.

In other words, society gives a business a right to pursue profit just as it gives individuals a right of free speech. The interesting and difficult practical situations occur when rights come into conflict. For example, what about our insurance employee who lobbies for an insurance bill that would eliminate private companies?

First, it should be noted that the law of agency is in conformity with the contention of my thesis that no employee can be required to perform some act which violates either law or a basic moral norm of society. The law of agency specifically states that "In no event would it be implied that an agent has a duty to perform acts which . . . are illegal or unethical . . ."

However, both the interpretation of rights claims and the adjudication among competing rights claims rest with the courts or with other appropriate procedural mechanisms—e.g., the collective bargaining process. Moral philosophers cannot provide correct solutions to conflicting rights claims—neither can anyone else for that matter. As employees begin to press these rights claims, management has only two viable responses. It can allow the court to resolve such matters or it can provide the mechanism for resolving the conflicts within the corporate decision-making process itself. It is interesting to note that a free speech issue analogous to the one in our insurance company example was specifically mentioned in the law of agency text. "A employed by P, a life insurance company, in good faith advocates legislation which would require a change in the policies issued by the company. A has violated no duty to P."

The alternative to costly litigation is some company grievance procedure. Such a procedure would be an excellent device for resolving the problem by the person who refuses, on grounds of conscience, to process payments for abortions.

In this section I have argued that all employees have the right to freedom. The chief difficulty is spelling out the extent of that right and of adjudicating disputes between the employee's right to freedom and the employer's right not to be harmed in pursuit of profit. I have argued that the answer to both difficulties depends on appeals to basic moral norms, to the Constitution and to the judicial and adjudicatory mechanisms society has provided for this purpose. Only in this way can the concern for worker dignity associated with the practice of individual rights be successfully incorporated into a competitive enterprise.

IMPLICATIONS

The final section of this report addresses some of the implications of the analysis presented above. First, the nagging individual free speech or life-style issues are not isolated phenomena but are tied together theoretically with a general human right of freedom which must be granted to all employees.

Too often, discussions of worker dignity focus on isolated phenomena—e.g., music in the shop, the right to argue with the foreman, and the worker's sense of importance, or lack thereof, in the productive process. I do not deny the importance of those items, but I believe that the theoretical unity provided by the conceptual links between responsible, autonomous employers, employee dignity, and employee rights adds substance to discussions of the particular issues.

Second, a classic approach which treats employees (labor) as just another of the factors of production, like capital, equipment, and buildings, is morally deficient. Since employers do not enter into contracts with such factors, it is evident that these entities are not moral beings. Employers do have contracts with employees and hence the status of employees is morally different from the other factors of production. These differences should become apparent in both corporate practice and corporate conversation.

Third, recognition that employee dignity is conceptually related to the employee's status as a moral being requires attitudinal shifts on the part of the employee as well. If the employee is no longer simply a factor of production, his relation to the company is no longer purely economic. A job brings with it a set of responsibilities and duties. The employee has a duty to do the job well. Part of what it means to be an employee with dignity and self-respect is that one performs well in his or her chosen line of work. Shoddy work is often evidence that the employee does not hold himself or his job as worthy of dignity and respect.

Fourth, the so-called law of agency must be revised to protect employees from being fired if they refuse to perform immoral or illegal actions. Right now the law of agency states that the employee has no duty to perform immoral or illegal orders, but employees faced with such orders have little legal protection against dismissal.

Fifth, the notion of loyalty to the employer must be suitably revised. Loyalty is a virtue which should be required of employees, but loyalty is loyalty to something. One should be loyal, but the object of one's loyalty should be morally appropriate. An employee who possesses dignity and self-respect will not accept blindly the person to whom or cause to which one is loyal. If worker dignity is to exist in the corporation, one cannot expect blind loyalty.

Sixth, and finally, corporations should be currently engaged in providing corporate mechanisms for resolving the conflicts between the pursuit of profit and employee demands for greater dignity and self-respect. The quest for worker dignity will add yet another complication in the management of a corporation. Yet such a complication is inevitable and morally necessary.

NOTES

1. Norman E. Bowie and Robert L. Simon, *The Individual and the Political Order* (Englewood Cliffs, New Jersey: Prentice-Hall, 1977), p. 78.
2. John Stuart Mill, *On Liberty,* Currin D. Shield (ed.), (Indianapolis: Bobbs-Merrill, Library of Liberal Arts Edition, 1956), p. 13.

Individual Dignity and Institutional Identity: The Paradoxical Needs of the Corporate Employee

*Charles W. Powers**

I want to start these remarks with a personal example, in hopes that it will lead into the issues that are covered in this amorphous topic, dignity in the corporation. I entered corporate life from academia in 1974. When I first told my graduate students at Yale that I was going to spend time on sabbatical at Cummins Engine Company, a number of them were quite upset. They were not worried about my commitment to keep up on my work with their dissertations, but they were worried about my soul. At a going-away party for me, they gave me a gift—a slingshot. On one side of the V was the word "profit" and on the other side of the V was the word "people." Along with the slingshot, they gave me six stones with the names of six corporations that they considered to be irresponsible. The message was clear: we want you to be a David; we don't want you to join the Philistines.

They were, then, somewhat disappointed when I came back in nine months referring to Cummins in the first person plural. I often spoke about it as "we" rather than as "they" or "it." I was proud of the institution and, in part, I identified with it. But my graduate students were horrified. They got more concerned about my soul. In the course of the next year of teaching, in 1975, I decided to go back to Cummins.

*Senior Executive Consultant, Temple, Barker & Sloane, Inc.; Former Vice President for Public Policy, Cummins Engine Company, Inc.

I felt an enormous loyalty to the organization and what it was trying to do. I spent a lot of time talking with these graduate students about the decision. I discovered that the concern that had led them to send me off with a slingshot had a different origin than I had first believed. It turned out that they could not imagine identifying with *any* institution sufficiently to talk about in the first person, and their concern was that while academics never talk about their employer as "we," corporations, on the other hand, engendered a different kind of loyalty in their management employees.

Berger, Berger, and Keller, in their book *The Homeless Mind,* include a chapter, "The Obsolescence of the Concept of Honor" which helps explain this reaction.[1]

I would like to quote that chapter at some length. The authors say:

> The concept of honor implies that identity is essentially, or at least importantly, linked to institutional roles. The modern concept of dignity, by contrast, implies that identity is essentially independent of institutional roles.
>
> In a world of honor, the individual discovers his true identity in his roles, and to turn away from the roles is to turn away from himself—in "false consciousness," one is tempted to add. In a world of dignity, the individual can only discover his true identity by emancipating himself from his socially imposed roles—the latter are only masks, entangling him in illusion, "alienation" and "bad faith." It follows that the two worlds have a different relation to history. It is through the performance of institutional roles that the individual participates in history, not only the history of the particular institution but that of his society as a whole. It is precisely for this reason that modern consciousness, in its conception of the self, tends toward a curious ahistoricity. In a world of honor, identity is firmly linked to the past through the reiterated performance of prototypical acts. In a world of dignity, history is the succession of mystifications from which the individual must free himself to attain "authenticity."
>
> The obsolescence of the concept of honor may now be seen in a much more comprehensive perspective. The social location of honor lies in a world of relatively intact, stable institutions, a world in which individuals can with subjective certainty attach their identities to the institutional roles that society assigns to them.
>
> In other words, the demise of honor has been a very costly price to pay for whatever liberations modern man may have achieved.[2]

But the authors also recognize the ambiguities of the honor-bound world they eulogize. Like my graduate students, they see the positive aspects of a world where people refuse to become immersed in institutions:

> On the other hand, the unqualified denunciation of the contemporary constellation of institutions and identities fails to perceive by just this constellation—the discovery of the autonomous individual, with a dignity deriving from his very being, over and above all and any social identifications. Anyone denouncing the modern world ... should pause and question whether he wishes to include in that denunciation the specifically modern discoveries of human dignity and human rights. The conviction that even the weakest members of society have an inherent right to protection and dignity; the proscription of slavery in all its forms, of racial and ethnic oppression; the staggering discovery of the dignity and rights of the child; the new recognition of individual responsibility for all actions, even those assigned to the individual with specific institutional roles ... all these and others are moral achievements that would be unthinkable without the peculiar constellations of the modern world.[3]

In this passage the authors have identified, it seems to me, the very heart of the paradox of contemporary people. It is the same paradox with which my students were wrestling. At the same time they reacted in horror at my being swallowed up and being able to talk in the first person plural about my employer, they were also reaching very desperately for *something* they could relate to themselves—a cause or a purpose or an institution with which they could identify.

What are the implications of this for this discussion of dignity in the corporation? I would like to illustrate how this paradox in contemporary people translates into the tasks of managers who would like to make their institutions places where people are respected and where they are treated with dignity. I hope to show that the "people versus profit" dichotomy symbolized on my slingshot is much too simple. Since we began with an Old Testament story, I will pursue this with another Old Testament literary form—the commandment. Listen closely now to six commandments for respecting persons in corporations; listen for the paradoxes even while you find yourself giving basic assent to the several imperatives.

1. A corporation that is concerned with the public good and the dignity of its employees should protect employee privacy by reducing employee information kept in its employee records to a minimum and by carefully controlling the access to that information. For example, it should maintain a rigid

separation between employee medical records and management decisions.

2. The corporation that is concerned about dignity of individuals and public good should ensure that supervisors know enough about their employees to take into account, in both assigning tasks and judging performance, the family problems, prior problems caused by excess, and so on. And the corporation should make the investment in employees to assure that they get the help they need to deal effectively with their personal problems.

3. A corporation that is concerned with the dignity of its employees resolutely tries to rid itself of all discrimination in its workplace, ensures equal treatment, and takes affirmative action to correct past discriminatory behavior.

4. A corporation that resolutely pursues the public good and human dignity is respectful of the strong personal views in its workforce and does not delve deeply into the personal attitudes beyond what is required to achieve the productive purposes of the corporation.

5. A corporation that serves the public good and is concerned about human dignity develops and enforces strong prohibitions against practices that violate the canons of straight commercial practice (bribery, unusual payments, large gifts to customers, and so forth) and aggressively enforces the prohibitions with effective monitoring mechanisms.

6. On the other hand, the corporation that is concerned with dignity and the public good not only gives its employees space to exercise moral discretion and make independent judgment about complex ethical matters, but also seeks to maintain a constructive ethos by not forcing employees to implicate each other.

My guess is that you found yourself largely in agreement with each one of these six corporate commandments. I put them in pairs for a reason. And when you begin to think about each pair, you begin to see how difficult it is to run an institution that meets both imperatives. For example, the commandment about privacy and the importance of limiting information kept in employee records tends to obliterate the informal information base out of which supervisors are able to make decisions that are empathetic to employees problems.

The statement about efforts to eradicate discrimination and pursue equal treatment for affected class employees implies an aggressive management effort. It suggests both training programs and work rules that are directed at changing the deeply held racist or sexist convictions of other employees. The same thing holds in respect to corporations and unusual payments. The corporation that takes a very strong stand on that issue, and lays out very specific rules about ethical practices proscribing that kind of activity, will be strongly tempted to require employees to testify about their knowledge about the wrongdoing of their fellow employees. Some corporations may find that there is no other way to monitor unethical practice effectively; but a context in which people are required to report on the conduct of others resembles a courtroom, not a place where loyalty to relationships or cooperation in pursuit of shared purposes is fostered.

Now those six commandments, presented in three sets of pairs, illustrate problems inherent in any organization. I think they are being made more severe by events that are about to develop in American corporations in the 1980s. Corporations have always tended to organize and distribute resources on the basis of meritocratic rather than democratic performance standards. I think the increased concern for productivity now at work in the society will accentuate this tendency. Organizational decisions and policies of every sort will tend to emphasize short-term organizational efficiency and effectiveness. This same drive will, I think, create incentives toward the "dignity" side of our pairs of commandments and—unless managements are very wise— tend to make honor even more obsolescent.

For example, policies that protect privacy fit beautifully with a corporation's concern for evaluation based solely on performance. If a corporation does not want to spend much time dealing with or being concerned about its employees' specific problems and specific stresses, and if its evaluation of employee capacity and potential is based on the narrower range of quantitative factors, the fact that the employee information records are skimpy due to privacy protection is a plus. When you turn to the "affirmative action" versus "hands-off personal values" pair, you see a much more complex set of issues. On the one hand, equal treatment is a process by which corporations are better able to evaluate people on job-related merit. It does not surprise me at all that corporations have outpaced most other societal institutions in achieving equal opportunity. When friendships and home-grown values get in the way of fair performance evaluation, the natural tendencies of corporate life help push them aside. But affirmative action, by contrast, requires a richer, less obvious conception of justice. And its implementation tends to set in motion organizational dynamics that require human relations development efforts of a much more extensive—and "inefficient" sort. For example, to say that people must be *treated* as people, not just hired and promoted as people—or to say that standards of evaluation may need to be adjusted to respond to past injustices in or outside the job—will bring tension to any workplace.

Basic attitude change must be fostered to make affirmative action policies acceptable. These are human relations processes that engender
real moral disagreement and delve deeply into the personal commit-
ments and loyalties of employees. In other words, they disrupt the existing hierarchy of "honor" and may well cause disaffection with the
firm. And they are "inefficient" either because they cause employee
dissension or require such extensive efforts as to reduce productivity.

What I have been suggesting is that at the same time that we have
developed a set of values that are modern—that raise the concept of
individual dignity—we maintain a deep sympathy with, and a yearning for, the types of relationships that only patterns of loyalty and
honor can sustain. We live with this ambiguity, often unconsciously,
in the way in which we define our responsibilities and relationships
with the institutions with which we are associated. We want to be
free; but we also want to be known by, and to know ourselves in relation to, the institutions in which we live. It is clear that we want to be
known to be different from the Philistines, but we aren't sure whether
we want to be David out there all by himself or one of the Israelites.

But the nuances of this *personal* ambiguity gets lost when we focus
on how we want *institutions* to relate to *us*. We do want the anonymity
and control of our own destinies that privacy brings, but we also want
the patterns of institutional care that seem to come only by way of
incursions into our privacy. We want the individual dignity that equal
opportunity concepts bring, but not the institutional actions to
achieve them if they break up group loyalties and expectation patterns with which we are familiar. We do want to be associated with
institutions whose practices are above reproach, but we want to be
free of the responsibility to break personal loyalties or to be required
to "rat" on others even if that is necessary to make the institution
honorable. Our preference for all six of my commandments—and I
could have provided twenty-nine—illustrate how equivocal our expectations are.

If, then, we turn the tables and look at the ambivalence of preserving individual dignity and honor from the point of what it means for
the task of institutional management, we see how extremely difficult
it becomes. Little wonder that corporations are tempted to resort to
the "amoral" categories of efficiency and productivity not because (or
at least not only because) of "profits," but because it is exceedingly
difficult to find policies that get the relationship of people to institutions right. Good managers are those who anticipate how dichotomous
preferences will yield dissension about both practice and policy. These
managers try to shave the sharpest edges off policies that favor either
individual dignity or honor alone. It is sometimes possible to build an

organizational ethos such that temptations to unethical payments are so low that "tell-all" requirements can safely be eschewed. It is sometimes possible to foster supervisor-supervisee relationships that yield voluntary communication about personal problems without extensive formal records. Affirmative action can sometimes be handled with sufficient skill to avoid harsh reactions.

These things can be accomplished in theory, of course. But every manager also knows that affirmative action conflicts are sharpest when business is down; that supervisor-supervisee relationships are most humane when business is on an even keel; that building a corporate ethos according to which unethical payments are routinely avoided is incredibly difficult unless the potential "payees" have grown to expect that extortion is futile. Exhortations to achieve respect for persons and to preserve human dignity in corporations are easy. But to implement them requires managerial competence and diligence of a very high order. It also requires some luck: The quest for respect for persons in corporations, as in any other institutions, is never ending. It involves a never-ending chain of paradoxes because we are complex beings and because the complexities grow exponentially whenever we are part of collectivities. But the fact that the goal is never fully achievable is no reason not to pursue it.

NOTES

1. Peter Berger, Brigitte Berger, and Hans Fried Keller, *The Homeless Mind* (New York: Random House, 1973).
2. Ibid., pp. 90–95.
3. Ibid., p. 95.

Discussion

Question: I'd like to address my question to Mr. Bowie. I am speaking as a philosopher to someone involved in management training, so I might have missed something, but you speak of reciprocity between employer and employee as a contract, and it occurred to me that the employer is often not an autonomous person. If, in fact, the employer is not really a person but an organizational entity, this fact must change your line of reasoning. When I make a contract with my employer, I'm making a contract with somebody who is not liable as a person. That's the result of the process of incorporation. Therefore I don't understand what kind of contract you're talking about. Can you explain?

Bowie: That's a tough question. The issue is, are you entering into a contract with an individual or are you entering into a contract with an institution? In either instance, I think the logic of the argument must be discussed in terms of rights. If your contract is with the employer, you would have rights vis-à-vis the employer; if your contract is with the corporate entity, you would also have rights. The metaphysical problem is, is the corporation the kind of entity that can be held responsible? My argument is that a corporation as an institution does have rights.

Powers: You're not talking about legal rights at this point, but moral rights?

Bowie: I think you can argue for the corporation having moral rights as well.

Powers: Give me an example.

Bowie: They have a moral right to pursue profit.

Powers: A moral right? What is moral about it?

Bowie: They have entered into a contract with society.

Powers: Then you have a contractual right, which, in this particular case, is specifically legal. But what makes it a moral right?

Bowie: What we need is an argument to show that all contractual rights are ultimately based on moral acts.

Powers: Well, I am not so easily persuaded. I'm happy to let you try, but I doubt that you will be able to demonstrate that.

Bowie: Notice what happens if you don't. You then have to talk about legal rights that are not grounded anywhere. There would be no ground for justification.

Powers: Some legal rights are grounded in moral rights and some are not. Some are grounded in various kinds of contracts and institutional arrangements that the society makes for a variety of reasons in order to accomplish certain tasks.

Comment: Some moral rights and obligations apply in the face of legal provisions.

Bowie: A good legal policy, which I think Chuck is arguing for.

Powers: No, not all legal rights are moral rights.

Comment: That may not be so. I think Cummins Engine is walking on thin ice arguing with a doctor of philosophy. There are philosophical problems with your argument because your position doesn't provide for the fact that for every right there are equal and concomitant responsibilities. Now it is that responsibility that no one on the panel has dealt with.

Bowie: That may be true. What we are trying to do with the argument is simply to show that somehow from the notion of a contract that an employee has with someone or something—how as a result of that kind of contractual relationship—the employee has rights.

Comment: And a responsibility.

Powers: My point had to do with the nature and basis of different kinds of rights, but you are correct: for every right, there is a concomitant duty sufficient to meet the right opened up.

Bowie: No, that is not true.

Powers: If that is not tautological, then at least I think it comes very close to being an axiological necessity. But the problem is that people who claim rights often do not tell you how or where the duties become specified. One of the things that I was suggesting by introducing the concept of honor, and the importance of people's ability to relate to institutions, is the stake society has in people feeling that they have certain kinds of obligations to institutions. We have all been reading about the "new worker," the employee who makes enormous demands on institutions. Such people feel that they have no institutional obligations at all. And that is not only a problem for institutions that wish to create a place for dignity and a sense of honor; it is also a problem for—a basic paradox for—contemporary human beings who want to identify with something. I expect all kinds of things in institutions, but in no sense am I willing to make the philosophical leap that suggests that because corporations have responsibilities, or because people have loyalties to them, they should have moral rights.

Comment: I don't see why we can't consider the corporation as a collection of individuals. It represents a collection of individuals, including the stockholder program, and not a fictitious entity.

Powers: In that analysis those individuals who have gotten together and gotten the government to grant them the limited liability of the corporate form suddenly acquire additional moral rights beyond those they individually have as persons.

Comment: It is an entity that represents a group of human beings who are all capable of acting as moral beings. So has not that moral entity, comprised of moral humans—real beings, not fictitious ones—the same problems as persons? The difficulty you are having in defining rights or responsibilities of the corporation stems from the fact that you're talking about a corporation as a fictitious being, and not as a legal being—or not really human.

Powers: I agree, if you are simply talking about the need for institutions to develop an ethos that creates a sense that the institution is itself honorable, and therefore capable of relating to constituencies in an honorable way. That's what I mean. We are very definitely lost without that. But to go on to suggest that the language that allows us to speak of a relationship *to* a corporation also commits us to acknowledging that corporations have moral rights is uncharacteristic of modern discussion.

Question: If a corporation has no moral rights, is it possible for a person to behave immorally toward the corporation?

Bowie: Only if you have a moral theory such that it is possible to violate obligations without violating rights. Now, most philosophers say that the class of moral obligations is wider than the class of rights. But you have to decide that issue.

Powers: If you are saying no more than that an institution can somehow embody worthy goals or that sometimes the harm done to it will bring harm to human beings affected by it, then yes. But I am not sure that an individual can act immorally toward an institution unless you go ahead and talk about the impact of the action on human beings who are dependent on the corporation. That is why I doubt that corporations have moral rights, although we do give them legal ones.

Bowie: The philosophy is wildly abstract here. Let's take a case. When I go in a telephone booth and I put a slug in the machine, I am cheating AT&T of whatever I owe. Now it seems perfectly sensible to me to utter the following sentences. First of all, I have wronged the corporation, AT&T. I have not wronged any individual in the corporation. Your question is, in a moral corporation, does that mean I have violated a right? Is that simply a legal right or a moral right? I would try to argue that it was a moral right, although it would be hard to do.

CHAPTER 9

A Peace Plan for Workers and Bosses

*Sydney Harman**

There has been much groaning of late about the slowed growth of American productivity, about how workers are turning out too little for every hour on the job, and about the profound effect of all this on inflation.

Various villains have been fingered—anemic business investment, more young and female employees who have less experience and therefore produce less, and meddlesome government regulations, to name a few. But there is still much head-scratching about why the rate of U.S. productivity growth is now trailing that of Japan and of virtually every other industrialized nation. "There are a lot of things about what has happened that we don't fully understand," as presidential adviser Charles Schultze has remarked.

What is truly difficult to understand, though, is why so little attention has been paid to a critical element of the problem: the adversary relationship between those who do the work and those they do it for.

Portions of this address appeared in an earlier form in *The Washington Post,* Sunday, April 15, 1979.
*Founder, Harman-Kardon, Inc.; Former Undersecretary, U.S. Department of Commerce; Special Advisor, Aspen Institute on Work and Industrial Policy

If workers feel (as most do) that they are just replaceable parts in the machine; if they operate on the idea (as they are encouraged to) that "they are out to get me—I'll get them first"; if the system is designed to generate tension on the theory that such tension produces positive results, then the workers' response is predictable. They will protect themselves, oppose pay guidelines ("I'll be paying for it all again"), and be isolated from a universe in which they are a prime factor.

Because we have built a system based on mutual distrust, workers simply do not identify global abstract problems of productivity and competitiveness as theirs. Where the adversary relationship has been replaced by mutuality and trust, where the emphasis has been on humans rather than on machines and systems, the result has been very different. Stunning reductions have developed in *total* costs—including the heavy price we pay for elaborate systems of quality control, supervision, product warranty, and other costs not included in traditional productivity measures—and striking gains have been made in output.

I have seen it happen in industry at Harman International, when I was chief executive of that manufacturer of high-fidelity equipment, auto mirrors, and other products. I have seen the idea adopted in the federal bureaucracy, where workers are active participants in the decision-making process in several Commerce Department units. And I have seen the idea gain acceptance in a growing number of other corporations.

Some managers may not like to face it, but experience makes clear that workers possess an enormous untapped inventory of knowhow. If ever they believed they were genuinely respected for what they know—if they were truly part of the action—they would jolt our economists, our pundits, and our savants with what they would produce.

I am not speaking about programs aimed at worker "motivation" or "job enrichment" or suggestion boxes, about piped-in music or employee swimming pools or other paternalistic benefits that "we," in our wisdom and generosity, provide for "you." Those are seen as ways to increase production, as the "carrot bastard"—which of course is what they are—and they do not survive worker suspicion. Rather, I am talking about workers sharing fully in making the decisions that design their lives at work.

Consider what happened at a Harman International plant in Bolivar, Tennessee. There, mutual trust led to early negotiation and agreement on a union contract that produced significant savings. The conventional negotiating process, conducted in a "hot atmosphere," invariably had generated deep tension and excess manufacturing costs. In the months before the contract expired, tremendous amounts of ex-

pensive and inefficient overtime would be worked to ensure an available inventory for customers in the event of strike. When an agreement
was reached, of course, inventories were too high and workers were
put on short work weeks.

In 1975 the company approached the union several months early
and said, "Look, we're going to build that protective inventory, and if
we have a strike we're going to go through the same damn mess we
did before. If we can sit down and work out our agreement early,
whatever we agree to we'll put into effect immediately instead of waiting until the expiration of the old contract." The local union said,
"Fine, let's take a go at it."

That contract was settled almost four months ahead of time. The
wage and benefit increases took effect four months before the old contracts expired. The wasteful inventory buildup wasn't necessary. The
work remained steady so that the madness of heavy and inefficient
overtime followed by sharply reduced work weeks was eliminated.

One might expect such a contract to have been rejected by union
members on the ground that if the union had held out longer, it could
have gotten more. But the three-year agreement was ratified by more
than 90 percent of the workers, members of a union shop in a right-to-
work state.

Of course it is not all that simple; that agreement was the product of
mutual respect that had been built over some years. Worker core
groups at the plant had participated in designing the plant production
system and in deciding what health and safety measures were needed.
The workers had even participated with management in developing
competitive bids for new business contracts—and the bids were
successful.

The productivity increases that resulted from all this were startling: Workers did in six hours what previously had taken them
twelve. They ended up with extra time, and they urged that a school
be started at the plant. The school offered classes in the arithmetic of
business so workers could understand better how costs were determined and what profit and loss meant. Other courses were given in
public speaking, welding, music, and a variety of additional subjects.

The point is that people need to know they really matter; life doesn't
add up to much when that's missing. When it is present, when the
worker is a genuine participant in designing the work and in shaping
the conditions under which the work is done—and when workers
share equitably in the reduced costs and increased profits that result—then mutual trust can develop.

What also develops is a deeper sense of worker responsibility, which
is what could be found not only at the Bolivar plant but at two Department of Commerce units, the publications shop and the auditor's of-

fice, where employees have been participating in production and policy decisions. The way those workers approach their jobs and the creativity and commitment they invest in their work—is markedly different from what one encounters in most other corners of the federal bureaucracy.

These are not isolated cases, not flukes. Last May, for example, as undersecretary of commerce, I walked through a relatively new Cummins Engine plant in Jamestown, New York, that builds diesel engines. Dick Allison, who runs the plant, explained that total manufacturing costs have been reduced by as much as 25 percent because the worker has become the focal point, because "the work is done right for the first time," and because supervision in the traditional sense has virtually disappeared.

General Motors and American Telephone & Telegraph, to name two others, have also begun moving in a similar direction.

But we are not doing anywhere near enough in this area. The government is not the central player, but it can provide leadership and it can sponsor and support such efforts in plants and communities. A bill to provide $10 million for this purpose, a measure that could finance the training of people to facilitate this process for those who want them, passed in the closing days of the last Congress. But the funds need to be appropriated in this Congress if the bill is to come to life.

Numbers of studies tell us what last year's coal strike cost the nation, and we'll be able to recite the impact on inflation of other work stoppages still to come. Has anyone ever studied the cost of traditional bargaining that does not end in strike—but that does create enormous unproductive costs in poor work, excess overtime, and damaged relationships while everyone concentrates on the negotiation and is distracted from the work? This is how the overwhelming number of contract negotiations proceed, and the effect of this process on inflation must be immense, regardless of the terms of the final settlement.

It will not be easy, of course, to overcome resistance to this thinking in the private sector, given the threat some managers will see, at least initially, to the nature and status of their jobs and given the suspicions of many trade unionists, who wonder if worker participation committees will undermine traditional union arrangements. Experience suggests, however, that such fears are essentially groundless and, considering the stakes involved, there can be little doubt that we should press ahead.

There is growing awareness that the old system doesn't work well for anyone any more. It was built on attitudes that may have been appropriate at the turn of the century but that are clearly inappropriate today. We must examine the extra costs generated by our tradition of adversarial relationships in the workplace—to say nothing of the needless waste of human resources and dignity—and we must move to change them.

While this cannot be expected to solve all our difficulties, it can make a significant difference in our economy and in our lives.

Let me speak for just a moment about the role of labor unions, of the labor movement in this kind of process. I grew up thinking that labor in this country truly represented the cutting edge of progressiveness. But as I grew older and as labor movements in this country changed, I came to reflect sadly on how bureaucratic so many of them had become.

What happens in business situations with which I am familiar— including my own company, in which the union has been active in the development of the sort of relationship to which I have been referring—is that unions have changed, and their relationship with the people they represent has also changed. If indeed it has been true that there has been a lack of trust on the part of the workers who have led unions and dealt with management, it has been no less true that there has also traditionally been a lack of trust of the workers by those who represent me. When the union has been courageous moving into the area that this conference has been concerned with today, however, I have seen a dramatic change in the nature of the relationship between the people the union represents and the union itself.

Discussion

Question: Have some of your observations been triggered by Jerry Wurf's view that labor-management relations must inevitably take the form of a power struggle?

Harman: Of course they were. What is change? Michael Maccoby talked about that this morning. Much has changed since the days Jerry Wurf's which observations, in my mind, throw back to. Years ago the working population consisted essentially of immigrants who came to this country to escape hunger or political or religious oppression. Today the people who work in our factories are well educated. They are frequently female. The composition has changed. Aspirations have changed. Their requirements have changed. You're a fool if you manage or run a business and fail to recognize this and fail somehow to respond to it. Industry is not composed of fools.

I spoke earlier about labor relations in the time that I grew up. I remember vividly Engine Charlie Wilson and his comment that what was good for General Motors was good for the country. Look at General Motors today, however, and you will see an absolutely stunning awareness of the cultural changes I've been talking about. I don't know if any of you know Dutch Lanton. He is one of the central figures in this remarkable development at General Motors, and he characterized leadership for me in this way. He said that at General Motors these days he finds himself chasing the workers down the hall screaming, "Wait for me, I'm your leader!"

Question: I think you've been unfair to Jerry Wurf. There is a tremendous lack of respect for, and a lack of trust of, government workers—civil servants. They are tremendously undervalued as a resource.

Harman: I don't know that I've been unfair to Jerry Wurf. I believe I can make every comment that I did earlier and agree with your observation that government workers are being attacked in a very unfair fashion, and indeed I do. The conventional wisdom in Washington is that the majority of our difficulties grow out of the civil servant. Indeed, the reorganization of the civil service is something worth examining because the whole emphasis of proposed service reconstruction is to establish a new elite core. This effort proceeds from the basis that people will somehow behave more effectively if they are treated with sticks and carrots. I think that is a fundamental failure. My own experience (and I now talk in terms of two fairly intense years in Washington) is that there is a yearning among the people who work in government to be able to work in circumstances and an atmosphere that permits them to make a significant and valued contribution, a yearning to feel some sense of personal value and personal worth. And sadly our system, our organization, the construction in government is such that it makes that very, very difficult to attain.

Question: It seems to me that the entrepreneur and the bureaucrat are very opposite creatures. I don't think the kind of cooperation you're talking about can work when a big bureaucracy is involved, whether that bureaucracy be the government, or the union, or the management. Shouldn't the effect of bureaucracy on labor-management relationships be studied?

Harman: I would probably be one of the first to sign up for such a study. I do, of course, think of myself as an entrepreneur, and the distinction I imagine is that I started my own company. I developed my own company and I ruled that company. I find a joy in that kind of work and would find no joy in running a very large company. Running a very large company is almost by definition bureaucratic in character. Indeed I remember a recent dinner with a one-time cabinet member who made clear that his view of himself and of leadership was somehow defined in terms of running a big company. That is not a job I would be interested in. I love the creative opportunities in entrepreneuring. I love the challenges in entrepreneuring. I love the poetry of it. I don't know that I'd do very well doing the other kind of work. I think, for example, that if you check on how well I did as a bureaucrat you'd at best get mixed reports.

Question: Say I wanted to bring workers into the decision-making process at my company. I don't think my managers would buy it. How would I start?

Harman: If you're interested in developing an arrangement or participatory democracy as opposed to participatory mediocrity, if you're interested in developing some new decision-making processes from the bottom up, the first piece of advice that I would give is, however paradoxical, you've got to start at the top. The mythology that the blue-collar worker is in plenty of trouble and managers are in great shape is a lot of nonsense. We continue to live in an age of such specialization that in organizations of any size—and this is true of medium-size companies no less than large companies—managers operate in very narrow and confined areas and I think for the most part live in silent terror. They know how to fix the things that break in the area of their responsibility. They haven't the first idea of how the whole thing works. They have a sense of the company as having a life, motion, and rhythm of it's own. They are passengers somehow desperately hanging on for the ride. If you want a new process to develop, start working through a colleague system among your managers. Start moving, for example, to get the engineers learning something about production, learning something about marketing. The best experience I had in my time in government was when I spent a period of weeks working in various agencies as a GS9; that's about halfway up the ladder. Time and time again I found that the people I was working with were bright, intense, devoted, eager, but seriously offended by the fact that they didn't have the faintest idea how the material they worked on came to them. They had no conception or exposure at all to what happened to the product that they worked on after it left them. This is precisely the same role as a machine on a classic assembly line. Working where the action is, sharing a knowledge of the other peoples' managerial functions, and getting a systematic sense of how the operation goes are prerequisites for beginning to understand how you can do anything vertically.

Question: If I were to tell my managers that I want our workers to have input to the management process, they would think I was telling them that they don't know how to do their jobs. How can you provide leadership among your managers? Isn't there potential for real resentment here?

Harman: I agree with that, but I'll also add that you don't provide leadership for the future in the present by suggesting that everything is perfect. The reality is that in every one of these situations there is a mix of hells and benefits. There is an enormous amount of work still to be done. It would be silly to suggest that somehow Michael Maccoby or I or anybody else has the answer. We are really just beginning to learn. I do think it is fair to say that the next decade is likely to be the decade that is crucial in that respect. Leadership isn't something that we can take a course in. I don't think he was fully serious, but Issac Stern some years ago offered what seemed to me an interesting perception. Someone said to this violinist that lots of people know how to play the violin and lots of people know how to play all the notes. What makes the maestro? Stern replied, "It's what we do with the intervals between the notes."

Question: I still think leadership is often resented. Maybe even more important, leadership is not often trusted. It's taken instead as self-serving criticism of others. Don't you think so?

Harman: It's tough to know when criticism is legitimate, and even tougher to know when criticism that may be accurate is nevertheless dishonestly intended. I don't trust people who exploit. I think leadership needs to be earned. Don't be discouraged. I urge you to stay with the items that you've got. I urge you also not to throw the baby out with the bath water. I urge you not to take for granted that everyone who speaks from a critical point of view is automatically somehow ripping you up, because that is simply not the case. The trick, it seems to me, is to draw a distinction between those who are taking advantage, using clever and manipulative language, and those who are acting out of a sense of conscience and social responsibility. If I respond in any way to what you say it is only in terms of suggesting that being suspicious of criticism may very well amount to turning one's back on opportunity for genuine profits.

CHAPTER 10

Labor, Government, and Corporate Views on Work Ethics in America

Quality of Work Life in the Auto Industry

Donald F. Ephlin*

In the program it was billed that Jerry Wurf was going to talk about how American labor views quality of work life, and he did a very good job of talking about business ethics other than work ethics, so to balance things out I'll talk about the quality of work life.

I did start working in Framingham at the General Motors plant many years ago, and then I worked in Detroit on the UAW staff for a number of years dealing with the major auto companies (General Motors primarily) and Rockwell International. In the last nine years, I've been involved in quite a bit of quality of work life activity. Steve Fuller from General Motors mentioned that in 1973 we formed a National Committee to Improve the Quality of Work Life, and I had the opportunity of being one of the two union members, along with Irving Bluestone. As Steve mentioned, there were two General Motors vice presidents. Irving Bluestone is a vice president of the UAW and at that time I was an administrative assistant to Leonard Woodcock. I did get a lot of very good experience in quality of work life programs, not only with General Motors but also with Rockwell International at their Battle Creek plant, with American Sterilizer Company, and many others. I've been involved for some years in these programs as

*Vice President, United Auto Workers

sort of a sideline to my regular duties. I must say that I am a firm believer in the concept, and, as we get into the questions later on, if anybody wants to talk about specifics in these kinds of programs, I would be very happy to respond.

Let me just give you a brief example, however, of what quality of work life can mean. I now am the regional director of the UAW in an area that covers all of New England and New York City up to Albany, New York.* Included in the region are three General Motors plants. Two of them are very similar, the Tarrytown plant in New York and the Framingham plant in Massachusetts. They are almost identical in that they are both assembly plants, have approximately the same work force, and perform the same jobs. Representing both plants, I have had the chance to go to one on one day and the other on the next day. A few months ago we had a quality of work life seminar in New York at which Tarrytown management and the local union leadership explained what they had done to a group of scholars and visiting management people. On that day in the Tarrytown plant (there are about four thousand employees in each of these plants), there were approximately thirty grievances. The same day in Framingham there were close to five thousand grievances. Tarrytown settled its local agreement before our national settlement with General Motors a few weeks ago. The Framingham agreement is not yet settled. Now I have the opportunity to be in the two plants pretty regularly, and there's no question in my mind in which plant the employees are better off. It's not a question of quality of work life giving anything away contractually as far as the employees are concerned. In my judgment, the employees in the Tarrytown plant have it much better than Framingham, and that's very painful for me because I come from the Framingham plant and would like very much to see it be the more successful of the two, but I have to say that it is not.

We do not have a quality of work life program in Framingham and for a very good reason. What we are doing is different in every plant. You can't impose a quality of work life program on a management or on a local union. The manager of the Framingham plant is a friend of mine. I've known him for thirty years so I would not want to say that it's weaker management that has the problems with the quality of work life, because I certainly would not characterize this man as weak, but his management style is not the proper one for quality of working life. The management force there is not structured for quality of working life. As a result, neither does the union committee favor a quality of working life program, since the union in any plant reflects

*Mr. Ephlin became a vice president of the UAW in 1980.

the management of that plant. As Steve Fuller said, if you're going to change things, management must change first. Try as I might, I've been unsuccessful in changing the Framingham plant as yet, but I have not given up and eventually we will have a program in Framingham also. We are starting a program at the General Motors plant down at Bristol, Connecticut, and there is no question in my mind that it will succeed there because we have the right atmosphere and the right support from both management and the union.

I'll leave that broad subject and talk about a number of little items, and perhaps some of them will lead to questions later. The question has been posed, quite a number of times, about the adversarial role of unions and its impact on relationships. It was said in such a fashion that you would think there was something wrong with being in an adversarial mode. I would remind the audience that our adversarial role at the bargaining table is a legal responsibility. By law that is our function and in fact we are subject to many lawsuits when people don't think we carry it out properly. The question of performing the adversarial role on one hand and collaborating on the other, we do not find inconsistent. When I say "we" let me point out that even in the UAW not everyone shares my view on this subject.

Irving Bluestone and I have been the leading advocates of quality of working life and because we both dealt with General Motors over the years more has happened there than elsewhere, not just through our efforts but because of General Motors' efforts. Jerry Wurf mentioned that quality of work life programs are just part of wages, hours, and working conditions. We, too, think they are covered by those broad terms, but we don't think most unions include bargaining on quality of work life in the negotiations. There was one thing Mr. Fuller didn't tell you. He mentioned the 1973 agreement but did not indicate that prior to that time General Motors was doing organizational development work in their plants and not talking to the union about it. In fact, the vice president of General Motors with whom we do deal would not even let us talk to Mr. Fuller and his staff; he said it was none of our business. But we insisted that it is an extension of working conditions and that we had a legal responsibility to be involved, and so we got involved. Ever since 1973 we have been working on quality of working life together with General Motors but separate and apart from our collective bargaining responsibilities. I don't think one has interfered with the other in any fashion. In fact, they complement one another.

If anybody in the audience is familiar with the history of bargaining in the auto industry, he will know that over the years we used to have local strikes following the national settlements. Only in hindsight now can we look back and know what the causes were. Those were the quality of working life problems. The people in the plant, having all their money in hand, the good economic settlement in hand, would still opt to strike over local conditions.

In many of the strikes it was hard to figure out what they were striking over. The press and the liberal community poked a lot of fun at the issues that arose in some of those negotiations. We, at one time, had a big issue at General Motors over putting doors on toilet stalls. People had a lot of laughs over that; the "toilet strike" it was called, and so forth. But when you're talking about quality of working life, what is more fundamental than a little personal privacy? We had another issue in a Baltimore plant where the workers demanded a covered walkway to the parking lot. Again, the press poked all sorts of fun at us. Well, it wasn't a covered walkway that the people wanted but the highest skilled hourly worker in that plant did resent the fact that, although he got to work first, he had to park the farthest from the entrance. First, we had all the supervision, then all the white-collar workers, and then the space that was left was for blue-collar workers. It had nothing to do with what time you got there or what your job was in the plant other than that you were a blue-collar worker. Fortunately, that's changing in a lot of places.

People do resent being discriminated against because they are blue-collar workers; the only thing they do is build the product. They make the money, but the white-collar workers and the management people used to treat them as second- or third-class citizens. They do resent that, but it's changing to some degree. In the Framingham plant from which I came, the management tried to bar me from entering the plant when I was the local union president. I came back a couple of years ago as the regional director, and I was invited to the plant to make a speech to all of the G.M. executives who happened to be in the area because they were interested in my views on quality of work life. We have made some progress.

There are a couple of other items that popped up at this conference that I do want to touch on. One of the speakers quoted Leonard Woodcock, but he quoted him improperly. We had the question about bargaining and the Bill Serrin article in the *New York Times* that said that the settlement in General Motors gave away quality of work life. That indicated a complete lack of understanding of what quality of work life is and how it works. What really happened many years ago, when quality of work life at that time was called humanization of the workplace, was that Leonard Woodcock made a response to the press that all of the workers in the plant are already human; we don't have to humanize them. There's nothing wrong with doing the production work in America because someone has to do it if we are to prosper as a nation, and the workers should be praised for it and not ridiculed. He went on to say that you cannot negotiate quality of work life for 150 plants covering 425 thousand people in crisis negotiations at the bargaining table on the fifth floor of the General Motors building. If General Motors had said to us—how do you want to humanize the workplace?—we wouldn't have a simple answer to give them. There's a good reason for that. If we are going truly to improve the quality of working life, it has to be done on a local basis, and we have to let the workers involved tell people what it is that they want. If we decide in Detroit in all our wisdom what's good for them, then it's no better than in the old authoritarian system. So what we are doing in General Motors occurs on a plant-by-plant basis. All we do is get the parties on the right track and let them decide for themselves what they want to do and then assist them as much as possible. In Bristol, Connecticut we now have the committee formed. We will stand back and let them work at trying to develop what they want to do at that plant. That is truly giving them something to say about their own jobs, and we find it much more successful to operate in that fashion.

Now, many of the things that Mr. Fuller said I obviously agree with, but I must point out to you that the thoughts he expressed are not typical of the auto industry. I had never heard Mr. Fuller make his speech before, but I want to pick up a point he made because I have been using it in a number of speeches, and that is the question that we face in America about our declining economic situation and the question that gets raised all the time—productivity. At the moment, all of our problems are blamed on OPEC, and everything it does, because of what those horrible Arabs did to the oil prices, and Mr. Hall will elaborate on that, probably. I think it is a copout on the subject we're talking about at the moment. Japan, Germany, and Sweden are all proportionately more dependent on imported oil than we are. Yet, all of them have less inflation, less unemployment, more growth in their economy, and their productivity growth is greater than ours. Our productivity is still the greatest in the world, but they have been growing faster than we have. If this is so, then we must be doing something wrong in America, and I think we certainly are wasting our most valuable resource—people.

One of the differences, I submit, is the role of labor and labor unions in the power structure in the economies of our countries. In each of the countries I mentioned—Japan, Germany, and Sweden—labor people are involved in the economic planning with industry, with government, and together they determine national goals and all work toward achieving those goals. Meanwhile, here in the United States, we dissipate most of our energies in useless struggles.

American industry still has not accepted organized labor. The struggle over labor reform a year ago was not just a battle over what the law was going to say; it was an effort to eliminate organized labor in America, and this is a serious struggle that still goes on. Only the larger companies, like General Motors, deal with us as though we are here to stay, and that is due to our relative strength in large multiplant companies. I happen to be working in Hartford, Connecticut dealing with many small enterprises, and, after those years in Detroit, I'm shocked and dismayed to find that many productivity problems in New England are due to management still operating the way it did in the 1930s and 1940s. Most of the problems are caused by inept management. Workers are no different today than they were, except that they are better educated and better trained. They have higher aspirations and so forth, but here in New England, particularly in the small enterprises, class consciousness has led management still to treat them like second-class citizens and to waste totally their talents.

Now, lest anyone think that my being favorably inclined toward quality of work life has diminished my militancy, some local companies in Connecticut would tell you differently, since we just settled three strikes that respectively ran twenty-one, twenty-four, and twenty-six weeks. Two of them were over important economic issues, but I can say without equivocation that all three strikes were prolonged to a large degree because management did not know how to bargain with the union. They treated the committee scornfully; it was difficult for them to talk with us, and it sure is hard to solve problems that way.

I had a meeting in the governor of Connecticut's office. There were three people present: the president of one of those companies; the governor of Connecticut; and me. When the company president left the meeting, Governor Grasso said to me, "Donald, he did not hear one word that you said." I said, "Governor, that's why we are on strike; he won't listen to what I have to say because it is beneath his dignity to pay any attention to me." That is why we had a twenty-four-week strike. It was a horrible sacrifice on the part of the people and costly to management, but it explains why their productivity is low. They don't work together. Workers are treated like part of the machinery and they react accordingly.

We could improve productivity a great deal if we could get together and start working cooperatively. Obviously, we have a stake in making these enterprises succeed because it is our jobs that are involved. We don't like to let inept management ruin our jobs. Workers, as a group, have a bigger economic stake in the enterprise than does the manager who can move on if the plant folds. We need to do a lot of work to get our system functioning properly. As Steve Fuller said, we have to get our act together. I couldn't agree more.

Chapter 10B

A Business View of the Work Ethic

*John R. Hall**

I cannot presume to speak for other industries or even all of the oil industry on a subject so intangible as the work ethic. However, I think many workers and managers would agree with the broad definition that the work ethic is "doing a fair day's work for a fair day's pay."

Twenty years ago, the work ethic was something taken for granted by both labor and management. The question of what exactly constitutes "fair" work and "fair" pay was generally decided in negotiations over such concrete matters as wages and work hours.

Today, largely as a result of the changes in values and perceptions that began in the 1960s, the question of what is fair in the work ethic has gone far beyond the question of wages and work output. The degree of personal involvement in one's work, and the satisfaction to be derived from work, are becoming just as much a part of the work ethic as is the traditional concept of fair wages and fringe benefits. The topics on the agenda of this conference—and the very fact that we *have* this national conference to discuss the status of the work ethic—are indications of this trend.

A case is often made that the shift in attitudes that began in the 1960s, with young people's rejection of the Vietnam War, and the

*Vice Chairman of the Board and Chief Operating Officer, Ashland Oil, Inc.

challenges to the limits of authority of such institutions as the school, government, and even the family, have led to a dramatic change in the work ethic in the 1970s. Surveys conducted by Yankelovich, Skelly, and White last year showed that 64 percent of American workers feel their work is not meaningful, while only 13 percent feel that their jobs have meaning. Yankelovich studies have further shown that in the 1960s, 58 percent of all Americans believed that hard work will always pay off in terms of personal advancement, but that in 1978 only 43 percent believed it.

This year, Pat Cadell's Cambridge Report organization did a special study of American attitudes towards the work place. In Cadell's survey, 51 percent of those interviewed said that they did *not* plan to be working for their current employer in five years.

At the same time we have such apparent dissatisfaction with work, the nation itself faces the severest productivity crisis since the Great Depression of the 1930s. Consider this statistic: in the 1950s, the United States accounted for 52 percent of the world's economic output, but today we account for only 35 percent of world output. The projection is that this will fall to 25 percent in the 1980s.

Coupled with this disturbing trend, today's wages are at an all-time high—as are federal transfer payments for social programs—and are going even higher with inflation. Even more ominous, an astounding 70 percent of the United States work force is employed in government or service jobs. Fully 20 percent of all households in the United States have no wage earner, living off either pensions or government payments.

The National Center for Productivity concluded that if we are merely to sustain the standards of living of 1978, output per manhour in manufacturing jobs will have to increase 3 percent a year in the coming decade. The total national work force itself, however, is expected to increase only 1 percent a year in the 1980s, because of the declining birth rates of the 1960s.

It is tempting to draw a direct correlation between the changing attitudes toward work and the lag in productivity, and to conclude that a major reversal of work attitudes is necessary. However, it would be a great injustice to the work force to conclude from the falling productivity rate that today's worker is somehow lazier or less concerned with putting in a fair day's work for a fair day's pay than was his or her father or mother.

If there has been a change in the work ethic, it has been in the perception of what is "fair." What today's worker sees as fair wages and benefits is vastly different from what his father wanted and expected. Today's worker feels such things as pensions, medical insurance, vacations—and a voice in running these programs—are *rights* rather than benefits. Today's younger worker also has much higher and different expectations of the intangible sense of satisfaction and accomplishment that should be gained from work.

Let me interject at this point that I do not think this is, in itself, a bad trend. It is a part of our western heritage for each generation to seek a broader and fuller life than that of its parents. During the past one-hundred years, the average work week in the United States has been reduced from seventy hours to forty hours—and in some cases less than forty hours. At the same time, we managed to increase both real wages and overall national productivity. How did we achieve this apparent miracle? It was not because we had discovered a super-vitamin to make workers exert themselves more, but because new equipment and new technology to make production more efficient was developed and put to use.

Today, the real answer to enhanced productivity must lie not in pushing employees to work harder for the same or lower wages, but in stimulating capital formation so that research and development programs can successfully generate new processes, and so that new facilities and equipment can be afforded. In brief, the answer is to enhance efficiency.

This is the area in which countries like Japan and West Germany are excelling, and in which the United States is lagging. Between 1970 and 1978, output per manhour increased 47 percent in Japan and 51 percent in West Germany, but only 22 percent in the United States. Japanese and German workers clearly are not supermen; they simply have the advantage of more R&D and new capital facilities. American R&D and capital formation have been stifled in this decade by the combination of inflation and government regulation.

While the opinion polls reveal what on the surface appears to be a deep dissatisfaction with jobs, this is not to say that there has been a decline in the effort that the individual puts into his work. When the pollsters ask narrower questions, we find strange contradictions in the perception of job satisfaction.

Cadell, for example, found this year that 97 percent of all workers cite money, rather than self-fulfillment, as the primary or secondary reason for working. Even though 49 percent of the people responding in Cadell's survey said they did not plan to be holding the same job five years from now, 69 percent said they are satisfied with their present jobs.

In another national poll reported in *Public Opinion* magazine, 61 percent of those interviewed said they place more emphasis in their daily life on working hard and doing a good job than on personal satisfaction and pleasure. The old "Protestant Ethic" of working hard and doing one's best, for the sake of working hard and doing one's best, thus appears far from dead.

As Studs Terkel found when he conducted interviews for his book *Working,* people generally seem to subscribe to the old theory that the grass is always greener on the other side of the fence. This does not imply that they are going to move to the other side of the fence, or that they want the real estate on their side levelled and relandscaped.

Specific studies and programs to enhance the workers' sense of satisfaction and involvement on the job are more in Mr. Ephlin's and Mr. Horvitz's area than in mine. In the refining and chemical industries, most work requires very specific and sophisticated skills, and the work environment itself is less flexible than that for most manufacturing jobs.

My company has not gone to the point of setting up such programs as rotating jobs or the team concept of production—although Shell of Canada has one chemical plant operating under a team structure—but we have initiated a number of programs to enhance worker-management interaction. We believe strongly in the concept of joint labor-management committees for identifying, discussing, and resolving problems. In fact, most of our labor agreements specify regular bi-weekly or monthly labor-management meetings.

If the work ethic itself is to be reinforced, I think we might begin by looking at the perceptions fostered by popular culture, especially television. It is a sad fact that on television and even in the schools, service jobs are glorified and production jobs are often pictured as undignified and unworthy.

If everyone here today were asked to name a blue-collar television character, I bet most of us would come up with Archie Bunker, who has come to be the composite stereotype of countless negative stereotypes associated with the blue-collar worker. At the same time, of course, we have the stereotype of the Ewings in the series *Dallas,* with the businessman portrayed as an amoral and ruthless wheeler-dealer.

Both these negative stereotypes are related to the general decline in respect for institutions that began in the 1960s. The 1980s promise to be a decade of greater challenges than the '70s, especially in the area of productivity and new technology. Unless these stereotypes are modified, we may find ourselves incapable of meeting the new challenges.

The means of tearing down the stereotypes must be worked out not only between labor and management, but in the schools and universities where the workers of the 1990s are being shaped today. As Daniel Yankelovich said in one of his most recent analyses of the problem, "The desire to do a good job is a value that people bring with them to the job; it's not something that can be created on the job."

Even though new approaches to labor-management relations and the quality of the work environment must constantly be explored, I want in closing to reemphasize that the greatest challenge to both labor and management today is not in the area of revamping the work environment, but in the area of revamping our technology and capital facilities.

Again, in focusing on the productivity problem I do not want to imply that everything is satisfactory in labor-management relations and employee job satisfaction. Although we need to enhance the worker's sense of job satisfaction, the more crucial problem is to preserve and create jobs themselves.

The challenge is to awaken all levels of the public to the productivity problem. Once the problem is recognized, I believe the American work force will respond by declaring, to paraphrase an old saying, "We will do the job if you will give us the tools."

Chapter 10C

Confrontation Politics and Fundamental Issues in the Collective Bargaining Process

Wayne Horvitz*

What do we see in the arena of collective bargaining with respect to such things as the work ethic? I think it's alive and well, it's just a question of how you put it together. What do we see as impediments in this society to the development of an ethical way of making arrangements between workers and their employers that have within them common goals and common value systems? What is it that is making it difficult for us to understand polls which say that the average American doesn't trust government, doesn't trust business, doesn't trust labor, and doesn't really trust our institutions?

One of the institutions that has been a part of the life of so many of us in this room is the institution of collective bargaining, which is uniquely American. The United States system has been essentially a voluntary system, despite the complaints that are made about government regulation, government interference, and government intervention. Certainly, that segment of government which I represent is a part of that voluntary system. The Federal Mediation and Conciliation Service is a service which is offered to the parties on a voluntary basis; they don't have to take it. That is purposely so. We are an independent agency and the parties are free to use our services or not to

Director, Federal Mediation and Conciliation Service

239

use our services. We are in a peculiarly interesting position to see from one vantage point how this institution of collective bargaining is struggling at the moment. This is the vineyard in which I work and I think that some of the things that I observe lead to the kinds of questions that you're struggling with.

Take, for example, the question just posed by Don Ephlin: why aren't more managements more responsive to these kinds of quality of work life programs? Why are not more unions interested in them? Why do unions view them with suspicion? I think you have to go back (and I happen to spend a lot of time with these kinds of problems) and look at the structure of the institution which we are using to build on for this kind of debate.

What I see is not terribly encouraging. Basically, the institution of collective bargaining, which is the institution on which we are trying to build these relationships between management and labor, because it's the institution which we have adopted in our society, has some very serious fundamental problems which the parties are going to have to address before they can begin to discuss some of the more difficult problems, such as defining common goals and defining a common ethic under which they are willing to establish a relationship with each other and be able to make that kind of relationship work. I hope that I'll remember, if not now perhaps during the question period, to relate some of the things that I'm going to say to the things that Sidney Harman said last night with respect to leadership. That kind of leadership is sorely missing, I think, in many of our institutional arrangements, including collective bargaining.

We have a very serious problem in this country, which has been around for a long time and which is unique again as compared with other democratic industrial societies. We have structured in the name of free enterprise a management system in this country which does not look upon the union relationship as one of a partnership or a collaboration on any issues, whether you distinguish between adversarial or nonadversarial issues or however you are willing to put these two things together. I am a supporter of the adversary system, but I would like to discuss briefly some of the things that are nonadversarial and can be dealt with in that way. After all, our whole system of justice is an adversary system.

I see in this situation, which I came into as a third party and also as an exmanagement representative myself, what I've come to call "Dover's Law." George Dover was a production superintendent I worked with about twenty-five or thirty years ago. George had a very simple view of life and that was—if he worked hard all week, was good to his wife and children, and went to church on Sunday, he would come to the plant on Monday morning and the union would be gone. George went to his grave believing that.

There are many managements in this country, and more and more in recent years, that want a return to a kind of nonadversary system of reaching agreement, but a system which nevertheless requires confrontation politics rather than adversary bargaining. Unfortunately, we are seeing more of that and I think that audiences like this one should begin to examine why that is so. If you don't understand that it's happening and you don't understand why it's happening, then you can't understand what you can do about it. You can talk esoterically about the quality of work life and you can theorize a good deal, but when you get into the situation where things are going to have to change to make them happen, you will find yourself coming up against this kind of stone wall. Being a good mediator, of course I don't reserve all of my criticism for management. On the union side, you find that the rigidity of the union as an institution is not atypical. The typical situation is one of the same kind of rigidity with respect to the changes that are occurring in society, the kinds of changes that are occurring with the thrust of minorities, the new demands that are made by the increase of women in the work force, etc. All of these things are being resisted by the very institutional arrangements under which you're going to have to build this new world.

I think that one of the things that I heard in the questions that came out of this audience is a feeling that these institutions, or the representatives of these institutions, the management representatives, the labor representatives, were somehow guilty of sins that the rest of the society didn't commit. The fact of the matter is that the workplace is nothing more than an extension of society. It's not unique in that respect. The workplace is not a place that somehow differs; the people that come to it do not have different views in the work situation than they have at home or at church or anywhere else in the kind of society that we have. They simply bring that orientation with them into the workplace.

When you accuse the unions of developing protective clauses to keep blacks out, or when you accuse the unions of collaborating with management, of not doing things that they should be doing if they are progressive, with respect to the environment, you're really asking more from them than the institution can provide because they have, as all of our institutions have, including the academic institutions which many of you are from, certain kinds of built-in rigidities, certain kinds of difficulties in making the system work. That doesn't excuse them, it simply explains them. As a friend of mine says in this business. "I didn't make the world, I'm simply trying to live in it." I

think you should be accusing them of something much more fundamental and much more important in terms of developing change and
progress in this world—this world of collective bargaining, this world
of the kind of economy we have, and this world with increased government regulation which is not going to go away. The accusation should
be that they are not themselves changing with the times by preparing
themselves for trying to reach new solutions.

What I see in almost every situation in which I have been participating in this particular job as a mediator, is that the parties come to
the table unprepared to deal with the real issues. They don't even
come prepared to deal well with the traditional issues because the
traditional issues aren't the same. The fact of the matter is that you
don't come to the table to bargain simply on wages and hours. Mr.
Fraser can say what he wants about the guidelines self-destructing. A
lot of other people don't believe that and they come to the table bargaining with respect for those guidelines. The guidelines are a new
element in the economic situation and we are going to continue to
have some form of them for a long time to come. Then if you move
from there to the really subtle issues, such as the quality of work life
and the kinds of things that are important to people in terms of their
jobs, there are few people sitting at the table today in the higher coun-
cils of labor and management who really come to the table either in
the crisis bargaining situation or outside of the crisis bargaining situation prepared to sit down and discuss those issues. Until you begin to
work on the fundamentals, you are going to have a hard job getting
from there to the next step.

I think that is the main point that I want to leave with you. I can
give you lots of examples. I'm not interested in pointing fingers or lay-
ing blame, but I'll say two things about it. One relates to a recent trip
to Israel. I was invited there to discuss improving labor relations at
the plant level. The five people with whom I had the most contact all
had done their graduate work in the United States. They know more
about quality of work life than probably anybody in this room, but
they didn't know the first thing about what was wrong with their
grievance procedures. They're in a mess over there; they don't need to
be talking about quality of work life. They need to be talking about
the fundamentals of the relationship between labor and management
at the plant level. They really weren't very interested in working on
that. When I told them that they were kind of unhappy, but I think it's
a fact and I think they now recognize it's a fact, although they are still
unhappy because they don't want to work on it.

The other final note I'd like to leave you with is this. I know what
happens in these situations, over the years, when the parties them-

selves will not work on the problems, whether that problem is pensions, or welfare, or quality of working life. I'll tell you what happens. I come from a town that abhors a vacuum and we don't have the Employee Retirement Income Security Act which covers pension funds because a bunch of senators and congressmen sat around reading Marx. We have ERISA today because twenty years ago the parties to those pension fund agreements did not live up to their responsibilities to the work force. That's not every party, that's not every pension plan, that's not every safety regulation that led to OSHA and that's not to defend the amount of over-regulation we have today.

By not dealing with the problems before them, pension problems and job-safety problems, the parties created a vacuum. And government filled that vacuum with the pension fund and job-safety laws as a result of pressures on Congress from their constituencies demanding action. Now the fact of the matter is that the parties created that situation. Management doesn't like it, labor doesn't like it, but that's what will happen if problems like these continue to be ignored by the parties.

Discussion

Question: I don't think that anybody would disagree that a major input into productivity improvement is new product investment and basic R&D. However, it seemed to me, Mr. Hall, that you were stressing that not to the exclusion, but perhaps from my point of view with an overemphasis, as compared with the question of modern management and labor relations. I am reminded of a couple of newspaper articles and articles in *Business Week* or one of the other industrial journals about what happened when the Japanese from SONY came to California and opened a plant for production with American workers and without any major innovations in capital equipment. The only real difference about the plant from a standard American plant was that it had two Japanese managers. The story is that they out-produced, with American workers in California, the competing American firms. There's something going on in Japan that we need to learn from. I don't think it's more R&D, newer capital equipment, or better physical technology. I think it is better management, and I think that American management better wake up to the fact that there is something out there that they need to learn, even though we have always prided ourselves on being the leaders of the world in management. The same thing happened in Macon, Georgia at another SONY plant. There is something about the Japanese knowledge of how to manage people and how to involve them in the day-to-day activities of the firm and how to make them feel a real part of the firm that we need to learn.

My question to you relates to your mentioning that the oil refining business is very technical and very complex and that there are highly skilled jobs. I wonder if you have had a chance to look into the history of some of the work that has been done by Shell Oil Company in England and Canada in their refineries along the lines of quality of work life programs? It can be argued, in fact, that the more complex, the more expensive capital equipment is, the more technical an operation is, the more risk there is to the company in having a worker who is turned off or bored or angry, because if that worker screws up it can stop a whole production process and cost thousands of or even millions of dollars. An argument can be made that it is precisely in those high technology, complicated process industries such as yours where it is most important to have good labor relations first; then second, a worker involvement, quality of work life kind of program. I have not been out to check on these personally. I have read articles about them and heard about them at conferences, but my understanding is that Shell Oil Company in England and Canada has done some very innovative things along that line.

Hall: Responding to your last point first: in my prepared remarks—which I left out in order to meet the time schedule—there was reference to the program that Shell of Canada has set up. It is a program that involves rotating jobs within a team concept; the team can rotate positions and, to some extent, can divide up the task that is assigned by the management. It certainly is an interesting concept. We have not yet tried it, but it is a program that we are studying.

It is difficult for me to comment on your first question because my primary experience is in a capital intensive industry rather than in more labor intensive work, such as television manufacturing may be. I think it is an interesting comment that perhaps the Japanese have techniques other than technology improvement that we should be looking at, and I'll certainly take the time to investigate it. It is having problems because the Japanese and West Germans have much better technical programs and facilities. There may be other factors within the work force, but not being in the steel industry I can't comment on it knowledgeably.

Ephlin: I'd like to jump in for a moment and comment on a few things Mr. Hall said, and the steel industry is a good example. When you mentioned that capital formation has been stifled by inflation and government regulation, it calls to mind a couple of very pertinent facts. Since the wage controls have been in effect, wage increases in America have averaged just slightly over 7 percent, and, as you all know, inflation is running at 13 percent, so it wasn't wages that caused the inflation. When we talk about government regulation, this is management's copout. The airlines were deregulated over the violent opposition of that industry. Even airline stewardesses were lobbying passengers that if this happens all sorts of terrible things are going to take place. The trucking industry is fighting deregulation with everything they can muster. Let's take the steel industry. They're wanting more government interference. They want the government to stop the unfair competition, and so forth.

The Ford Motor Company happens to have a steel plant in Dearborn, Michigan. They are among the highest paid workers in the United Auto Workers. They not only make enough for themselves, they sell it to others. They are not making steel there because they like to be in Dearborn. They are doing it because it is profitable. What's the difference? They put some of the profits into buying modern equipment and modernizing the plant, etc. The steel industry took all the profits, didn't reinvest, and now they are saying that Uncle Sam should protect them. They want government regulation when it's to their advantage. In that matter I might point out that much of this new technology, in Europe particularly, is financed with American capital and American technological knowledge, much of which was subsidized by American taxpayers. We've run over there because we've found a new place where we can make a faster buck.

Speaking about government regulation, we're talking now about one of the big issues that is going to come before Congress in the next year or two which is going to be a big battleground—legislation over plant closings. Every management person who hears about this issue goes into a frenzy. They scream that this is the worst thing that could possibly happen. But every place in Europe where these same companies build plants there is legislation already in place covering plant location, plant closing, and so forth. Obviously, it isn't the regulation that they oppose because they run to the countries that have far more restrictions than we propose.

I have one last item to mention. I happen to know a little bit about the Shell operation in Ontario. It's not a full refinery; it's a partial one. I do not know the proper term for it. One of the reasons that they were able to accomplish what they did was that there was recognition of the union before the plant was built. This is a little unusual in America, even in Canada. I have to quickly give you an example. I went to Sweden and Volvo was planning to build an assembly plant in

Virginia. They asked my opinion as to how to build the plant to make it better for the workers, which is the way they do things in Sweden. I was very excited about the chance to have some input. We even had transatlantic phone conversations about how it would be best to construct this plant to make work a little easier in an automobile assembly plant. But then they came to America and hired an American manager and American lawyers, and, as Michael Maccoby can testify, they were forbidden to talk to us about it because they were told it would have been a violation of the law, it was a violation of the relationship here in America. They didn't want input from the union. They didn't want the workers to have anything to say about it. Maybe that's why Volvo never finished building the plant.

Horvitz: I think there is one other point that relates deeply to the kind of things you have been discussing at this conference. The question of productivity and the relationship of capital to that has an interesting aspect which bears on the point that the first questioner was making. Much of the problem in the United States doesn't have to do with increased capital investment, but with the acceptance of technology that was created by the capital now invested. One has only to look as a citizen at the enormity of the transportation problems in this country, particularly with respect to moving goods, forgetting for a moment the problems of moving people. If you look deeply enough at that—and I have because I came out of that industry and spent some years on the problems of introducing containerization—what everybody finds is that all of the technology that is needed is on the shelf, but it is the institutional arrangements, including the relationship between labor and management, and labor, management and government, and management and government, and labor and government, that are inhibiting the possibilities for more efficiency and for more productivity. There have been a few examples, one of which I participated in, namely the development of the mechanization and modernization fund with the West Coast longshoremen. That is a very small example in a very large arena in which the people who are going to change that fact of our industrial life are the people who are working with the institutional problems, including the problems of the relationships between management and their workers, and particularly under collective bargaining. Without that you can not change the institutional arrangements which now inhibit the growth of productivity in all of those institutions.

Question: I'd like to take up this issue of productivity and ask if it's possible to raise the question—is productivity for the sake of productivity good? Shouldn't we raise the question of what is produced as it was raised in a book called *Toward a Human World Order?* In that book it is suggested that we are not going to solve these kinds of problems completely because our hands are tied in a lot of ways by national security decisions. It suggests that we look at some of the think tank models that are composed for global concerns and some kind of global means to get security questions settled. Then we won't have the problems that bind our leaders and tie our leaders' hands so that there is a big gap between what they know is good or what they think is good and what kinds of decisions they can make and bargain for on the basis of security issues. I'd be interested in what your response is to this. Do you see areas in which you as leaders, or a leadership that you see, are bound and limited because of national security concerns that would hinder development on these more micro levels?

Horvitz: I can give you a quick answer: no. You've really opened up a global question. Seeing this from the vantage point of someone who works with industries and unions which are, many of them, deep into defense and national security work, leads to the conclusion that if it became possible to relieve the enormous amount of our gross national product that is being committed for these purposes, obviously we could use those funds for more productive and peaceful purposes. Other than that I wouldn't know how to answer your question.

Question: A great deal of ideological obfuscation has lifted while I've been here and I'm very grateful for the conference for that. It seems to me what I've learned here is that the basis for quality of work life improvements is collective bargaining relations between unions and management. And I think a very strong case has been made that indeed that is the only way that it really will work without being potentially very exploitative and a gimmick and a trick and speed-up and so forth. But then I think that only 25 percent of the American work force is unionized. Only 25 percent and that percentage is declining constantly. Also I came from Louisiana. Just within the past two years a right-to-work law was passed because it was supposed that prosperity would be right around the corner if we pass the right-to-work law. I thought it was a lot of baloney, but the people of the state bought it and there is very little possibility of overturning right-to-work. Not only that, I think by state law all high school students in Louisiana have to take a course on the free enterprise system in Louisiana, not on labor/management relations or problems of work, but on the free enterprise system with the clear implication that we can't structure and regulate labor/management relations, rather we have to go back to the market. The market will solve all of our problems. A key thing that comes out of the conference, besides the importance of collective bargaining, is that the crisis of productivity is a crisis of management. I think that Mr. Horvitz has expressed it very well that it's the institutional arrangements and people not facing the real problems. I would really like to see someone write a major article or cover story for *Time* magazine on this issue of the crisis of management as at least part of the crisis of productivity.

Ephlin: If I could make just on quick comment on Louisiana. There's a development in the last few years. General Motors opened a plant in Monroe and our problems in organizing that plant were not with General Motors, but more with the people of the area. We won the election. Wages went up to two dollars an hour immediately because that was the going rate at General Motors and now they pay it even before we organize the plants. Now the citizens of Monroe think that the union is really not so bad because they are all enjoying that extra money and the merchants and all are getting fat, and, so maybe, their opinion will change on this matter. Recently, the New York Stock Exchange published a very fine booklet on productivity. On page one of the booklet it listed all of the items that go into making productivity increase. It talked about the fact that you need to have a motivated, satisfied work force, properly trained, and so forth. After several pages of graphs and charts about how productivity is not going up, they described all the things that have to be done and they never mentioned people once. I had the opportunity to go to New York and talk to the people at the New York Stock Exchange about that booklet. They said they didn't mention people because they didn't know anything about those problems. I am very happy to say that they now have engaged some experts to try to find out what can be done in this area that would contribute to improving productivity. We are making a little progress, but it's not good copy for the media. Strikes are much bigger news than these kinds of constructive activities.

Question: To Mr. Ephlin and Mr. Horvitz: how concerned do each of you think we should be by the clearly antiunion activities that are going on? I don't mean violence or anything; I mean the organized activities among certain consulting firms to sell services to enable smaller corporations to avoid union formations. I'm just curious what your own reactions are to how serious that is. I don't recall the name of the movement, but every month I see their address in the *New York Review of Books* showing some worker and saying you don't have to join the union and that sort of thing. How much of a serious threat do those kinds of activities pose?

For Mr. Hall: it has been said in reply to the claim you and other oil company executives have made about government regulation stifling R&D that the oil companies themselves are making decisions to invest capital not in R&D, but in other areas where there will be a higher return, and for this they have been criticized. I wouldn't criticize them from the point of view of their own interests; this may be wise. But the data for this assertion comes from the business publications themselves and I think that there even is legislation pending in Congress now to try, in a direct or indirect way, to control some of the investment freedom for just that reason. I wonder if you think that it's just false that the investments have been going in that direction or whether it's true. Also do you think that it's not the place for the rest of us to be concerned about it or what?

Horvitz: There is some cause for concern, of course. We all know about these consulting firms who claim that they will improve your employee relations when in fact it's a course on how to keep the union out. We know who they are. I have to feel that this, somewhat like the percentage of union membership, is cyclic. If I didn't I suppose I'd go out of business. Management attitudes could be called tougher, or whatever phrase you want to use to characterize this. While all this is going on General Motors and the UAW have just changed that letter of neutrality to an accretion clause. There will not be another Oklahoma City and that's an enormous concession, one which obviously is going to set a pattern for other industries.

The neutrality letter was a major issue in the rubber strike because the auto people had given it, and at the same time, after a long and bitter struggle, Newport News, Virginia has now been ordered and is in fact bargaining with the steel workers. That's been going on for years. Five years ago the prediction would have been that they would never get that plant. These things go on at the same time.

I spoke a year or so ago at the third annual meeting of the Evansville, Indiana Labor/Management Committee. There were 350 people there all paying ten dollars apiece. It was obvious to me that they didn't pay ten dollars to hear me. I wondered who they were. It turned out that all 350 people in the audience were actively engaged in some way at some level in labor/management cooperation efforts in that community, either as shop stewards, city officials, officers of unions or companies, or on the committees themselves in the plants. Everyone in that audience had some role to play at some level in that community. That very same night I was handed a copy of the local paper and there was a picture of Wayne Kirkland on the front page and it was the time that he made the statement at Arden House that we are returning to class warfare. I suggest to you that we are a big country and what happens one place doesn't necessarily govern what happens in another, so don't give up.

Ephlin: The antiunion movement that is a food is a very great concern to me, though not from its impact on our union. Our union has been growing rapidly and the success of this antiunion movement is not in heavy industry; it's usually in smaller plants where the people need the union the most because they are the most underpaid. But most importantly, I think it is bad for our union, as I mentioned. While we are engaged in this no-win warfare, we are losing the economic war to Germany, Japan, and other places.

Hall: I said in my comments that capital formation and investments in new facilities are being limited by inflation and government regulation. When I mentioned inflation I did not mean inflation in workers' wages. I simply meant the inflation that triples the costs of building a new plant. And keep in mind that the depreciation you can take against the facility, which is the method of forming the capital to replace it, is based on what the facility cost when it was built.

As to government regulation, in Ashland, Kentucky, a small town of 35,000 people, Ashland Oil has eighteen local government auditors. They have moved to our town to be sure that we accurately follow the price regulations. We estimate that we have somewhere between four and five hundred employees whose entire work effort is dedicated to filling out forms and interfacing with the personnel of OSHA, DOE, EPA, etc. Our country is overregulated. Perhaps we were underregulated at some previous time, but today we are overregulated and it's going to strangle our industry if something isn't done about it. And I think even President Carter, as a liberal Democrat, is one of the people who is aware of this.

To answer your second question, a lot of our research and development efforts go into improved processes for manufacturing petroleum products. We also are spending research money in other areas. The reason is very simple: I hope to be working twenty or thirty years from now and I hope to be working for the same company. I don't think the oil industry twenty years from now is going to be where it is today. So if we are going to survive as a corporation, we've got to begin to enter new fields.

CHAPTER 11

Humanization of Work: Ethical Issues in Converting Ideology to Practice

*Stanley E. Seashore**

I want to stimulate discussion and promote understanding concerning the ethical issues that arise from programs to humanize work and workplaces. The Bolivar Case provides an account of one such program.[1] I will give some collateral information and opinions, and suggest some basic issues, to complement the facts about the specific case. Four topics will be treated: the state of the work ethic in America; some results from the Bolivar experience that enlarge upon the case report; the impediments to undertaking such projects; and the ethical issues that must be confronted.

To explain this choice of topics I must mention that I do not think ethical behavior results from interpretations of divine law (e.g. turn the other cheek), or of natural law (e.g., big fish must eat little fish). Instead, I regard ethical behavior as being defined and redefined continuously in the course of exchanges among persons (or organizations) who are in some way dependent upon one another and who stand to achieve mutual benefits if their behavior rests upon notions of reciprocity, justice, equity, and mutual respect. These criteria are elusive. They are not absolutes, but are expressed in ever-changing norms and standards. Viewed in this way, ethical issues are never

*Program Director, Institute for Social Research, University of Michigan

permanently settled, although workable temporary arrangements emerge. Thus, the "work ethic"—once rooted in religious dogma and the reality of harsh economic necessity—now is rooted in beliefs concerning the personal and social benefits (aside from immediate necessities) that accrue from being employed, being productive, and being cooperative. On the other side, the employer's ethic has been changing from hard, short-run wage bargaining to include notions of responsibilty for the welfare of the employee off the job as well as on, over his or her life span, and the welfare of the employee's family and community as well. New, changed ethical norms do not arise without strain. Humanization of work programs challenge the prevailing conceptions and operative rules for ethical behavior, and, therefore, are often profoundly disturbing to both employers and employees.

THE WORK ETHIC IN AMERICA

It is sometimes alleged that there is a decline in the force of the work ethic in America—people are said to be less attracted to effective and productive work, less willing to accept the constraints of being employed, more attentive to receiving economic rewards as a matter of entitlement rather than fair exchange. The evidence offered seems to me anecdotal, episodic, and unconvincing. There is evidence to the contrary, and I provide some examples.

Table 1 shows that employed Americans attribute very high importance to their work, and to the standard of living that it provides, as sources of their life satisfaction. In a national survey, people distinguished seventeen domains of their lives which, in combination, account for most of their variation in overall life satisfaction. Work is near the top of the list.

In a number of national surveys, employed Americans have been asked the following question: "If you were to get enough money to live as comfortably as you'd like for the rest of your life, would you continue to work?" About 75 percent of the employed mean and career women respond with a confident "Yes." This figure has been stable for two or three decades. The proportion is considerably higher for young people (about 85 percent for those in the 21–35 year range) than for older people. One may discount as he wishes for the possible bias in such responses to a hypothetical question, but the stability of responses over many years is impressive. The figures remained high even during recent years while the prevailing level of job satisfaction has been declining and the proportion is rising of employed people intending to quit their present jobs to find a better one. People, other than those

Table 1.   The Role of Work in Individual Well-Being

Domains of Life Evaluation	Percent of Variance Explained
Nonworking activities	29
Family life	28
Standard of living	23
Work	18
Marriage	16
Savings and investments	15
Friendships	13
City or county of residence	11
Housing	11
Amount of education	9
Neighborhood	8
Life in the United States	8
Usefulness of education	8
Health	8
Religion	5
National government	5
Organizations	4

Source: A. Campbell, P. E. Converse, and W. L. Rodgers, *The Quality of American Life* (New York: Russell Sage Foundation, 1976). The figures show the proportion (R^2) of the variance "explained" by each domain. Figures add to more than 100 percent because some domains overlap in their reference (e.g., marriage and family life).

approaching retirement age, have difficulty imagining a good life without working, even though they may dislike the job they have now.

In national surveys of employed adults, conducted over a period of years, information has been obtained about the characteristics of their jobs and work environments, and also about their degree of job satisfaction. The more satisfied people have jobs that, most importantly, provide some challenge (e.g., chance to learn, variety of activities, responsibility, or use of one's best skills). The second most important factor concerns having the resources needed to do the job well (e.g., suitable supplies and equipment, enough information, and help when it is needed). Of far lesser force in generating job satisfaction were the factors of economic reward (including fringe benefits and security), physical comfort and convenience, and good relationships with other persons at work. This regard for the challenging aspects of work, and for the provision of conditions that allow effective work, holds similarly, although in varying degrees, for virtually all kinds of employed people in all levels of educational and occupational status.

Perhaps people talk well about the work ethic but behave contrarily. One clue lies in the hours they choose to work, when they have a choice. During the last five years, the proportion of employed people who work more than forty hours per week on their main job has continued to rise. The proportion who choose to moonlight—that is, to have a second job—is rising and has been rising for at least a decade. People who are self-employed, and, therefore, choose their own hours, work more hours than those whose work schedule is set by an employer. These facts do not suggest that Americans have an aversion to work.

When asked how much effort they put into their job performance, 97 percent of all employed adults asserted that they "put in *more* effort than the job requires." This may be as much a commentary on the prevailing low level of job demands, or on the poor design of jobs, as on the motivations of the job holders. In any case, the American people do not perceive themselves to be withholding effort. They respond similarly, although with less consensus, when asked about the effort given by the other people with whom they work.

If taken at face value, these observations about the work ethic in America suggest that the effective performance of worthy jobs is integral to, not antithetical to, the humanization of work life.

WHAT HAPPENED AT BOLIVAR?

A humanization, or quality of work life, program such as that at Bolivar should be assessed primarily with reference to the aims of the people on the scene. As it worked out, some of the early expressed aims were rather global and abstract. Different people at different times conceived various more specific aims. Outside observers claimed to detect some implicit aims that were never expressed by the participants. I think this state of affairs is characteristic of humanization programs, and for good reasons. Initial consensus on purposes may depend upon those purposes remaining somewhat idealistic and ambiguous. Specific aims come to be defined later within the limits of what seems feasible at the time, and the estimates of feasibility keep changing. Unplanned good and bad side effects emerge, and themselves come to be the focus of explicit intentions or aims. The events can unfold in surprising ways.

Certain global aims were early formulated in writing and agreed to by management and employees' representatives. These were:

Security: The creation of conditions which give all employees who are doing their jobs freedom from the fear of losing those jobs, creation of a system in which there are healthy working conditions with optimal financial security, based on higher productivity.

Equity: Fair rules, regulations, and compensation; the end to discrimination based on age, race, and sex; and the sharing of profits based on higher work output.

Individuation: The concept that each worker is to be treated as a unique human being, rather than as an interchangeable cog, with maximum opportunity for learning and for practicing craftsmanship. The job should be designed, where practicable, to maximize the jobholder's control at the person's own best pace and style.

Democracy: Where individuals have a say in decisions affecting them—starting with their own jobs—and in which the rights of free speech and due process are part of the industrial experience.

An unusual arrangement was made, with the Ford Foundation subsidy, to allow some of my colleagues to observe the events at Bolivar, prepare an independent account of them, and to attempt to document the degree of achievement of these aims as well as any other aims or outcomes that might help to understand such humanization programs.[2] I will give some results from that work to supplement the information you have been provided from other sources. First, some "hard" data from the records maintained at Bolivar should be reviewed. The data cover a five-year period.

Security for Employees

Freedom from fear of losing one's job: More jobs were created, as the employee roster rose 55 percent. Involuntary turnover rates (discharges, jobs eliminated, scheduled retirements, etc.) declined 57 percent, while voluntary turnover rates also declined by 72 percent.

Healthy working conditions: Minor accident rates declined 20 percent even with the presence of many new and inexperienced employees. Rates of absence because of illness declined 16 percent. OSHA accident rates declined 61 percent. However, not all was favorable, as the rate of minor illness rose 41 percent and the rate of medical leaves rose 19 percent. (Comments on the employees' reports of their own health appear later.)

Optimum financial security: The wage rates for hourly employees remained quite constant over the period, when adjusted for inflation, and the wage rates relative to community standards did not change. (Note that for the country as a whole there was no gain in real wages over this span of years.) The fringe benefit package was improved.

Security founded on high productivity: Output per hourly employee-day in inflation-adjusted dollar value rose 23 percent. Net product reject cost rates declined 39 percent. The rate of customer product returns was down 47 percent. Some of these gains are attributable to technological and capital inputs. There was a significant gain in the index of employee productivity relative to standard, but also in the rate of unscheduled machine downtime. Supply usage variance (excess over budget) rose 22 percent.

In sum, the evidence is that jobs objectively became more secure, productivity rose, and quality performance improved; accident rates were moderated (but not illness rates); and employee earnings held steady.

Equity for Employees

Equity is in the mind of the participant or observer, not in the objective records, so there are no hard data to report on the fairness of rules and regulations, of compensation, and of discriminatory practices. Note that there is an employee stock ownership acquisition plan in operation under which the eligible employees can benefit from distributed profits and stock appreciation. Proposals for the introduction of a gain-sharing compensation plan (a negotiable issue) were brought forward but none were adopted during the period of study, nor since.

Individuation and Democracy at Work

As with the case of equity, these aims do not lend themselves readily to assessment through the usual existing record systems of organizations. It was possible, however, to get information directly from the Bolivar workers. This was done through systematic interviews on two occasions widely separated in time. From these interviews we derived thirteen indicators of the employees' experienced quality of working life, (QWL), and twenty-four indicators of job and job environment (organizational) characteristics known to be associated with a higher quality of working life. Tables 2 and 3 give a highly condensed summary of some changes that were found at Bolivar through this method. These data refer not to all of the Bolivar people, but to a panel of individuals who were interviewed on two occasions (June 1973 and November 1976) and who consented to be identified so we could match the changes to their own unique exposure to the Bolivar program.

The impression given by these tables is that the areas of gain are more than offset by areas of loss or no change. It should be taken into

Table 2.   Changes in Thirteen Quality of Work Life Indicators

Gains	No Change	Losses
Treated in a more personal way	Job satisfaction	More report of physical stress symptoms
	Alienation	
Job involved more use of, or higher level, skills	Job offers opportunity for personal growth	More report of psychological stress symptoms
Job is more secure		
	Working conditions	Less satisfaction with pay level
	Fairness of work load	
		Less satisfaction with pay equity.
	Fringe benefits	

Table 3.   Changes in Twenty-four Work Environment Characteristics

Gains	No Change	Losses
Supervisors more participative	Supervisory favoritism	Supervisors are less work facilitating, supportive, respectful
	Supervisory feedback to workers	
More work group participation		Less satisfaction with work group
	Work group feedback	
More worker influence on task decisions	Employee influence on work schedule decisions	Less association between work performance and rewards received (four indicators)
More adequate work resources	General organizational climate	
More work improvement ideas provided by employees		Less job feedback
	Number of work improvement suggestions made	

account, however, that over the period studied there occurred also some unmeasured changes in the aspirations and expectations of the Bolivar employees, such that the later conditions were probably judged more critically than the earlier conditions. When asked a series of questions of an evaluative sort, the Bolivar people gave generally positive opinions about the beneficial impact of the QWL program upon the employees, upon the effectiveness of the union-management relationships, and upon the ability of their union to represent member concerns.

During 1979, the Bolivar management, with consent of the union, decided to discontinue the provision of on-site professional staff support for the program. The joint committee continues its work, but at a reduced level of activity, and could become entirely inactive. However, it is my opinion that the Bolivar organization will not return to its original, preexperimental condition but will instead incorporate in its normal activities the values and some of the methods of working together that have been learned. The emerging array of ethical norms and standards may prove durable.

CONTRACTS, SOCIAL NORMS, AND HUMANIZATION OF WORK

It is useful to regard programs for the humanization of work as purposeful efforts to redesign the existing norms of ethical behavior which govern relationships at work. The Bolivar case, like most others, included explicit intentions to enlarge the range of both "goods" (e.g., individuation) and "bads" (imposed work pace) to be taken into account, and to alter the weights given to the factors that enter into a reciprocally balanced understanding between an employer and the employees. Specifically, the aim was to address jointly some matters that seemed unsuited for the established bargaining, contract, and grievance management arrangements, and to try out some supplemental ways (implicit contracts, oral agreements) to enhance mutual benefit. At Bolivar, it plainly was not a situation in which one party proposed to "give" something of value to the other without some expectation of offsetting benefits.

The difference between such implicit bargaining and balancing of interests, and the established contractual relationship, lies in three factors:

1. Most of the goods and bads to be altered are ambiguous as to the forms they may take, the scope of their impact, and their side effects,
2. Many of the proposed changes rest wholly upon voluntary acceptance and compliance, with little or no possibility for enforcement of the (initially ambiguous) understandings,
3. Some of the proposed changes defy assessment in terms of a balance sheet of gains and losses, of risks and potential benefits.

For example, the paid personal time arrangement was committed without confident advance knowledge of its scale of application, its effect upon employee job stress, its effect upon product quality, its impact on equity among employees, its cost to supervisors, its contribution to the quality of life for those who tried it. It was an act of trust and acceptance of risk by all parties. It violated certain established norms of behavior in the hope that some new norms would emerge to govern behavior in the redefined situation and steer toward collective benefit.

Earlier I suggested that social norms of ethical behavior arise from consensus among people (or organizations) concerning the terms upon which they will manage their real mutual dependencies. When the *real* dependencies are altered—as in the instance of the paid personal time program, and in the absence of explicit and enforceable contract—all depends upon the emergence of new norms. Such norms of behavior induce people to do things that are beneficial to the collectivity, to themselves, even though they have no certainty—only a trustful hope or expectation—that a reciprocal benefit will eventually come, either to themselves personally or to themselves indirectly through the maintenance of a more humane collectivity.

All this leads up to three observations. First, successful programs for the humanization of work are rarely bargained in the traditional sense, but rest upon some workable levels of mutual trust and upon the acceptance of some risks. Second, successful programs for the humanization of work depend upon the emergence, often very slowly, of new social norms appropriate to the objectively altered interdependencies and, as well, on the disturbing violation of some existing norms of ethical behavior. Third, it takes a long time; the Bolivar case is typical in that it has not yet "settled down," even after six years.

These matters seem to be well understood by many people even when they lack the words and the logical facility for describing them. That is why spontaneous humanization of work initiatives are so rare, and why so many such initiatives, whether by managers or by union leaders, are subverted. The risks seem immediate and palpable, while the gains, however great, are distant and lacking in certainty.

SOME ETHICAL ISSUES FOR DISCUSSION

The humanization of work (viewed broadly to include allied notions such as "new forms of work organizations," "industrial democracy," "participative management," and the like) is widely accepted as a desirable goal. It is becoming widely practiced at the local initiative of firms, individual managers, and union leaders. In some states, and at the federal level, the matter is being elevated to the status of public policy.

While humanization of work is variously approached and practiced, there are three common basic themes: (1) collaborative planning and action between management and the employees and their unions; (2) redesign of jobs and work environments; and (3) enlarged areas of individual self-determination or participation in workplace decisions.

The motives of the initiators are often mixed. There are forces stemming from political or economic ideology, from social welfare values, and from old-fashioned entrepreneurial self-interests. Occasionally the initiative arises from some individual's private impulses toward advantage, self-protection, and survival in a harsh world. The ends sought usually include improvements in the quality of work life for the employees, improved effectiveness in work performance, and accommodation to desired or unavoidable environmental changes.

The Bolivar case is unique in important ways, as all specific cases are, but it serves to illustrate some pervasive issues of ethics, and issues concerning the "work ethic," that are common to many such efforts to humanize work.

1. Work ethic: The idea of the "work ethic" carries a load of meanings, which have changed and developed from the last century to this one. Work formerly was often individual, physical, performed to time standards, and quality controlled by the worker. Under technological advances and some humanization programs, work more often emphasizes collaboration, work system management and control, collective action, surveillance of work flows, nonrepetitive initiative and ingenuity, and the like. Who now wants or needs hard work, long hours, imposed time standards for accomplishment and evaluation of the work ethic in terms of acceptance of hardship, suffering, and inconvenience? Can we invent a new conception of the work ethic, and a new calculation of the reciprocities that are involved?

2. Gain sharing: Who "owns" (should own) the product of labor, of capital, of managerial inputs? As a society we are of mixed view. Congress legislates tax advantages to firms that take steps to share ownership with the employees (e.g., ESOP plans). The Profit Sharing Foundation reports some increasing use of sharing plans. But, some managers have been sued by shareholders for squandering potential profits on costly employee or community projects. When gains accrue from humanization of work programs, how can they most ethically be allocated? (Note that in the Bolivar case virtually everyone appeared to benefit in one way or another, but the terms for sharing remain ambiguous, elusive, and controversial.)

3. Voluntarism: Many humanization programs, including the one at Bolivar, emphasize voluntarism. Still, a good deal of persuasion and (one suspects) of subtle coercion took place in initiating and advancing the program. Bolivar is by no means unique in this respect. Must voluntarism be imposed? Can a humanization program proceed without coercion?

4. Role of experts: The theory, value orientation, and often the action intentions as well, in humanization programs, emphasize the importance of the principle of mutual self-help. Experts, particularly outside experts, usually try in all good will, to do no more than encourage and assist others in doing what the others want to do. Still, most humanization programs do involve very influential expertise. Is this unavoidable? What ethical problems arise when expertise is applied and the expertise goes beyond assistance in social change technology to include the promotion of the expert's own social goals and social values? How can we develop suitable professional role definitions and ethical norms for such experts?

5. Costs, risks, and benefits of social change: Any significant change in an organization is bound to carry risks, costs, and benefits, particularly during the transition period. Ideally, the risks and costs should be moderated, and should be shared equitably among people in some proportion to their prospective benefits. In humanization programs, are there some people, because of the positions they occupy, who are put at inequitably greater risk than others? Some say that this is so for supervisors and middle-level managers, and for union leaders. Note the advance assurances provided in the Bolivar case. Were they adequate? Could more be done?

6. What is a "humanized" job like?: Most humanization of work programs start with some rather fixed ideas about what jobs *should* be like. For example, there is mention of opportunity to learn, opportunity for self-determination at work, relief from onerous physical conditions and arbitrary pacing of work, etc. But not all people want the same things with like priorities. In the Bolivar case, was the principle of *individuation* realized? If not, could it have been? What ethical considerations can help resolve conflicts between the requirements of an integrated work system and the surrounding economic constraints, on the one hand, and the ideal of humanizing

work in individualistic ways? Who deserves priority—the individual
or the collectivity?

NOTES

1. Karen S. Henderson, *Bolivar.* Cambridge: Harvard Business School, 1977, pp. 30,
   multilith.
2. A report, *The Bolivar Quality of Work Experiment,* by Barry A. Macy, G. E. Ledford,
   Jr., and Edward E. Lawler III, was scheduled for publication by Wiley-Interscience in
   1980.

Discussion

Question: Could you give an example of an ethical norm that was upset by the Bolivar experiment and the new norm that came in to replace it?

Seashore: Equal pay for equal work, to name one. Another example is "A fair day's work for a fair day's pay". Some Bolivar people were going home as much as four hours early and getting paid for eight, the person on the next machine not having that advantage. Norms of equity were disrupted with equity coming to be defined by output instead of time at work. There were changes in what people did, what you could count on them to do, and their reasons for doing it. Accommodation was difficult, and still incomplete after a couple of years.

Question: What makes those ethical principles rather than economic principles?

Seashore: Is there much difference? I suggest that all ethical rules rest on some real dependency which one person or organization has on another. The values at stake may be economic or noneconomic. They may be altruistic.

Question: What is the possibility of an adversary relationship work-ing alongside a cooperative one? Life is dispersed with that type of relationship almost at every turn. An example would be competition within an athletic team. I don't feel that they are mutually exclusive; they have to live side by side. I'd like to get your opinion on this.

Seashore: This is a matter of some debate among union leaders and others. My personal view, without much evidence to back it up, is that the two modes of relationship can coexist, and that there is benefit in their coexisting.

Question: Getting back to the differential number of hours worked in a day. Could it be said that an eight-hour day is possibly imposing a variety of structural inefficiencies in job design, and when you remove the requirement for eight hours on the job, then people can find ways to improve their efficiency?

Seashore: Yes, but not everyone wants to be time-efficient, and the eight-hour norm is protective against norms of excessive effort. It is relevant that, in our recent survey of employee adults, 93 percent said that they gave more effort to their job than the job really requires. I think this is as much a commentary on the poor design of the jobs as on the aspirations of the workers. Some studies of time use, including time use not only at work but also at home, suggest that most people choose to expand more effort, not less, when the activity seems worthwhile.

Question: What is your personal prognosis about the future in terms of the spread of humanization of work?

Seashore: There is a faddish note in the phrase "humanization of work" which may disappear, but I do not think this implies any dimi-nution in efforts to make collective production work more humane and more effective. The phrase does reflect some new ideas about means for advancing those goals. I expect humanization to spread; many peo-ple have a stake in seeing that it does.

Question: How is the work ethic related to the ethics by which people live the rest of their lives?

Seashore: Michael Maccoby was addressing this point in his remarks yesterday. I would add a few points. He was treating the general theme that the conception of the work ethic which people act on has been changing. I would go further to suggest that, possibly within the lifetime of some of the people in this room, the demarcation between work and nonwork will vanish. Am I working now? I'm not getting paid. I'm enjoying it. More people than ever before are doing, for income, things that they would do voluntarily, without a requirement for pay. It is a long way from where we are to that kind of idealistic condition of "work life" for everyday but, more and more, work is going to take on some of the attractive attributes of leisure activity. We already have some useful occupations where people actually pay for the privilege of doing the work.

Question: Could you give me an example of altered real dependencies in the Bolivar case that violated and gave rise to a change in ethical norms?

Seashore: The paid personal time program. Also, the educational program which was only partially work-oriented.

Question: I have been appointed to a committee at my university, and here at this conference it looks to me like a "quality of work life" committee for the faculty. It surprises me because I don't think the faculty had any right to expect quality, but now that I am heading for this problem, may I ask you if you know anything done by academicians to explore quality of work like arrangements?

Seashore: I have heard about such programs but I have no personal knowledge of any.

Question: I have heard of shareholder suits in regard to excessive compensation in respect to top management, but I have never heard of any suits in regard to altered compensation arrangements on these humanization of work programs. Are there any examples?

Seashore: None that I know of. I suppose there are two reasons for this. First, there are often offsetting cost benefits to the firm. Second, the costs and risks to the shareholders' interests are generally modest. Some people raise strong ideological protests, but none leading to civil suit, as far as I know.

CHAPTER 12

Joint Labor/Management Activities: A Workshop Discussion

Michael Brower* and Richard Balzer**

The following list of lessons from the Massachusetts Labor-Management Center and the American Quality of Work Life Center and of other joint labor-management and quality of work life programs was prepared by Messrs. Balzer and Brower for the Third National Conference on Business Ethics at Bentley College. The list was presented to initiate and stimulate the discussion that followed.

1. It is essential to have the full support and active involvement of top management.
2. It is essential to have the full support and active involvement of the top union leadership.
3. Joint ownership of a joint program should be created as early as possible. Both sides should be involved in discussing and determining the goals and the ground rules for a program. When management unilaterally initiates a program, the longer it waits to involve the union as an equal partner, the harder it will be to develop a truly joint program.

*Executive Director, Massachusetts Labor-Management Center
**Director, American Center for the Quality of Work Life

4. A program cannot work if management does not accept the basic legitimacy of the union, or has any hidden agenda or hope of using the program to weaken or destroy the union.

5. A joint labor-management or QWL program is *not* a substitute for any of the following:
—A strong competent management leading the organization toward clear goals.
—A strong competent union exercising its basic duties to protect the interests and rights of its members.
—A good fair contract worked out through standard collective bargaining.

6. At the core, the program should be task oriented. There is no reason for management to deny or hide its very real concerns with lowering costs and improving quality and organizational effectiveness. Denying these goals will only lead to suspicions among union leaders either that managers are trying to hide the truth or that they are not functioning as competent managers.

7. At the core, the program should also be people oriented. Management and union leaders should share a genuine interest in utilizing every employee's talents to the fullest extent possible and in making the organization a better place to work for all employees. When programs work successfully towards these objectives, the effectiveness of the organization also increases.

8. If the organization has not already implemented a considerable program of training for management at all levels, from top through middle to bottom, such a training program usually should be initiated prior to, or parallel with, a joint union-management QWL program. Good up and down (and horizontal and diagonal) communications systems, ability to form and work in teams, and ability to diagnose and solve problems are among the skills that are needed for a successful QWL program—*and* for a good management operation.

9. The active involvement of first-line supervisors and of union shop stewards is essential. If either of these groups feel threatened by the program or build resentment towards it, it will be difficult or impossible for the organization either to benefit from suggestions of rank and file workers or to improve the quality of their work life. The program should seek to improve the work life of the foremen and stewards and to utilize *their* talents more fully; it should be a program as much for them as for anyone else in the organization. They will probably need some new training programs, perhaps conducted separately for

a time (if that is necessary), and then together whenever that becomes feasible.

10. Middle managers should also be involved and not overlooked. Some programs focus first on top management and then on first-line supervisors, bypassing middle managers. This is a mistake. A program cannot in the long run succeed or survive without the active and growing involvement of all levels of management and of union personnel.

11. Whether or not to use an experienced outside professional third-party consultant to facilitate the development of a program is a question which should be openly addressed and considered by the participating parties and not simply ignored or decided automatically. Such outside assistance can be especially helpful for starting a program and for helping it over early difficult times. Good outside facilitators will work towards developing strong internal ownership of the program and growing internal skills and competence to function with decreasing outside assistance.

12. Management, which has greater economic resources, and which stands to reap economic benefits from a successful program, should be prepared to pay the greater proportion of the costs of a joint program.

13. The union should also make some financial contribution to the cost of the program, in order to increase the joint ownership of it.

14. The top-level labor-management committee (whatever it is named) will need competent staff support to allow it to do a quality job of setting goals and priorities for the program, developing and implementing action plans, reviewing progress, and revising objectives over time.

15. A QWL program is *not* a canned "quick-fix" program. It is a slow, gradual process to: develop more cooperative working relationships, increase the willingness and ability to jointly solve problems, and systematically involve a growing proportion of the employees in finding ways to make it both a more effective organization and a better organization in which to work. All of these can be accomplished but they cannot be accomplished rapidly. Hopes and expectations can and should be raised by the launching of a new program. But responsible leaders should make every effort to keep expectations realistic by stressing the slow unfolding nature of the program. A great deal of patience and long-term commitment are needed!

Discussion

Balzer: I am the Director of the American Center for the Quality of Work Life, a nonprofit organization located in Washington, D.C. We only work in unionized settings. We help put unions and managements together to set up quality of work life programs. We have worked with General Motors and the UAW, the steel workers union, and so on. We are presently trying to work out a program with Kaiser. We work with small and large corporations around the country. We are funded about 35 percent from either government grants or private foundations and 65 percent from client organizations. Both management and unions contribute to any program we are involved in. We have six people in our Washington Office and about fifteen people around the country who work with the center on a program-by-program basis.

Brower: I am the Executive Director of the Massachusetts Labor-Management Center, a nonprofit organization that operates only within the boundaries of Massachusetts. Representatives of organized labor, business, government, and other neutral representatives serve on our governing board. We used to run a series of conferences and seminars and publish a newsletter, and will do so again when we can find the time. We are basically an action organization. We work at a variety of levels in the state of Massachusetts, assisting labor and management to come together in programs similar to those of the American Center. We are working with municipal unions and municipal management in a number of locations in Massachusetts. We are working with a number of private organizations and their unions, and in the last year we have put an increasing amount of effort and attention into assisting several Massachusetts cities to establish area-wide labor–management–government committees. Some of you are possibly familiar with the exciting work that has gone on in Jamestown, New York, where they turned that city around from 10 percent unemployment, and rising, to 4 percent unemployment, and dropping. We are trying to do that here.

Question: What about programs like this in non-union companies?

Balzer: I should say the following. First, we are approached for our services by three times as many, on the average, non-union firms as union firms. Part of my answer relates to the type of values we have. What we basically believe is that quality of work life is an attempt to set up structures in which management and unions are able to work more effectively together for the benefit of management and employees. Our experience suggests that in order to set up a relationship that has the characteristics of equity and fairness, you need two strong parties present. The presence of trade union ensures a certain kind of strength, and what we say is, once you've got a collective bargaining agreement, you ought to be able to figure out lots of ways to work together more effectively, and we want to encourage unions, just as we like to encourage management, to look at quality of work life. We want to encourage the labor union movement and we found that a lot of labor union leaders are reluctant to enter these programs because they feel that many of these programs are out in part to destroy the labor union movement, and in many instances, in our opinion, a lot of consultants are in fact determined to keep unions out.

There are non-unionized firms that want to make progress, that are concerned about their employees, and would like to set up appointments. We don't oppose them, but we feel that we have a special function, and that is not our function. We think that everybody's quality of work life should improve—the work life of employees, managers, non-union people, and unionized people,—but we think the real need is to work for better cooperation between unions and management; that is why we restrict ourselves to working only in unionized organizations. In addition, a completely different set of companies are trying either to bust unions or to keep unions out. They are setting up, in the guise of labor-management committees, what is basically a company union.

We are ideologically opposed to such activities, and therefore obviously we wouldn't become involved.

On a practical basis, to reemphasize it once more, we find it is as hard to convince unions as it is to convince management of the benefits to be gained from the quality of work life programs. As long as that's the real situation in this country, we think that that's enough work for us to pursue. We do not discourage anybody from pursuing quality of work life. It began from a philosophical point of view. For quality of work life to exist as a long-term process to involve people, there has to be a certain kind of equality of power. I am not convinced that you have that equality of power when you have one organized group—a management that represents shareholders and the management philosophy—but you do not have an equally strong union group.

I'd like to make one other comment: we have been invited many times by unions and management to enter into situations. I recently was invited to Ohio by a company's management to look at a plant and consider a work life program. In the end, we told management that we felt that they were not strong enough at this time to enter into a cooperative collaborative program. What they really needed was a lot of traditional management consulting, getting a team concept together to manage the business better. You need to do your fundamentals before you try to enter this kind of program, and we have also entered situations in which it would be inappropriate for the union, from our point of view, to enter a program, because there are preconditions that are not met yet.

Question: Mr. Brower, do you have the same working principles?

Brower: Not quite. I agree with practically everything Dick said, but when our center was set up our board of directors discussed whether we would help a non-union corporation to set up a quality of work life program. The board said we would. Three-fourths of the labor force in Massachusetts is non-union, and we got public support from state and federal government money. However, as a practical operating matter, I share all of Dick's concerns. Four years ago—and still very much today—this whole movement was seen as an anti-union movement. Many of the changes in work structure were being effected, under the name of job enrichment or something similar, in non-union companies; the American trade union leadership was seeing this as a real threat, and for good reasons.

As a practical matter, I ask my board, and especially the union members, before I go beyond an initial conversation with a non-union company, what do you think of that company? What do you think

about getting involved there? What are the risks? What is their reputation and image in the labor community? As a matter of fact, in the
four years we have been in existence, we have not done any work in a
non-union firm. I suspect it will be at least another year before we do.
We feel it is necessary, especially in this northeastern part of the
country, that these programs work with major unions before we make
any major efforts to assist even the more progressive non-union ones.

Question: I don't discount the right of either of your organizations to
select its target. But the question being discussed still remains how
quality of work life programs work in non-union settings, whether or
not your organizations happen to attend to it. I am concerned to find
someone to tell me what is really going on in these organizations, and
second, whether there is anything to your premise that you need two
power groups. I say that is an unexamined premise. Is anybody going
to examine it? There are companies that seem to be doing some of
these things that do not have two power groups.

Brower: Absolutely. I can tell you about a number of very successful
programs in non-union firms.

Balzer: In fact, a lot of what's been learned about quality of work life
has been learned from the work that has been done in non-union settings. People such as Fred Foulkes and Richard Walton at Harvard
Business School have done a great deal of tracking of these programs.
If you want examples, Polaroid for a number of years has had a lot of
programs. One of the most famous quality of work life experiments is
at the General Foods pet food operation in Topeka, Kansas (which
some of you are familiar with), which is now not continuing at the rate
that it was before. One problem is that a number of companies consider their programs and their developments to be classified information
and hence don't want to share them. It is just like any technological
breakthrough. They will talk in very indirect ways about what is going on in the company, but not specifically about how performance has
been improved, how productivity has been improved, what has happened to absenteeism, and other kinds of indicators.
   Professor Walton wrote a piece basically making an assessment of
quality of work life programs after ten years. It is a very good and
thoughtful piece. Essentially, his point of view is that you cannot force
the kind of human objectives of quality of work life programs on the
business objectives of a company. I would say that he would say to you
that programs are more effective in a non-unionized setting. I think
on that issue you have to have a time perspective, which is to say what

is more effective now will not necessarily be more effective ten years from now.

Question: I agree. I know Walton. As a matter of fact, we have used him as a consultant for Business Roundtable. I think our problem is just what you pinpointed. How do you know what works with an awful lot of people claiming all sorts of things?

Brower: I think in some cases it will work very beautifully for a couple of years and then phase out. Then it may come back a year or two later, or it may not. That is a point I want to make: the problem is institutionalizing something. You can get something going and you can have some pretty good results—maybe not the first year but the second or third year—and then the question is, can you keep it going? Management turnover is one of the biggest threats to a successful program because American corporations like to rotate their managers every couple of years. That is another reason why a joint program, where there is a union, may be more successful over the long run. Unions are very often a much more stable institution than management, though not always.

Balzer: Some of the problems that the Topeka pet foods plant came up with were over the productivity gain sharing issue. The measurement issue is another tough one. The American Productivity Center spent 1.5 million making a very complicated measurement system. I guess our sense is that measurement is an issue that should be left up to the labor-management committee involved, to determine what it is that needs to be measured. It is very difficult. What we are trying to talk about is basically developing a strategy for a process that will have a life span. Beginning with the Hawthorne effect in the 1930s and then the introduction of MBO, and appraisal centers, you'll find that somebody keeps discovering a new approach to productivity and developing a new program. Then you have a productivity increase for a while and then it goes back down, until somebody comes up with a new idea and you keep on having this kind of up-and-down motion. Can you change that? Can you move to a more systematic kind of change that affects the nation and the operation of the business world generally?

Question: What were the preconditions for establishing a program that were mentioned earlier?

Brower: One clear precondition is top management leadership involvement.

Question: Do you have problems in Massachusetts that make it necessary to reduce labor-management conflict and labor strikes in order to retain and build the economic climate and prevent loss of industry? Isn't that a big part of, and a necessary prerequisite for, a quality of work life program?

Brower: You are touching on one of the motives why business, labor, and government leaders founded this Massachusetts Center. Our industry base will not survive unless we can develop both better labor relations and better utilization of the full talents of all our workers. The labor relations issue is most operative in a citywide program. That is one of the strong motivations in Jamestown and one of the strong motivations in other cities. Managers will come out and join and work together, and so will union leaders who are not ready to set up an in-plant committee because it is still too threatening or too unknown an idea. But for the sake of their city they will get involved in such programs on a citywide basis. Then later they will be willing to work together in their plants.

Question: Would you deal with a firm that has a company union as opposed to a national union?

Brower: I would not, although we will occasionally work with large, independent unions. Where they are border line, it is a difficult decision. We are working with one independent union now, but it is a fairly tough, large union, and there is a big difference between that and a company union. The other distinction I want to make, to get back to the earlier point, is that if management takes the initiative to do something for the workers' benefit, as well as for the company's benefit, some short-term effects will be produced. But nothing has been changed fundamentally, except the way the worker is doing his job. What is new about this field that we call quality of work life—and here I have to go back over to the union settings—is two things. One, it is an attitude of respect by management toward the union to say, "you are here to stay, we are not trying to get rid of you, we are not going to try to undercut you. We want to deal with you as a partner." Second, it is a new attitude of respect for the worker to say, "you, our workers, are intelligent adult human beings and we are going to start treating you like that, and furthermore, we want to start getting the benefit of your knowledge, ideas, and creativity because we, the organization, need that for our own health and survival." Now the first of these things cannot be done in a non-union firm, because there is no union unless you want to invite the UAW in to organize one, which in my opinion is a very intelligent thing to do. The second thing can be done in a non-union firm. You can go to your employees and say, "By God, you people have a lot more in terms of smarts, knowledge, and experience to contribute to this organization and we want to set up a process, committee, or whatever it is called to tap into that resource which is our employee."

Balzer: I'd like to get to the question of why some people need an outsider to help. Some people don't need an outsider. I think quality of work life is both simple and complicated. The simplicity of it is its attempt to build a process and its attempt to build a problem-solving capability. It is task-oriented. It tends to get people to look at problems. I think that can be done in unionized or non-unionized settings, and I think that experience has shown that there are successes in both settings.

Right now I am working with an institution, the World Bank, that employs a lot of professional and well-qualified, talented people. I'd say from my experience of working with them that they could use some training sessions on how to run a meeting. When I try to suggest that to them, their reaction is that they are professionals and that they run meetings all the time. I think there is a lot of technical assistance that joint labor-management committees can gain. I think there are a lot of strategic questions that have to be faced. How do you start a committee? What is it that you want to do with it? What are the issues you want to get to? How do you not build up expectations too quickly? How do you get rid of the kind of blockages that have been interfering for years and years? I think that often takes the care and attention of the skilled outsiders. Firms that don't think they need it ought not to get skilled outsiders. Firms that think they need it ought to look for assistance and they should also try to build up an internal competence so that they will not become dependent on an outsider.

It has also been my experience that organizations often don't allow insiders who have the same or more information to say things that they will allow outsiders to say. Ultimately, someone will come up to me after a meeting and say, basically, "I knew that." And I say, "I thought you did, but why didn't you say it?" They say, "I do say it but nobody listens to me."

Another question that was brought up is "can there be independent groups in a non-unionized setting?" I think that is open to debate. You really have to look at quality of work life as a long-term investment in changing the organization and the nature of relationships. That is a twenty-year process, and I think we are at the infantile stage of understanding what the developments are. I would suggest to you that there has been a lot of leadership in non-unionized organizations making changes and people have learned a great deal from them. But it is my own belief that there are organizational problems in the structure of those organizations, or in the power relationships, that in time will become more difficult.

Question: I guess your comment regarding generating respect toward the union and toward the workers generally raises in my mind how far you could be willing to go with this. For instance, would you go to the point of favoring union or rank and file representation on the corporate board of directors as the ultimate evidence of an enlightened attitude?

Brower: My own view is that on the whole those are gimmicks. One or two workers or a union representative on the board of directors probably does not change company policy at all. On the other hand, they may serve to open up a little bit more information flow regarding the financial status of the corporation. Let's ask Donald Ephlin, Regional Director of the United Auto Workers, to comment on that and the earlier questions.

Ephlin: With regard to non-union firms: at most of these seminars the vast majority of management speakers are from non-union firms. Even where national companies such as TRW have done a lot of things in their non-union plants, they have not been very successful in their union plants. One of the reasons is that it is more difficult to conduct a program in a union plant because you have someone else to contend with.

But when we are talking about industrial democracy or bringing democracy into the workplace in typical non-union settings, even though they may do quality of work life programs, there is no real democracy. Management people decide what is good for the workers, and although they may do good things, they still make the decisions.

One of the questions mentioned Polaroid. In the past I attended a Polaroid seminar, as the company wanted to hear union representatives talk about how to do their plant because they wanted our experience. But the companies that have done the most in these fields, like Polaroid and others, have been in rapidly expanding industries that have plenty of money and could afford to do unusual things. They were not in the most competitive places or higher labor intensities like the auto industry. To change the auto industry from what it used to be to a more enlightened one is a tough job for anybody. But the unions are involved because you are dealing with tougher work. There is no chance for advancement, such as there is in the IBMs of this country, so you are dealing with a much tougher situation.

As to the question why do you need an outsider, most of the time you don't. The best consultant is the guy who gets out of there the quickest. You will find that large corporations—General Motors, for example—may have a great staff of their own. I've gone into situations where I have asked them to send in a particular staff guy who was skilled at bringing together people who had not talked to each other in a long time. Once he got them to talk, he slipped away and was gone. That is the key to consulting, not staying there. This is one of the problems when you hire outsiders: sometimes they get in and they don't want to leave. The best program is what the people in the plant are doing without outsiders from the unions, corporate levels, or other firms. They are doing it themselves. This is a real change.

Somebody raised the question of community organizations. The only thing that a community group can do is to get the plant manager to come to meetings with the union because in the plant he doesn't do it. All that the city wide groups can do is to get everybody committed to these new approaches. If you can get the plant manager and the union people talking in the plant about their own problems, then you have made a major step forward, and that is all you can achieve in a community-wide organization. You get them interested in working together. For the most part, they have got to do it themselves.

On the question of what is different from this and the fads: many social scientists claim to have quick fixes for management, and mostly they are phony. The first meeting that I attended was in Washington in 1971, and I asked, "What role does the union have to play?" One social scientist said that the unions have failed and that now the social scientists are going to correct all the problems of the world. There were a lot of gimmicks and they hurt this effort and this is why most unions are opposed to them: because of the quick-fix artists and the gimmicks.

It isn't going to solve anything overnight. It does take time to change. The first things that have to change are relationships. You have got to start talking to one another about problems, and this is not always easy. Then you gradually make changes. One of the reasons some managements resist these changes is that if you turn people on to true industrial democracy and give them the right to make decisions, it is very difficult to turn them off. Management people are afraid that if they gave away these rights, then they won't be able to control their organization. If workers have been involved in these programs, very few of them want to go back to the old system. We have had experiments within plants that were temporary to begin with, and when they ended the workers involved wouldn't go back to their old jobs. They said they found out that there is a better way to work and live and "I don't want to go back to the old system." That is a hazard that people have to recognize. Union people, too, resist because they may feel that once you turn people on, such programs may interfere with the unions' authority. Many people think they do and for that reason unions do resist. Irv Bluestone and I and others think that if the unions give leadership to these programs we are better off for it. Sidney Harman said that last night. His plant is in Tennessee, which is a right-to-work state, and after the quality of work life program in that plant was in effect for a few years, union membership was higher than it had ever been. We had a better union there then they had ever had before. You have to work a lot harder at it. That is true for both management and the union, and that is why there is resistance from both sides. But once you do turn workers on, there is an effect that is more lasting than what some people try to tell you.

Question: No one has mentioned the examples of corporations that installed quality of work life programs long ago by firms, for example, the Lincoln Electric Company. That is an excellent example of a long-term program that doesn't die after its own success but actually grows on the basis of success.

Brower: That is an excellent point. Let's move to curriculum: What are the implications for graduate or undergraduate business curricula? What do you think the implications are and what needs to be done? Do you need a special course in the curriculum about these new approaches? Or are these concepts that need to be built into a wide variety of courses?

Comment: I built mine into a personnel administration course on the graduate level. I have two courses in organization theory and personnel administration that are really taught to middle-management people averaging between thirty and thirty-three years of age.

Brower: Turning to the final question we can handle today, why should management get involved in these programs? Well, a whole host of activities are going on in our corporations today that are very expensive. There is turnover, tardiness, absenteeism, machine downtime, waste of raw materials, production problems, sabotage, grievances, and anger that is built up in a workplace and denied the opportunity to be heard where workers are treated as just another factor of production. That anger comes out in a dozen different ways, including strikes. Every successful quality of work life program that I know about has led to improvements in at least some of these dozen or so costly behaviors. The second kind of gain that Sidney Harman talked about last night is that while it is a lot of work for a manager it is also a lot of fun. There is a joy involved in being in or leading these programs.

CHAPTER 13

The Work Ethic Is Alive, Well, and Living in Cleveland: The Lincoln Electric Company

*D. Richard Harmer**

American industry is in the middle of a productivity crisis. In one industry after another, we have fallen behind our world competitors. Some believe the problem is primarily one of capital formation. With infusions of new technology, they say, we can regain our lead in world markets. Others see the problem more deeply rooted in a decline of the work ethic. American workers seem no longer prepared to put in a day's work for a day's pay. They seem no longer to care about the quality of their work. Still others believe our underlying problems rest with how we approach the task of management in the United States. They assert that we are finally going to have to get serious about how we manage private enterprise. For many years, they claim, we were under little pressure to do so. Our technological superiority over other world competitors allowed us to incur a lot of waste in the use of our human resources and still maintain a competitive edge. We could tolerate the adversary relations between employee and employer on which collective bargaining is based. We could afford the Parkinsonian bloat of multilayered management heirarchies. We no longer can, these people argue. We can afford to waste our human resources no longer. We do need up-to-date technologies; but technology alone

*Assistant Professor of Management, Bentley College

283

can no longer bail us out. We must develop approaches to industrial enterprise in which management and workers work together for their own good, for the good of the enterprise, for the good of their customers, and ultimately for the good of society.

Voices from all sectors of society are calling now for a new social contract between capital, management, and labor. Some point to Japanese organizations as models for us to copy. But there are deep cultural differences between the United States and Japan. Many question whether the Japanese model can be transferred to the United States. Can we not look within our own boundaries for models? Can we not find within the United States itself organizations whose success with alternative approaches to industrial enterprise might help us rethink the U.S. model? We can. One such organization is the Lincoln Electric Company (LEC) based in Cleveland, Ohio.

* * *

The Lincoln Electric Company—a company of about twenty-five hundred employees—is the world's largest maker of equipment for arc welding, the art of fusing metals in the white heat of an 8-10,000°F electric arc. The bulk of the company's sales is split between welding machines and electrodes, the metal rods consumed in the electric arc that help form the welding bond. The company accounts for more than 40 percent of the arc welding products sold in the United States.[1]

One industry observer has written of the company:

> The Lincoln Electric Company of Cleveland . . . ranks as one of the most unusual business organizations in any industry. In its general management concepts and their application to production operations and employee relations, Lincoln has followed a path that represents a considerable departure from prevailing practices elsewhere. But this unorthodox approach has paid off handsomely.[2]

Lincoln's approach to management has paid off in creating one of the most productive manufacturing organizations in the United States today. On nearly any measure, compared to more conventionally managed organizations, Lincoln Electric's performance is truly impressive. For over fifty years, LEC has been the price leader in its industry, selling quality products at prices so low that some industry giants (such as General Electric) have abandoned the market altogether, while others have retreated to specialized niches. One would expect Lincoln's low prices to be reflected in low margins; but that is not the case. One good measure of a company's profitability is its operating margin. That is the difference between sales revenues and all operating costs (all production costs plus general, administrative, and sales expenses). Lincoln Electric's operating margins generally range between 25 and 30 percent of sales. The range for more conventionally managed manufacturing companies is closer to 10 to 15 percent. With its low prices, Lincoln is still two to three times more profitable than its more conventional counterparts.[3]

How is that possible? In a word, it is because The Lincoln Electric Company, for nearly a half century now, has consistently produced two to three times the sales value of product per employee than similar manufacturing organizations. How has Lincoln been able to do this? Is it a corps of engineering geniuses who know how to reduce the labor content of any manufacturing process to zero? Is it a work force that is willing to see its jobs eliminated and that has forfeited labor's traditional prerogative to restrict output? Or might it be some set of management techniques that repeals Parkinson's Law?

Mitchell Fein, a prominent U.S. industrial engineer has pronounced the company an "enigma." According to Fein,

> Very little is known about its inner operations, except that the will to work of the entire work force down to the lowest skills is not matched anywhere in the world. . . .
>
> Its employees' man-hour productivity is unsurpassed. . . . A manager from the outside would drool on witnessing employees of The Lincoln Electric Company at work.[4]

No behavioral scientist has yet made a systematic study of the Lincoln Electric Company. Lincoln Electric's approach to management runs counter in some important ways to ideas which have dominated the thinking of many organization development experts. LEC's facilities have been visited, however, by many businessmen and journalists, some of whom have written about what they found. Casewriters from the Harvard Business School have also written cases on the company in 1948 and 1975. In addition, James Lincoln himself published books about the company in 1946, 1951, and 1961. This case draws on all these sources, both to provide a glimpse inside one of the most unconventional and most successful industrial organizations in the U.S. today and to look at what James Lincoln himself came to believe accounted for that success.*

---

*James Lincoln died in 1965. In 1972, he was succeeded as chairman of the board of directors by William Irrgang, who had joined the company in 1929 and had served as LEC's president and general manager since 1954. Since 1972, George Willis, who joined the company in 1947, has served as president.

* * *

According to Lincoln Electric's management, no one thing can account for the company's impressive record. Rather, they attribute their success to a combination of practices, involving market strategy, their approach to technological innovation, their personnel policies, their management practices, and their overall philosophy of private enterprise. Perhaps the best first cut in describing these practices is along external/internal lines—that is, to describe Lincoln's strategy in relating to its external markets and then to describe the internal practices LEC has adopted in support of that market strategy.

PROMOTING MARKET GROWTH

James Lincoln decided quite early that Lincoln Electric's involvement with arc welding would not be a short-term affair. Lincoln had a vision that many different industrial applications could be found for arc welding—applications which, by cutting manufacturing costs on a broad range of products, could help to improve the standard of living in society as a whole. In pursuit of that vision, Lincoln committed the company for the long haul to the arc welding market, and committed its resources to active promotion of the market's growth through the discovery of an ever-broadening range of applications for arc welding.

From the time it entered the arc welding business, The Lincoln Electric Company has acted aggressively on a number of fronts to encourage steady growth in its markets. Early in World War I, James Lincoln tried to convince the Department of the Navy that it could build stronger and lighter ships faster by substituting welding for riveting in their construction. Lincoln was rebuffed, however, by an Admiral who turned him away, saying "Welding is all nonsense, Lincoln. You can't weld ships. I could kick off with my boot any weld that you will ever make."[5]

World War II proved Lincoln right and the admiral wrong. After the war, in fact, Franklin Roosevelt personally acknowledged the welding industry's contribution to the war effort, noting that the size of the Liberty Fleet and the speed with which it had been constructed would not have been possible without the benefits of arc welding.[6]

Between the wars, The Lincoln Electric Company had also been active on other fronts, promoting new domestic applications for arc welding. LEC was instrumental, for example, in the construction of the first welded steel building in the United States.[7] It sponsored design competitions, essay contests, and seminars on welding applications. Indicative of Mr. Lincoln's flair for promotion, the winners of one contest in 1932 were paid with welded steel checks, which Lincoln later "cancelled" with a submachine gun. (One of these checks can now be seen at the Smithsonian Institution in Washington, D.C.) In the late 1930s, Lincoln also set up a foundation to promote the development of programs in welding engineering in colleges around the United States, and to promote the development of arc welding through publication of technical reports, welding texts, and handbooks. LEC has also operated its own welding school since 1917, so that once it has lead engineers and businessmen to recognize arc welding's potential as an alternative to other joining processes, it can also offer them inexpensive expert training in welding theory and techniques. Over sixty thousand graduates have diplomas from Lincoln Electric's welding school. LEC continues to encourage education, technical publishing, and other long range programs which foster growth in the arc welding industry and, thereby, generate new market potential for the company.[8]

LEC'S MARKET-CORE STRATEGY

Lincoln Electric's top management long ago rejected the idea of growth through wide-ranging diversification and conglomeration, a route which seems to experience a revival in fashion in the United States every decade or so. It has chosen instead to concentrate the company's attention on doing a few things as well as it can "rather," in Mr. Lincoln's words, "than many things not so well."[9] In point of fact, LEC does not even go after the full spectrum of the arc welding market it has done so much to develop. Rather, the company aims its efforts squarely at the broad center of the welding market. It concentrates its research, development, and manufacturing talents on meeting the major needs of the metalworking industry, developing and improving a line of standard, no-frill products—ones that can find use in a wide range of welding applications and that will be used in large volumes. LEC has consistently left to its rivals the more specialized niches of the market.

Often such a heart-of-the-market strategy is linked to a follow-the-leader approach to product innovation, allowing others to shoulder the trial-and-error costs of new product development. Not so at Lincoln Electric. Product innovation is an ongoing fact of life at LEC. The company works continually to improve its established products. It has pioneered in the introduction of many new products representing significant contributions to the welding industry. In 1979, nearly 75 percent of LEC's product line had changed in the last ten years.[10] According to Lincoln management, those changes are not cosmetic. Each represents a solid improvement in the product.

Product changes and new products are not brought on stream at LEC on whim or caprice. Before a new design makes it into Lincoln's line, it must have proved itself on some tough criteria. For example, it must represent honest progress in offering greater utility to the user—in terms of new applications, greater dependability, ease of use, or lower costs. It must also address a broad enough need in the market to justify high volume production.[11]

LEC's approach to pricing its products is simple and straightforward. Lincoln has rejected the idea of trying to "optimize" its prices in interaction with market forces, both in the old-school sense of "all that traffic will bear" and the B-school sense of pinpointing that price/volume combination—whether it's a low volume at high prices or a high volume at low prices—that yields the greatest overall profit. Instead, the prices on Lincoln products generally represent a standard markup on overall cost of producing and distributing them. Generally this results in lower prices than its competitors. In contrast to some of its rivals, LEC does not offer discounts; it holds firm to its published prices.[12]

CUSTOM SALES FOR STANDARD PRODUCTS

Lincoln Electric complements its no-frills product line with a highly customer-centered approach to sales. While most competitors either sell through distributors or employ business graduates as salesmen, LEC fields a sales force of engineers who can personally demonstrate to potential customers how Lincoln equipment can meet their needs as well or better (and often at lower costs) than rivals' sometimes more elaborate models. According to LEC's vice president of Sales Development, "For many companies our people become their experts in welding." Lincoln salesmen are expected to know each customer's needs and they should be prepared to put on a headshield and show the customer how to meet those needs with Lincoln equipment.[13]

To prepare for that role, Lincoln's sales engineers go through a seven-month training program in which they take classes in welding, metallurgy, and equipment design at the company's welding school; do a stint in the head office learning how orders are processed; and work out in the factory on the production line on which machines brought in from the field are rebuilt. Before they graduate, trainees must find some way to improve on the manufacture of the product and they must each make a presentation to Mr. Irrgang, chairman of The Lincoln Electric Company, as if he were an important new customer.

Lincoln management believes its investment in custom direct selling has paid off well and, as metalworking becomes more technical each year, will continue to do so. Once LEC is "in," they claim, it seldom loses a customer. As a result, sales costs per unit for LEC are often as much as 50 percent lower than those of its competitors who sell through jobbers.[14]

LEC'S INTERNAL STRATEGY: HIGH EFFICIENCY IN OPERATIONS

Lincoln's management could not have adopted, or at least could not have continued for long, a market strategy that combines low prices with high product quality and high customer service, were it not for the very productive use LEC makes of the technological and human resources available to it. We shall look next at how LEC does this.

No Frills, No Perks, and Hard Work

A visitor to Lincoln Electric is immediately struck by two things that unquestionably contribute to LEC's low costs and high per-person output. One is the absence of many of the amenities that have come to be associated with "progressive" management. The other is how hard Lincoln employees work.

In regard to amenities, one finds no bowling alleys, no swimming pools, no Muzak wafting through the loudspeakers. The company's windowless one-story plant sports no exterior landscaping to speak of. Everyone enters the plant through a common entrance and down a flight of stairs to a subterranean tunnel whose outlets deposit employees within two hundred feet of their work stations. Locker rooms and sanitary facilities opening on to the tunnel are austere. No lounges, no saunas, no steambath, no recreation rooms. The factory itself is not air-conditioned.

LEC's administrative offices, located in a windowless, one-story cement block smack in the middle of the plant are no less Spartan. No designer-label, color-coordinated offices there. Most of the staff work in large open rooms at old, worn desks lined up side by side. Department managers are often thrown in there with them. One notes the absence on these desks of such niceties as personal coffee pots, potted plants, and the like. The few private offices afforded to middle management are small, have no carpets, and are separated from each other only by green metal partitions.

Top management fares little better. The office of the president of the Lincoln Electric Company, Mr. George Willis, is slightly larger than the others; but it too retains a modest air. Only one office in the plant has a carpet. That office is one pressed on Mr. Lincoln many years ago by his subordinates. It stood empty for five years after Mr. Lincoln passed away. It is now used by the board of directors, the company's advisory boards, and Mr. Irrgang, Lincoln's successor as chairman of LEC.[15]

LEC's no-frills policy extends to still other kinds of perquisites to which higher-level managers in more conventional organizations have long become accustomed. For example, top executives at LEC are denied such trappings of their office as reserved parking spaces and exclusive dining facilities. LEC's parking lot works on a first-come, first-served basis. Employees of all ranks eat together in the same company-operated dining room. Except for one small four-person table in the center of the room reserved for Mr. Irrgang, Mr. Willis, and their guests, people may sit wherever they want. It is not unusual to see management personnel sitting and talking with factory workers.[16]

There is also little question that Lincoln Electric employees are diligent in their work. Visitors to the plant report that LEC operators work at a brisk pace. One seldom sees LEC workers goofing off on the job. In some quarters in Cleveland, Lincoln Electric has a reputation as a "sweatshop." One hears stories of Lincoln workers pressuring newcomers who fail to come up to speed according to schedule. Each year enough new recruits leave the company after only a few months to keep that reputation alive.

A Flat and Lean Organization

Spartan facilities, no perks, and hard work are perhaps some of the more obvious ways LEC keeps its costs down. Another way—one that might not be so obvious to a visitor at Lincoln Electric, because he would see no organization chart hanging prominently on a wall or even under the glass on someone's desk—has to do with how *flat* the Lincoln organization is. While traditional management principles call for a span of control of five or six at upper management levels, at LEC nine people report to the company's chairman and another fifteen report to the president.[17] One of these fifteen, Mr. Don Hastings, vice president of sales, has thirty-eight district sales managers (DSM) reporting to him. More conventional practice would have these thirty-eight DSM's reporting to four or five regional sales managers, who would in turn report to the vice president of sales. Mr. Hastings estimates that, including their office support, that extra layer of regional managers would cost LEC roughly an extra $500 thousand each year.[18]

Our visitor would not have seen an organization chart at Lincoln Electric because the LEC organization does not use them. James Lincoln felt quite strongly about organization charts and the kinds of authority relations he believed they fostered. Lincoln wrote:

> It is impossible to have an efficient organization with anything like military lines of authority. That kills, and obviously is designed to kill, any possibility of initiative from below.... The detailing of all duties to the last act and order ... and (producing) a chart that shows who has authority in all functions and under all conditions ... will stifle progress probably as completely as the shop politics that it engenders.[19]

Present LEC management still sees little constructive use for formal organization charts. Many positions in Lincoln Electric's organization structure have no bureaucratic life of their own. Vacated positions are not automatically refilled. For example, it is not uncommon when a person retires for his work to be parceled out among others and the position he held to be eliminated. James Lincoln liked to argue that industrial progress boiled down to the elimination of jobs.[20]

This practice of allowing for positions only to match the press of work and not to fit some set of scholastic abstractions about division of labor and functional authority is also reflected in how *lean* the Lincoln Electric organization is. Few staff departments feel they could not easily use a few more bodies. But top management keeps a tight rein on staffing, forcing departments to make the best use they can of the manpower they have, allowing them little room to become immersed in trivia or to make work for each other a la Parkinson's Law. As one LEC executive puts it, "We are very successful in overloading our overhead departments. We make sure this way that no unnecessary work is done; and jobs which are not absolutely essential are eliminated."[21]

Some departments take a certain pride in the fact that they get along without what would be considered a normal staff contingent. Clyde Loughridge, LEC's personnel director, boasts that, while his department's responsibilities go beyond those of a typical personnel department, he employs a staff of six, in contrast to a normal contingent of about twenty for a firm LEC's size.[22]

Some departments also get along on no budget *per se,* undermining the need at year's end to rush to spend what's left, just to insure that the next year's budget will not be cut. Mr. Loughridge again: "I don't get a budget. There would be no point to it. I just spend as little as possible. I operate just like my home. I don't spend on anything I don't need."[23]

AN UNORTHODOX APPROACH TO THE ORGANIZATION OF PRODUCTION

Lincoln Electric's failure to observe the orthodoxies of "proper" management practice in its executive ranks has been matched only by its unorthodox approach to organizing its production operations. Manufacturing operations tend to be set up along the lines of one or the other of two basic models of production organization. One is the "functional" model; the other, the "line-flow" model. In a functional approach to organizing production operations, workers operating similar types of equipment and doing similar kinds of work are organized together in the same department under the same foreman. For example, a typical functional organization might consist of a machine shop, an assembly department, a paint shop, an inspection group, and a stock room. Where it is justified by the volume of work, a machine shop might itself be split up into several departments, with lathes, milling machines, punch presses, and drill presses each under a different foreman. In contrast, in a line-flow approach to organizing production operations, departments are organized around the flow of the work, rather than around the type of work done or the types of equipment workers are operating. In an automobile assembly line, for example, each foreman is responsible for a segment of the line—which may include welders, grinders, drillers, fitters, and assemblers—rather than for a group of operators all doing the same kind of work on the same types of equipment.

Each approach has its advantages and disadvantages compared to the other. One advantage of a line-flow approach to production is that the patterns of work flow tend to be fairly simple. In a functional approach, they can become quite complex, as work-in-process must be moved from one department to another (and sometimes back again), depending on the types of work that must be performed on it and the order in which that work must be done. To deal with the complex patterns of work flows associated with functional layouts, organizations must often employ a combination of in-process buffer stocks and sophisticated inventory and production control information systems to try to minimize slack in production schedules.

On the other hand, except in extremely long lines designed to handle very large volumes of work (such as automobile assembly lines), a line-flow approach can go against the well-accepted principle of specialization in the division of labor—the principle by which each man and the equipment he operates is kept constantly busy at a fairly narrowly defined piece of work. Except in very long lines, compared to the functional approach, a line-flow can also require extra investment in equipment and greater costs associated with training each employee in more than a single task. It can also lose the advantage, attributed to the functional approach, of having (in the foreman) an "expert in" each type of work directly overseeing all operations of a particular type in each department.

Comparing the advantages of one model over the other, the wide majority of U.S. manufacturing companies have opted to arrange most of their production operations according to the functional model. Only about 5 percent of the industrial workers in the United States work on line-flow assembly lines like those used in the auto industry.

Lincoln Electric has gone against the crowd. Early in LEC's history, Lincoln management turned the company away from a functional approach to production organization in favor of a line-flow approach. In 1951, when LEC built its first new plant from ground up, Lincoln management incorporated this line-flow model directly into the plant's design. Materials and components coming into the LEC plant enter through receiving docks that stretch the full length of one side of the building. They never go to a central stock room. The plant has none. Instead, by a complex system of overhead cranes and hoists, materials are carried directly to the work stations where they will first enter into production. To the extent practicable, work flows directly across the plant floor to shipping docks on the opposite side of the building. Production departments are organized, not by type of work, but by product line.

In those respects, Lincoln's production system is similar to the auto assembly line. But there the similarity ends. Auto lines are machine-paced; all work at LEC is man-paced. Where the auto assembly lines tend to be very long to take advantage of specialization, Lincoln Electric's lines are much shorter. Where the division of labor on conventional assembly lines results in the assignment of each worker to no more than a few simple tasks at most, on Lincoln's lines work is divided in ways that often result in a single worker's performing a number of different tasks which may require a variety of skills. In fact, many Lincoln workers operate in effect as independent subcontractors in their own "shops" along the line, performing all the different tasks that fit the next stage of production in the work that reaches them. Clustered around each work station are all the necessary equipment, materials, and components with which an operator (or in some cases a small team of operators) does his own set-ups, puts together a complete subassembly, and performs his own in-process inspection. For example, performing operations that in a conventional organization might be split up among perhaps half a dozen workers in as many departments, one LEC operator fabricates complete gasoline tanks in a variety of sizes. He spot welds and seam welds sections of the tank together, solders on fittings, pressure tests each tank, makes necessary repairs, inserts bushings, spray paints each tank, cleans the finished tanks, and sends them on for final assembly in Lincoln Electric's gas-driven welding machines.[24] At another station, one worker operates five different machine tools to transform a blank into a rotor shaft. He runs a tape-controlled engine lathe, a tracer lathe, two small milling machines, a hydraulic press, and does all his own inspection. At still another station, a team of two men makes covers and guards for welders. To do this, these men are provided a forming roll, a spot welder, an arc welder, a degreasing tank, and a paint booth.[25]

Self-Management at the Operator Level

LEC workers are encouraged to act on their initiative in caring for their equipment, in monitoring inventory around their work stations, and in responding to emergencies and helping others. Lincoln workers also take personal responsibility for the quality of their work. Workers run their own checks to insure their work is meeting established specifications. Whatever work does not pass final inspection is returned to them to correct on their own time. To a large extent, LEC workers are expected to supervise themselves in their day-to-day work activities.

James Lincoln felt quite strongly that workers at the bottom levels of an organization should be able to direct and control their day-to-day activities in the carrying out of their work. In other words, each worker should be his own manager. In 1951, Lincoln wrote:

> It becomes perfectly true to anyone who will think this thing through that there is no such thing in an industrial activity as Management and Men having different functions or being two different two kinds of people. Why can't we think and why don't we think that all people are Management? Can you imagine any president of any factory or machine shop who can go down and manage a turret lathe as well as the machinist can? Can you imagine any manager of any organization who can go down and manage a broom—let us get down to that—who can manage a

broom as well as a sweeper can? Can you imagine any secretary of any company who can go down and fire a furnace and manage that boiler as well as the man who does the job? Obviously, all are Management.[26]

Comparative Advantages

At first glance—on paper at least—Lincoln Electric's short line-flows, complex production jobs, and operator self-management may appear more costly than a functional, more specialized approach to production. Lincoln's approach appears more costly mostly due to the higher direct, easily allocable costs it should incur, including a greater investment in equipment and more extensive training for workers. Lincoln management concedes that in some cases (but not all) these one-time costs are greater under their line-flow approach. Granting that, LEC management still maintains that its approach still ends up saving money in the long run. This is due in large part, they argue, to the way the line-flow approach keeps down many of the *indirect* costs associated with production—costs which are often more difficult to predict in planning production and to allocate once they have been incurred and which, therefore, are often given little weight as choices are made between different configurations for organizing production.

These more indirect costs include a number of costs associated with materials handling, inspection, production control, supervision, and the paperwork that accompanies them. Compared to a functional approach to production, LEC's straight-through work flow requires 1) a much smaller production control staff; 2) many fewer materials handlers; and 3) susceptibleness to fewer bottlenecks and line-balancing delays. Visual inventory control by workers themselves and the overhead crane operators who deliver materials to work stations has led to the near complete elimination of work-in-process and raw material record keeping and all the staff personnel required to do it. In-process inspection by the workers themselves means a smaller inspection department. Self-supervision by workers reduces the number of foremen required to maintain high production. Paradoxically, Lincoln management claims to get better supervision with fewer supervisors and better quality with fewer inspectors.[27]

COST REDUCTION: THE ROLE OF INGENUITY

Of the measures we have looked at thus far which LEC has employed to reduce its costs, most have limits. With each, there is some point beyond which no *further* savings can be made. Once the perks are gone, there are simply no more perks whose elimination could result in new cost reductions. There is probably a limit to how few foremen a production system can accommodate, even if that limit is theoretically zero. There are physical limits to how fast, how hard, and for how long people can work. In many cases, LEC probably reached what were to be its limits in these areas years ago. Once these limits had been reached, no new cost reductions could be achieved, no new savings won, were it not for the penchant exhibited by people at all levels of the Lincoln Electric organization to keep a constant lookout for new, different, better, and more efficient ways to do their work.

James Lincoln liked to say that the direct labor content of any manufacturing process could eventually be reduced to zero.[28] Statements like that could prompt a cynical smile, were it not for the achievements of some LEC employees in nearly doing just that. One of the key articles of faith at Lincoln Electric is the idea that

> every design can be bettered, every method can be improved, every skill can be increased, every material can be replaced by a better and/or cheaper one. The only question is how soon and by whom the progress will be made. . . . It is only our inhibited mind that keeps us from seeing the obviousness of new inventions. . . . Our minds are so dulled by habit that often they do not recognize and accept a new or better idea soon enough.[29]

LEC management has made finding the better, the more efficient method a way of life in all aspects of the company's operations. LEC's ongoing drive to cut the costs of operations reaches to all corners of the company—to the plant, purchasing, distribution, credit operations, and sales. It seems no stone remains unturned for long in the firm's unrelenting search for economies wherever they can be found.

Cost Reduction in Product Design

At Lincoln Electric, for example, the process of cutting costs on the manufacture of a new product starts even before it leaves the drawing board. Early in the design stage, methods staff and plant engineers (who are responsible for tooling) are brought in from Manufacturing to analyze the initial drawings and prototypes engineers in the Design Engineering department have produced. The people from Manufacturing are told to ask for any changes in the product's design which they think can reduce their production costs or, for that matter, costs involved in such things as shipping and warehousing. (Tooling costs, for example, can vary a great deal, depending on sometimes quite minor differences in a product's design.)

The design engineers are expected to adopt those changes which will lead to reduced *total* costs, when all factors are taken into consideration, without interfering with the final quality or performance of the product. According to Mr. Irrgang, who keeps a close watch over much of this process,

> Some [requests] will be accepted, and some will be rejected [by the design engineers]. However, when any idea is rejected, a reason has to be given. And it has to be a sound reason, not just a matter of personalities.[30]

The design group transfers "custody" of the product to Manufacturing after the representatives from Manufacturing and Design Engineering are both satisfied with the new product's design. Lincoln management believes this early getting together between departments before the design group has committed itself to a particular design and set of specifications helps insure that the company not get locked out from important potential economies down the line and, in addition, helps avoid many of the territorial battles that commonly arise between design and manufacturing groups.

Cost Reduction in Equipment Design

While Plant Engineering and Methods are getting together with Design Engineering over product design issues, they also work with each other to find, adapt, and/or develop the equipment on which the new product will be manufactured. LEC engineers themselves design a good share of the company's equipment. Lincoln engineers also modify much of the equipment LEC purchases from outside vendors to increase its production capacity. (Not all of these engineers' handiwork is available for public appreciation. For example, the plant where electrodes are manufactured is off limits to all but those who have passes signed by Mr. Irrgang or Mr. Willis.)[31]

LEC management once required a five-year payback on new equipment.[32] That is, it would not authorize requests for new equipment which would not pay for itself in five years or less. (Five years is on the short side for this type of industry.) Top management later shortened the payback requirement to two years. They did this to direct employees' attention away from the " 'easy solution' of purchasing new *machines*" to focus more on using their ingenuity in developing "new *ideas*" to solve their production problems.[33]

That move has paid off handsomely for the company. Faced with bottlenecks, delays, and other inefficiencies in the flow of production, Lincoln engineers (and even workers on the floor) invariably come up with new attachments, jigs, fixtures, and tools that materially increase the output of Lincoln's manufacturing equipment. Some pieces of equipment run at two and three times their originally rated speeds. Pieces of equipment ten, twenty, and thirty years old are rigged up to yield higher outputs than newer models designed to supercede them.[34]

Now LEC employs a one-year payback on equipment required for cost reduction. To replace equipment short of that, the Manufacturing Maintenance department must certify that it can no longer return the equipment to productive status, an admission that department is seldom eager to make. In cases which involve new equipment for a product for which demand is growing, paybacks of up to two years are sometimes allowed.[35]

Cost Reduction in the Specials Department

Work on equipment design, methods, and work allocation continues after new products leave Design Engineering. From Design Engineering, new products do not go straight into regular production. They go instead to what LEC calls its "Specials Department." There, Methods staff and some of LEC's most imaginative workers try to uncover and rectify manufacturing problems that could crop up later. They also work together to figure out the most efficient work methods that can later be applied in regular production.

Pilot runs in the Specials Department range from half a dozen to 500 units, depending on the type of product. Some units are tested in LEC's own labs; others, in the field under actual operating conditions. (Depending again on the type of product, testing may last six weeks to six months.) Standard costs are set on a product and the product is turned over to a regular production line only after Lincoln management (1) has hard evidence that a new design is dependable and will present no unforeseen problems for the customer, and (2) is satisfied that Methods has gone as far as it can at that point in devising the most efficient techniques of production.

Cost Reduction on the Shop Floor

Even after products go into regular production, LEC's drive to develop better methods and cut manufacturing costs continues. Methods staff are still expected to keep trying to think up better work techniques. LEC workers are not expected to devise their own work methods from scratch. The prime responsibility for that rests with the Methods department. However, workers are not bound by those methods. They are expected to draw on their experience to try to improve on the "official" techniques prescribed by Methods. And they often do.

Sometimes workers have made discoveries which have more than doubled their output over night. For example:

> Lincoln machinists were among the first to discover that the heat created by the use of tungsten carbide cutting tools could be eliminated, and work expedited at the same time, by increasing the speed of the machines. The chips carry away the heat. Monarch lathes that whirled at 600 r.p.m. were geared up and have been used at 1200 to 1800 r.p.m.[36]

Sometimes these breakthroughs are the product of a single person's insight. Just as often, they are the result of several minds working together. An idea may originate with one worker, then get developed further in conversation with others, his foreman, or staff from the Methods department. Or the idea may start with the Methods man, then be improved on by suggestions from the operators who will be called upon to implement it in their work.

Most often single improvements will be less dramatic than the one cited above. Much of the progress on the shop floor represents finetuning—small, gradual improvements in a number of different aspects of production. When they are made with regularity, however, and when many of them are made in all facets of operations, together they can add up over the course of a year to a significant improvement in overall efficiency.

Cost Reduction in Overhead Departments

Lincoln Electric's drive to develop better, more efficient ways to get the job done is by no means limited to its production facilities. For example, an ongoing search for shortcuts in LEC's administrative offices has eliminated much of the paperwork that can bog down such operations. Forms have been combined to eliminate duplication. Credit and billing procedures have been streamlined to minimize paper flows in handling customer accounts. Access to that most fecund machine, the Xerox copier, is restricted.

In the purchasing department, employees' tasks go beyond looking for raw materials and components at the lowest prices. Purchasers are also called on to find ways to combine orders from neighboring vendors, to save on inbound shipping costs. They are also expected to work closely with the various engineering and manufacturing departments to keep them up-to-date on new advances in components that might find application in LEC equipment designs or manufacturing processes.

Purchasing also plays a major role in LEC's "make or buy" decisions. Lincoln Electric has not per se ruled out self-processing any of the raw materials it purchases or fabricating any of the components it buys. On a regular basis, LEC executives take a hard look at the company's purchases to see where new economies can be won by transferring work into the company. As a result, LEC has gradually "back-integrated" in a variety of directions, by making rather than buying more and more of the components that go into LEC products. Lincoln's employees can often offset vendors' economies of scale. For example, the company found that it could purchase engine blocks and other components for gasoline engines and assemble them in-house at a lower total cost than by purchasing them from the same supplier already assembled.

The results of LEC employees' ingenuity in finding ways to cut costs can also be seen in the company's Traffic and Shipping departments. Lincoln Electric was one of the first companies to adopt palletized shipping. On the shipping dock, loaders use what one industry observer calls an ingenious hairpin-shaped C-hook, as long as a semitrailer, to place welders with speed and ease in the far-most reaches of covered truck bodies.[37] Lincoln shippers have also figured out how to load welding machines double-deck in trailers, permitting shipping loads of 40,000 lbs. vs. single-deck loads of 24,000 lbs. Through the use of satellite warehouses and a system of staggered shipping "windows," LEC's Traffic department is able to consolidate orders so that over 85 percent of what leaves Lincoln's docks goes as a full railcar or truckload. Most companies average around 50 percent. In the face of increased shipping rates and other operating costs, LEC's traffic department manages to hold freight and warehousing expenses to around 7 percent of sales, compared to a national average of about 10 percent for its type of business.[38]

A PHILOSOPHY OF MANAGEMENT AND PRIVATE ENTERPRISE

That is a cursory view of what people at The Lincoln Electric Company have done—what top management, middle managers, engineers, salesmen, production workers and purchasing, traffic, credit, and other administrative staff all have done—to make the company a very efficient and profitable enterprise for better than half a century.

An explanation of Lincoln Electric's success in strategic terms boils down to two interrelated strategies: one in relating to its markets and one in relating to its people.

> Lincoln Electric's market strategy has been simple and unwavering—to promote the growth of the arc welding industry and to capture the broad center of that market with a combination of basic, high quality products, low prices, and superior customer service.
>
> Lincoln Electric's internal strategy has also been simple and unwavering—to get its people to work diligently and efficiently, in Spartan surroundings, under very little supervision, and to get its people to apply their individual ingenuity in finding better, more productive ways to do the company's work.

At one level of understanding, that explains The Lincoln Electric Company's success. On another, it begs for further explanation. Especially that company's internal strategy. Lincoln's market strategy is based on the seemingly optimistic assumption that back in the plant people will maintain the very high levels of productivity required to sustain that strategy—that they will work hard, that they will cooperate with each other in getting the product out, and that they will accept and adapt to technological change—not for just a year or two, but year after year after year.

That assumption is one few managers can make in many organizations. Many top managements have had to reconcile themselves to the idea that the natural state of affairs in a company of any size is for the employees at the lower levels to take work life as easily as they can, to avoid responsibility, to restrict output, to withhold cooperation, and to resist any kind of change. They have had to reconcile themselves to the idea that the natural state within the managerial ranks is for some middle managers to invest much of their energies in hatching plots and counterplots against each other, while others are most active when weaving themselves sinecures in webs of red tape.

How has Lincoln Electric been able to avoid these syndromes? How has top management been able to keep its people diligent in their work for so many years? How has it been able to sustain a level of cooperation among its people over that time which few managements are able to maintain for even a few years at best? How has top management been able to induce employees at all levels of the company to apply their ingenuity in favor of LEC's interests rather than against them? How has it been able to ward off resistance to change, to avoid stagnation, to resist falling victim to the dry rot that inevitably seems to overcome an organization with age? It is to these kinds of questions that we shall turn our attention next.

To be sure, Lincoln Electric's management makes no claim to have batted even close to 1,000 in any of these areas. It does not claim to have completely done away with restriction by workers; it does not claim to be completely free from empire building and infighting among its managers; it does not claim that all in the organization embrace every technological advance with open arms. To the contrary, Mr. Lincoln himself referred to the company's achievements as "only a few halting steps in the right direction."[39] Still, both the pattern of results the company has achieved for nearly fifty years *and* observations by visitors to LEC's facilities suggest that, compared to more conventional organizations, the Lincoln Electric Company has encountered fewer of these problems and has made impressive progress in fostering a spirit of cooperation among its employees and in reducing management-worker friction, interdepartmental warfare, and resistance to change.

JAMES F. LINCOLN'S CONCEPTION OF ORGANIZATIONAL MAN

In his later years, James Lincoln looked back on his own experiences with the Lincoln Electric Company, comparing them with the way he saw more conventional industrial organizations operating. Lincoln attempted to explain what caused the LEC system to work as well as it did, putting down some prescriptions for what he thought a top management must do (and what it must avoid doing), if it is to create and maintain an organization as highly productive as his own.

Lincoln's prescriptions were influenced very much by his ideas about the nature of man and how man relates to his brother. The son of a fervent and quarrelsome Congregational minister, James Lincoln employed the same conception of man to guide his thinking about how a company should relate to its markets, how a management should relate to its employees, and how organization members should relate to each other as he did to prepare for the Sunday School classes he taught. That was a view of man as a soul torn between higher and lower natures. Lincoln saw man as capable of virtue, but prone to vice; capable of growth and development, but inclined towards indolence and rationalization; capable of supporting, helping, and serving his brother, but more apt to dominate, oppress, and exploit him; sensitive to the injustices he suffers at the hands of others, but indifferent about those injustices he inflicts on others. Lincoln saw the struggle between man's two conflicting natures as a recurring, life-long affair. In the conduct of their lives, Lincoln believed, men aspire to the challenging, the beneficial, and the good. But weak, victims of their own avarice, pride, and sloth, Lincoln believed men more often ended up embracing the expedient, the injurious, and the evil. Lincoln held out a very hopeful vision of the growth and development man *could* achieve, for the good that could become of man. But he also pointed to man's innate capacity for sin—a capacity which, Lincoln believed, a management could ignore only at its peril.

This conception of man as having a dual nature, in conflict with oneself, is in itself not new. It has been part of the Western tradition since at least Augustine and Aquinas. But as a model of man it is much more rich—with important implications for the practice of management—than the models employed by early management thinkers or, for that matter, than models in fashion among present-day students of organization theory. Let us take a closer look at Lincoln's conception of man and the implications it has for the conduct of organizational affairs.

Man's Brighter Side

James Lincoln had an almost romantic vision of what man could become, both on his own and organized together with others. Recognizing that there are often great differences in the latent abilities with which people are born, Lincoln argued that each person could still achieve a greatness of his own. He maintained, in agreement with William James, that a person's latent endowment is seldom the limiting factor in his achievements. Lincoln once quoted James as saying:

> The human individual lives actually far within his limits. He possesses powers of various sorts which he habitually fails to use. He energizes below his maximum and he behaves below his optimum.

Without discounting the importance of careful selection in hiring, Lincoln argued that the actual human resources available to a company was determined much more by the development which can be accomplished in people after they join it. He went so far as to say:

> The personnel of any organization has inherent in it the making of a company of unique and outstanding ability, if only their environment will stimulate in its members a desire to develop their latent abilities.[41]

Lincoln also believed that it was possible to create and manage an organization in ways that

> self-developed men enthusiastically (joined together in) spontaneous . . .
> eager, wholehearted, vigorous and happy cooperation. . . doing their
> best in useful production, . . . rejoicing in their mutual success.[42]

Lincoln believed that the development of latent abilities, though often accompanied by stress, was "natural"and could bring much satisfaction. "After we develop a latent ability,"he wrote, "we see how natural that ability was."[43] Lincoln maintained that a "deep satisfaction" came "from proving our competence to ourselves and knowing that others recognize it." Self-respect and status—the respect and admiration of others—were, to Lincoln's way of thinking, "the incentive that almost completely determines our efforts in life."[45]

Man's Darker Side

James Lincoln was also no Polyanna. While he had seen how high man could reach, he had also seen how low he can stoop. He had seen the acrimony, the wretchedness, the malignancy that characterizes much of the relations between men. He had seen how callous, how mean, how vile man can be in his actions toward his brother. He saw it in the attitudes companies had towards their customers. He saw it in the posture stockholders took towards their "holdings". He saw it in relations between managements and their workers. He saw it in the relations between workers themselves, and in ways some people approached their work.

Lincoln had seen how few people, left to their own devices, could endure the stress and keep themselves under the pressure necessary to develop any but their most basic latent abilities. He had also seen how people could find any number of ways short of self-development to win status and some form of self-esteem for themselves. Lincoln believed that the natural propensity among the largest share of the human species was, on balance, towards taking a metaphorical "low road". Given the opportunity, he believed, too often individuals and organizations would rationalize their way into taking easy routes to quick profits, unearned status, and unjustified position among their peers, rather than limiting themselves only to rewards gained through ethical service and real personal development. Lincoln saw these phenomena in the people's relations with each other. Lincoln pointed out how readily people would refer to differences in race, ancestry, wealth, and taste to help themselves "feel superior (to others) no matter how thin the claim of superiority might be."[46]

Lincoln saw this happening in business's dealings with its customers when, taking advantage of situations where demand outstripped supply, firms grabbed themselves easy profits by jacking up their prices. He saw it in the common practice of consumer product companies to exploit their customers' baser motives, advertising supposedly new products whose only improvements over earlier models are engineered changes in fashion. For this Lincoln specifically upbraided Detroit's auto magnates, writing in 1961:

> It was the industry's hope that it could inflate the customer's vanity, stimulate his envy, make thrift seem shameful, and overcome prudence so that he would go into debt to buy a new car every year, since the design and appearance changed that often.[47]

Lincoln believed professional managers were often taking the low road to profits when they took the route of conglomeration, polishing a corporation's image, inflating its stock, then using that stock to acquire the profits of less glamorous businesses. He believed conglomerator's interest in growth had more to do with the size of their empires than with more or better service they might provide the public. He argued that the large multiple company would fall behind its more simple and compact competitors, becoming of less use to both society and its own stockholders. By then, of course, the professional managers have taken their money and run.

James Lincoln saw managers and stockholders alike taking the low road when they exploited their employees in the name of "free enterprise." When times were good and the enterprise was successful, they took for themselves what Lincoln thought rightfully should have been the employee's share of the profits. Basing their decisions primarily on financial considerations, when work was short they turned their employees out into the street.

Lincoln maintained that when a firm became more profitable, the stockholders seldom deserved the credit. Therefore, they seldom deserved the profits. He argued that the idea of stockholder as "owner"of a company had in many situations become an anachronism. Stockholders were just another source of financing for the business, like bondholders or lenders. Lincoln pointed to the absentee shareholder who

> buys the stock today and sells it tomorrow . . . has no knowledge of or interest in the company other than getting greater dividends and an ad-

vance in the price of his stock . . . [and] does no useful work himself [on contributing] to the efficiency of the operation.[48]

Lincoln believed most workers more than agreed with him on this point; that stockholders' assertion that theirs was a legal right meant little to the people who did the work; and that "most would be glad if the stockholder never got a cent."[49]

Lincoln also felt quite strongly about what he saw as a very casual attitude on the part of industrialists towards the plight of the workers they laid off. In 1961, Lincoln wrote:

> The industrialist will fire the worker any time he feels he can get along without him. The worker has no control over his future. His need of continuous income is far more urgent than that of management, yet he has no recourse. Only management is responsible for the loss of the worker's job. Only management can follow and develop a program that will bring in orders. The worker can't. Management, which is responsible, keeps its job. The man who had no responsibility is out. Management failed in its job and had no punishment. The wage earner did not fail in his job, but was fired. No man will go along with such injustice, nor should he. This is still true, in spite of custom which completely sanctions such procedure. . . . The fact that the usual management will fire the worker when he runs out of work has had more to do with production limitation than any other circumstances. No man will willingly work to throw himself out of his job, nor should he.[50]

Although James Lincoln saw collective bargaining as a serious obstacle to creating a highly productive organization, he understood how many in the work force had been almost forced to organize. He wrote:

> Use of layoffs and improper use of profits are abuses to which the hourly worker has been subjected by custom . . . The worker has had to go to the union to get the increase in the standard of living and status that he should have gotten from management automatically. . . . The abuses of labor union power are the natural reactions of human beings to the abuses to which management has subjected them. . . . If managers were treated as unjustly as much management has treated wage earners, they would also fight back as the unions do, by any means at hand.[51]

Lincoln also saw managers taking the low road in the pattern of privilege, domination, and general oppression that he saw in the conventional business organization. Lincoln observed that in much of private enterprise, as in the military, "authority is of much greater importance than results."[52] He saw superiors pull even day-to-day decisions up into the hierarchy as high as they possibly could without bringing the organization to a grinding halt. Superiors seemed to need to retain all but the most routine decisions to themselves, denying their organization the wisdom of many minds. Lincoln also noted how, in many organizations, bosses tightly restricted their subordinate's access to information, keeping them dependent on their superiors. He observed how, in many organizations, subordinates concerned for their careers must maintain a subservient posture towards their boss in all their relationships; how they must be careful not to suggest ideas that might "stop some of the prerogatives of top management;" how they must sometimes go through extreme contortions to insure that the boss thinks a new idea was his; how many times their jobs boiled down to just "show respect for the boss and pass the buck at the right time."[54]

Lincoln noted the injustice employees had to endure in seeing the savings resulting from their efforts being "frittered away" by selfish managements. Lincoln believed that most employees, especially those at lower levels, kept careful track of the doings of their bosses. They often had some difficulty, he thought, understanding how their bosses' high salaries were justified by work that entailed "many luncheons, banquets, speeches, and cocktail parties . . . several months' vacations, . . . [and] five hour days."[56]

Of course this pattern of privilege, domination, and oppression was nothing new. Lincoln traced through a tradition of such social relationships—between the master and the slave, between the lord and the serf, between the upper classes and the lower, between the industrialist and his employee. In each case, Lincoln believed, the powerful had endeavored—sometimes with open force, sometimes less obtrusively—to rob the weak of opportunities to grow, to restrict their development, and to keep them in their place. In that way, by comparison, the powerful could appear superior.

Lincoln saw this happening at all levels of society and at all levels of organizational life. The dynamic was to be found working its effects all the way down the line. Not only did top management try to keep middle managers in their place, middle managers worked to keep supervisors down. Supervisors were determined, in turn, to keep workers in line. And Lincoln was no romantic when it came to the work force. He saw the same process going on there. Through a variety of both organizational and social devices, skilled workers were careful to keep a good distance between themselves and their unskilled counterparts. Senior workers resorted to seniority clauses and strict job progression rules to keep an advantage over junior workers. Unions sought to formalize production quotas far below the capacity of their members, so the old-timers could avoid the embarrassment of being outperformed by younger, more capable men. In nonunion shops, senior workers were quick to show newcomers the ropes, which in many cases bound them to norms of low performance, denying them any opportunity to distinguish themselves.

While at every step down the heirarchy these restrictive actions had some people silently (and sometimes not-so-silently) screaming "You can't do this to me!" many others were only too willing to go along with strict limitations on their work roles. Of this "failure of the individual's ambition," Lincoln wrote:

> He is willing to be sidetracked. He will not pay the price of success by developing his abilities. He is very willing to trade any chance of development if someone will only remove responsibility from him. He is anxious to trade any chance of development of greatness in himself if someone will but promise him security.[57]

It seemed, however, that even those who initially willingly cooperated in their subjugation could not be counted on to remain docile for long. Eventually, they too would rise up against their masters.

The Low Road: Long Term Implications

In short, Lincoln saw people at all levels of organizations (and at all levels of society) as generally disposed to trying to get away with taking the low road in their relations to their work and in their dealings with others. He saw them trying to gain profits, advantage, and standing by taking shortcuts, often exploiting and oppressing those with whom they came in contact, rather than seeking rewards through their own personal development and through legitimate service to others.

James Lincoln was the first to admit that low road shortcuts often lead to immediate gains, sometimes sizeable ones. When the customer really needs your product, he'll pay when you jack up the price. Professional managers are definitely successful sometimes in parlaying their glamour stocks into industrial empires, riches, and prominence in the public eye. Marketeers can take the customer in often enough to win the quick profits necessary to get that fast promotion. Even workers make fools of management often enough to win the acclaim of their peers.

But Lincoln also argued that passage on the low road could often become more and more difficult (so that it changed from being the "easy" way), that the low road was often shorter than it originally appeared (so you couldn't get very far on it), and that it was often a one-way street. (Once you started down it, it was difficult to come back.).

Acquired forms inevitably go into decline when their founders sell out and either leave for Florida or stay on only to retire at their desks. Conglomerates are eventually revealed as the house of cards they often are, and falter. The conglomerate falters. A marketing strategy of "all the traffic will bear" turns into a game of wits between buyer and seller. Distrustful, resentful, and alienated, the customer condemns the seller and, at first opportunity, turns to another source. Managers who lead a firm in chasing the siren call of easy profits, once they attain high office as a reward, frequently lack the vision and skill to return the firm to those fundamentals which assure its longer term viability. Finally, Lincoln asserted, a low road strategy eventually weakens a firm's position with its external markets because it diverts management's attention away from those internal tasks that speak to the real, lasting needs of the customer.

Lincoln believed a low road strategy also weakened a firm internally. Taking advantage of a customer or exploiting his more ephemeral needs is an ignoble strategy with which many employees, especially those at the lower levels of an organization, will have a hard time identifying. That is made even more difficult when the chief goal of those strategies is to maximize profits that are to go into the pockets of top management and absentee stockholders. Lincoln maintained that stockholders and top managements alike were deluding themselves if they really believed that

1. It was possible for a top management to build and maintain among its employees for any length of time a strong desire to be more productive, when the profits resulting from that higher productivity were to go to absentee stockholders and/or to top management in the form of higher dividends, bonuses, and finer perks. Or, failing that

2. A top management might be able for any length of time, to exact high productivity and the concomitant high profits from employees through strict supervision and formal controls.

Lincoln argued that when it came to the prospect of being exploited, the employees of a firm were not that much different from its top managers or its stockholders. They did not like that prospect; many would recoil from it. To be "played for a sucker" was, to Lincoln's way of thinking, one of the worst of fates—for which most would avoid at all costs, even economic costs. Therefore, when the rewards of a firm's improved operations were primarily to benefit stockholders and/or top management, Lincoln believed it would be nearly impossible to get industrial workers to push themselves to increase their output, that it would be very difficult even to get them to adjust to new technologies and working arrangements, but that it would be quite easy to get them committed to resist innovation and to apply their best thinking to finding ways to keep production down.

Scientific Loafing

James Lincoln called such activities "scientific loafing."[59] Scientific loafing consisted of reducing one's level of output and working at the lowest level one could get away with without incurring serious punishments, such as getting fired. The objective of scientific loafing was to work at that level that allows the organization only enough revenue to keep you employed but not to deliver up surpluses of any magnitude to stockholders and top management. To many workers, that point seemed to be just above the point at which management started firing people. Of course, sometimes parties miscalculated, the firm went under, and everyone lost their jobs. But for workers who had no guarantee against being laid off next week or next month, it still seemed a prudent strategy for the short term. In fact, by stretching out the immediate work, scientific loafing probably helped ward off layoffs.

Lincoln was convinced that when workers set their mind to it they could be much better at scientific loafing than their bosses could be at scientific management. Lincoln thought managements only deluded themselves when they assumed they could achieve much success in preventing restriction and in exacting high output from their workers by means of formal controls and close supervision. Such tactics lead only to a losing battle for management.

Two Offenses and an Expensive Defense

In this battle, workers had two excellent offenses. The first pitted the individual worker against his foreman and the time-study man. In the second, workers banded together as a power block against management. If the first offense sometimes did not work, the second nearly always did. But the first offense often worked only too well.

The worker's advantage, according to Lincoln, is that he is "the expert on the job he is doing. He knows much more about it than any other manager when he really wants to." As a result, Lincoln argued, a single worker can often restrict his output "with little difficulty."

He knows enough about the machine that he is operating so that he could curtail output to any desired point without the usual boss being conscious of it.

When a man dug a trench with a spade, any boss could tell if he was working and how hard. No boss can tell accurately now whether a man operating a ditch-digging machine is doing his best, trying to limit output, or is actually wrecking the machine.[60]

Should the individual offense fail, however, workers can always join together against management, either formally through a union or in an informal conspiracy. Either way, standing together, workers can do a lot over the long haul to bargain down standards, to resist technological innovation, to undermine management initiatives, and, generally, to make a game out of getting away with doing as little as they can. Under such conditions, Lincoln maintained, managements end up spending a great deal on extra control systems and supervision to achieve seldom better than a standoff with their work force, at a level of production far below their operation's true potential.

In spite of its prevalence, Lincoln believed that resistance to efficiency in production was not normal in men. He once wrote, "We normally strive to increase our efficiency in every way we can, when we play a game or when we work for ourselves."[61] To Lincoln, such resistance could be as frustrating to the "loafer" as it was costly to the enterprise and to the customer. Workers were driven to resistance and restriction of output, he believed, as a defense against what they saw as exploitative goals on the part of top managements and stockholders who employed them. Simply the expectation, the prospect, that those who had a so-called legal right to the profits of the enterprise might gain from their efforts lead workers, Lincoln believed, to doom most of private enterprise to a life of internal friction and operational inefficiency.

In sum, Lincoln argued that while sometimes the nimble and the lucky were successful in parlaying one low road expedition into another, more often taking the low road eventually made everyone the loser.

Society was denied the productive efficiency that meant more of the good life for all.

Stockholders seldom got the high returns of their avaricious dreams, at least not for long.

Customers failed to get quality products at low costs.

Top management, if it wanted the regard of the people it managed, seldom got that.

Workers often ended up living shallow, stunted lives—"their god-given abilities staying dormant"—feeling resentful and hopeless about their lot.

Taking the High Road

Because he was convinced that business did not have to be conducted that way, Lincoln saw low road strategies as a tragic waste. Relations between the producer and the consumer did not have to be a game of wits, leaving both wary of each other. Relations within the enterprise did not have to be characterized by "grudging, distrustful, half-forced cooperation of men who must earn wages and men greedy for larger salaries." Rather, he was convinced, "A new conception of the relationship between so-called management and workers" could be made reality—one that "results in both wanting to work together for a common and very useful end."[62] In the accomplishment of this end, Lincoln believed, both could "fulfill their basic desires for recognition and pride in their individual abilities and worth."[63] In other words, man could be redeemed. He could take the high road. And everyone could profit from his having done it.

What exactly did it mean for an organization to take the high road? Basically, it meant forsaking exploitative postures in all organizational relations—

in the relation of the producer to the customer;
in the relation of the stockholder to the enterprise;
in the relation of the manager to the managed;
in the relationships among the employees themselves, and;
in the relationship of the employee to the firm.

In the realm of producer/customer relations, Lincoln's definition of the high road was clear and direct. Industry must have as its goal: progress, improvement in the ways of living, better lives for everyone. That translates more specifically for a manufacturer into "The proper responsibility of industry is to build a better and better product at a lower and lower price."[64]

Lincoln rejected as moral bankruptcy and strategic foolishness the adoption by individual businessmen of the Western capitalist dictum (espoused by philosophers and economists from Adam Smith and John Locke to Milton Friedman) that private enterprise should seek first to maximize its own profits. Adam Smith had argued that individuals accidentally serve the common good while seeking their own private interests. The individual considering only his own gain is led by an "invisible hand" to promote an end which was no part of his intention.

For Lincoln, that did not excuse the individual's failure to aim at the common good. It often also led the entrepreneur down those perilous low road paths.

Lincoln argued instead that the top management of a company should eschew all low road profit strategies and should discourage its subordinates from even considering them. Lincoln had no difficulty with profits per se. He was not antiprofits, as many critics of business seem to be today. He never questioned the need for private enterprise to make substantial profits. He saw them as necessary to pay stockholders a just rent on their capital; to provide seed money for a firm's expansion; and to reward managers and workers for their contributions to a company's success. Lincoln believed that, for a company to remain viable over the long term, it had to make a profit and it ought to be a healthy one.

However, Lincoln argued, a company should allow itself to make profits only as a direct result of providing service to its customers. On this point he was adamant:

> The goal of the organization must be this: to make a better and better product to be sold at a lower and lower price. Profit can not be the *goal*. Profit must be a *by-product*. . . .
>
> That is a state of mind and a philosophy . . . that takes ability and character.[65]

Lincoln maintained that, if a company were to adopt as its central strategy the *duty* to serve its customers—that if a company were to allow itself to make profits only in that way—that such a strategy would keep the company's attention directed towards the real needs of its customers. By concentrating on finding better ways to meet those needs, he argued, the company would assure itself stable and rewarding markets for its products.

Taking the high road in stockholder/enterprise relations basically meant that the owner of shares in the enterprise accepted a role as a source of funds, not unlike other sources such as bondholders and lenders, with similarly limited claims on the profits of the enterprise. Because of the greater risk stockholders assumed, standing in line behind lenders and bondholders in their claims on a firm's resources (its operating profits, as a going concern; its assets, on liquidation), Lincoln held that stockholders should receive a greater return on their investment than lenders or bondholders. But he also maintained that the enterprise's obligation to stockholders stopped at preserving their assets and paying them a return commensurate with their risk. In the case of a healthy, established company, because the stockholders' risk was slight, Lincoln argued that they should expect and should receive a dividend at a rate only slightly higher than that of a high grade bond.

In relations between people in the enterprise, taking the high road meant the forsaking of both formal and informal practices that allowed some, at whatever level in the organization, to block the development of others and the just and fair recognition of the contributions each person made to the success of the enterprise. Executives were not to dominate, but were to lead. On the shop floor, men were to give up restrictive practices in favor of letting each person best develop his skills and make his best contributions.

Finally, in the employee's relationship to the firm, taking the high road meant that each person strive to develop his latent abilities and apply them in service to the enterprise. Although men often aspired to taking the high road, left to their own devices, Lincoln believed, most would be hard pressed to keep it up for more than short periods at best. The obstacles preventing them were rooted, as has been said, in three characteristics inherent to most men: 1) their inertia; 2) their inclination to try to get ahead the easy way, even if it were at the expense of others; and 3) their fear that others might get ahead at their expense and determination to prevent that.

Out of his own experience with The Lincoln Electric Company, James Lincoln came to the conclusion that, for an organization to travel along the high road for long, it would require a strong leader at the top to put in place and to maintain a management system in which

1. traditional practices by which people dominate, oppress, or exploit each other would be either eliminated or neutralized;
2. new organizational practices would be instituted which assure all members of the organization that such abuses not go unchecked;
3. each member of the organization would be recognized for his contributions to the success of the enterprise in ways that are seen as just and fair.

Under such a system, Lincoln believed, people could come to deal with each other as do players on a well-coached athletic team. Together they work in "eager, wholehearted, vigorous and happy cooperation . . . rejoicing in their mutual success," while at the same time each is competing with the others, trying to perfect his own skills, trying to win for himself greater recognition, standing, and position within the group.[66]

When no one is allowed to hold another back, Lincoln asserted, each can then develop his latent abilities more closely to his potential. And while some will end up behind others in the internal contest, most will have distinguished themselves in some way that secures them a position of respect within the group.

THE LINCOLN PLAN

The management system developed by James Lincoln and others in The Lincoln Electric Company has fared well in meeting the three criteria listed above. Some aspects of that system have already been described in earlier contexts.

For example, Lincoln management believes the benefits to the company from a flat and lean organization extend beyond the cost savings of fewer administrative positions. It also keeps superiors from meddling in the work of their subordinates. Subordinates do more of the initiating, at times when they want and can use the input of the superior. According to Mr. James Clauson, New England district sales manager, "Top management sets the broad policies. Within them, we manage our own operations. That's a good way to work."

The same dynamic applies to many jobs on the shop floor in the plant. Compared to a functional design, the line-flow design greatly reduces the extent to which workers are dependent on and subject to unilateral initiation from "superiors" of every stripe—including inspectors, set-up men, and their own foremen. Most operators' jobs require skills which can earn the regard of fellow workers. Some jobs are designed in ways which offer a good deal of complexity and variety to operators who look for that in their work.

LEC's policy of no perks for those with high organizational rank also takes on new meaning in this light, reflecting top management's care in emphasizing the social worth of every Lincoln Electric employee. According to Mr. Irrgang,

> We have a very high regard for people as such. . . . There are no unimportant jobs. . . . There are no such things as unimportant people. . . . That has to be recognized.[67]

Promotion from Within

Turning to other important features of the Lincoln Plan which have not previously been mentioned, LEC holds fast to a strict policy of promotion from within. James Lincoln believed that a company ought to be able to create its own executives. With very few exceptions, mostly in highly technical areas, everyone at Lincoln Electric starts at the entry level, whether in sales, in engineering, or in the plant. According to Mr. Irrgang, who started with LEC on piecework in the armature winding department, "We feed in from the bottom and develop people here." Mr. Irrgang is convinced that to do otherwise would be a serious mistake: "There is nothing more discouraging, I think, than for somebody to work hard for a particular job and then, when a vacancy occurs, see somebody brought in from outside to fill it.[68]

There are no definite lines of promotion within Lincoln Electric. People are not expected to spend their work lives in one department or in one functional area. At least one job is reserved for management trainees in the inspection, time-study, and production control departments. Although LEC does not pick up the tab, Lincoln employees are encouraged to seek outside training in areas that can be of use to the company. At one time, Lincoln Electric boasted more enrollments in various night schools around Cleveland than any plant, regardless of size. Even when skills completely new to LEC are required in some position, they can usually be found among the members of the organization. For example, when LEC put in its first computer in 1973, they needed a programmer and a systems analyst. Twenty LEC employees who had training or experience in computers applied for the jobs. The organization got computer people who already knew LEC and its business.[69]

Outside of special cases requiring very specialized skills, such as some research positions, all job openings in the company (including those for top level positions) are posted on several dozen bulletin boards around the plant and in the offices. Anyone who wants to—regardless of seniority and present position—is welcome to apply. This often results in time-consuming interviews with many applicants. But Mr. Irrgang feels the extra time is worth it. "It's very useful," he says, "and we get some real surprises in the people who apply and turn out to be very qualified."[70] To this point, LEC's steady growth, combined with its policy of promotion from within, have assured that the company's employees have had substantial opportunity for advancement.

The Advisory Boards

Top management at Lincoln Electric subscribes to the principle that all promotions in the company should be based on merit alone. On this point of company policy Mr. Lincoln left no doubt about his feelings:

All men should know that the best man rises because he is the best man, for no other reason. . . . Advancement depends completely on ability of those chosen for advancement compared to all others and on nothing else.[71]

Top management is closely involved in most promotion decisions in the company. In most cases, they have more than a dossier and an interview to go on in making their decisions as to who is best qualified to take on new responsibilities. This is partially due to Lincoln Electric's advisory boards.

For many years, top management at Lincoln Electric—the chairman, the president, often both—have met on a regular basis with elected representatives of managers, and workers at all levels of the organization to discuss issues before the company. One board, made up mostly of middle managers meets once each month. The other advisory board, made up mostly of elected representatives from each department, meets with top management every second week. One important by-product of these meetings is that top management (and everyone else at these meetings) gets a fairly good reading on the level of intelligence, good judgment, and knowledge of the company's operations each member has to offer the company.

The advisory board goes back to the first days after James Lincoln took over the general managership of the company. James had just turned thirty and nearly all his business experience had been in sales when he took charge of the firm from his ailing brother, John. James had very little hands-on knowledge of manufacturing. He knew that; and he knew that the men in the plant knew that. At Ohio State, James had had more success as a tackle and captain of the football team than he had had as an engineering student. (The year he captained the Ohio State team, no opponent crossed its goal line.) Drawing on that experience, James resolved to turn the Lincoln Electric organization into a "team."

He called together the people of the company and asked them to elect representatives from each department, who would sit with him on an advisory board to raise issues and make recommendations concerning any aspect of the company's operations. The advisory board's role continues to be essentially the same today. For his services, each representative to the board receives an honorarium of $100 a year. Departments elect representatives each month in rotation so that the board changes gradually. Only employees with two or more years service are eligible and no member can serve more than two consecutive terms.

The duties of the representatives to the advisory board, as described in the *Employee's Handbook,*

> shall be to bring up and discuss the grievances and complaints of those they represent, to make suggestions regarding the improving of working conditions, and to pass upon plans for the welfare and safety of the employees in this plant. This elected board shall be empowered by the employees to represent them in dealing with the management in any matters necessary, due to changing conditions affecting the employees or management.[72]

Advisory board meetings are chaired by either the chairman or the president of Lincoln Electric. Often both attend. At board meetings, top management notifies representatives of important developments affecting the company, including market conditions, business prospects, programs of competitors, as well as the general state of plant operations. Lincoln management follows the policy of full and prompt disclosure to the advisory board of all important developments affecting the welfare of the company. James Lincoln believed that it was better for employees to get news—good or bad—from the company leadership first, before they learned it from outside sources.

Representatives to the board are encouraged to bring up whatever issues their constituents want addressed. Most issues brought up by representatives at board meetings are either resolved on the spot or are referred by memo to the responsible executive, who is expected to respond by the next meeting. Minutes of each meeting are posted on bulletin boards throughout the plant; and representatives are expected to answer questions about the board's actions for other workers in their departments.

The advisory board stops short of the kind of decision-making body prescribed by more ardent advocates of worker participation and industrial democracy. It does not act as a board of directors, with a final say, for example, over the company's market strategy. It does not review and pass on the promotions of key personnel. It does not make capital allocation decisions. LEC's regular board of directors does that. Formally, the advisory board's role is advisory. Top management retains the right to the final say on all decisions. In practice, top management seldom resorts to exercising that right explicitly. It does not flaunt its power. Most issues around which there may be some depth of feeling are resolved within the board by working consensus. According to Mr. Irrgang, when top management does reject a direction the board is taking, it is careful to explain its reasons, usually rooted in the longer-term effects on customer relations. As Mr. Irrgang points out, "Our people expect management to object if they are asked to do something that is not the right thing from an overall view."[73]

James Lincoln had no apprehensions that bringing workers into an advisory council would lead to struggles between labor and management over the control of the organization. He saw a big difference between workers wanting to be free from overly close supervision and domination by others, wanting to be left alone to manage their own day-to-day work activities, and workers wanting to take on the job of—or even participate in—making the myriad decisions relating to policy making and the overall management of the firm as such. In regard to the latter he said, "Labor does not want to manage."[74]

Lincoln Electric workers have yet to attempt a coup to take over the management of the company. That is not to say, however, that today's workers are no different from their predecessors, especially in their attitudes towards authority. According to Mr. Willis, "Today's workers are different. They're more outspoken. They are more interested in why things are being done, not just how." Still, that difference has created few problems in the conduct of the advisory board because, according to Mr. Willis, "We have nothing to hide and never did. So we can give them the answers to their questions."[75]

Besides the board's effectiveness in continually confronting top management with the workers' point of view, it has also helped broaden the perspective of many LEC workers. Some workers come to understand how considerations outside their own purview can legitimately preclude courses of action which make sense from their own operations-level perspective. Lincoln management believes the board meetings have also been effective in reassuring the workers of top management's sincerity in honoring and protecting their interests, even when management sometimes makes decisions with which they do not agree. On occasion, workers have also elected some of the more vocal skeptics among them to act as representative to the advisory board, as a way of bringing them around. It has usually worked.

The Guaranteed Continuous Employment Plan

One of the more revolutionary features of the LEC management system to emerge from deliberations of the advisory board is the company's Guaranteed Continuous Employment Plan. Adopted on a trial basis in 1951 and established as a formal policy in 1958, the plan guarantees year-long employment to all Lincoln employees who have at least two years service.

Even before then James Lincoln had expressed his feeling that an organization "should originally take its men from school and then keep them until their working life is over and they are retired."[76] The company had generally followed that policy on an informal basis since its beginning. During World War II, Lincoln Electric was one of the first companies to voluntarily set aside six months' severance pay for temporary workers who were in jobs that would be reclaimed by LEC regulars upon their return. (So new a practice was this that the IRS challenged it, accusing LEC of trying to avoid payment of income taxes.)

After the war, one of the more pressing questions relating to industrial practice that came to be debated on a national level was what U.S. firms and the U.S. government ought to do to ensure greater economic security for American workers, especially in the face of the kinds of security offered by our emerging ideological opponents, the socialist states. Many in the United States favored private firms' supplementing workers' unemployment benefits. Others, notably Peter Drucker, advocated guaranteed employment, whereby an employer, based on business forecasts, would guarantee his workers a certain number of hours employment each week for the next quarter or half year. Hormel Meat, Nunn-Bush Shoe, and Procter and Gamble had each operated under similar plans for many years.[77]

Eventually, the automotive and rubber industries opted for supplemental unemployment benefits (SUB's); others soon followed. James Lincoln held to the idea that the guaranteed employment approach made more sense, both morally and pragmatically. Later he wrote about this issue

> Wages cannot be properly given the worker for work that he does not do.
> If we pay such unearned wages, we are robbing the customer, who is the
> only source of wages. We have no right to waste his money.[78]

With sizeable layoffs in some industries depleting companies' SUB reserves in recent years, others have come to question the practicality of that route chosen in the early 1950s. Lincoln also argued about layoffs that they are "more a product of habit that they are of necessity.... They are often an escape mechanism for the ineffective manager."[79]

Lincoln's guaranteed employment plan guarantees all workers with two years service employment for at least 75 percent of the standard work week. (In 1951, that was thirty-two hours; now it is thirty.) It guarantees no specific rate of pay. Workers must also be willing to transfer to other jobs as conditions require. They must also be prepared to work overtime at times of peak demand. The overtime provision and the guarantee allow for a fluctuation in regular workload of about 36 percent.

LEC has gone through several significant business slumps. The more serious of these were in 1958 and 1971. At those times, operations were cut back to four-day weeks, projects were taken off the shelf—including work on tooling, new methods, and product development—and no one was laid off, even those employees with fewer than two years service.[80]

Distribution of Operating Profits

The aspect of the Lincoln Electric management system that gets the most consistent attention in the press is the way the company distributes profits at the end of each year. It goes as follows:

1. Top management sets aside a share of operating profits as "seed money" to be used for future expansion and purchase of new equipment. How much is set aside depends on the level of current operations and plans for future growth.
2. Dividends are paid to the company's stockholders. The dividend rate is usually somewhat more than the return from a safe investment in high grade bonds.
3. The rest of the company's operating profits are distributed to all of the employees in the firm as a year-end bonus. For close to fifty years now, that bonus has averaged about 100 percent of the regular annual payroll of the company—that is, each person in the company on the average receives each year a bonus equal to his pay for the previous year.

Since the early 1940s, the size of the bonus pool has ranged from 78 percent to 129 percent of the annual payroll.[81] The company generally plans its strategy so as to yield a 100 percent bonus. Profit performance higher or lower than planned results in the fluctuations in the bonus pool. In 1978, the bonus pool was 103 percent. On the average, each Lincoln employee—not just top managers, nor selected middle managers, but everyone: secretaries, salesmen, every man and woman on the shop floor—took home a bonus the size of that year's paycheck.

This is on the average. Everyone does not get the same flat percentage. Some get more, some less. Who gets what percentage in relation to his base pay, who decides that, and how it is computed have all changed over the years. Mr. Lincoln's first try at a bonus was a flop. For a number of years the company went without one. The origin of the company's present bonus plan is itself quite interesting. This one was not Lincoln's idea. It originated with the advisory board. During the first years of the Depression, Lincoln Electric experienced the same kinds of difficulties other manufacturing organizations faced. Sales were hard to come by. Hours were sometimes short. In 1933, through the advisory board, Lincoln's employees asked for a 10 percent wage increase. James Lincoln turned down their request, justifying his refusal in terms of the company's uncertain profit picture. The workers returned to Lincoln with a counterproposal for a year-end bonus, if through increased productivity and lowered costs, the firm's profits at year's end were larger than Lincoln had projected.

Mr. Lincoln's first reaction to this proposal was less than enthusiastic. In 1918, the first year that LEC had been able to pay dividends to its stockholders, James Lincoln had unilaterally also given his employees nearly as much in the form of a bonus. The bonus had amounted to about 3 percent of their earnings. It lead to little discernible improvement in their efforts at work, a disappointment to Mr. Lincoln. He concluded that the bonus had not meant much to his employees. However, in 1933, the workers were bargaining for a bonus *in exchange for* their improved productivity. Mr. Lincoln eventually agreed to try it for a year on an experimental basis. If the workers could *earn* a bonus through improved productivity, they were welcome to it. That year everyone pitched in to cut costs. Sales also improved. To everyone's surprise (including Lincoln's), at the end of 1934, after Lincoln paid his stockholders a 25 percent larger dividend, and after seed money was set aside to provide for the firm's growth, enough profit was left over to hand out bonuses averaging $350 per employee.

Lincoln employees have received annual bonuses every year since then. Between 1934 and 1942, the bonus pool grew to about 80 percent of the yearly payroll. During the Depression years, the bonus was linked for most employees to a low base pay compared with going rates for the trade. This was to permit the company, in Mr. Lincoln's words, to "skate through a tough period without going broke."[82] This arrangement did help the company get through a tough year in 1938. During this early period, the size of each person's bonus was personally determined by Mr. Lincoln himself and he asked employees not to disclose to each other the amounts of their bonuses. (Among some key executives, bonuses were as high as 750 percent of their salaries.)

Much of the secrecy around the bonus distribution came to an end after 1942, when the full scope of the bonus plan became public record. The IRS accused Lincoln of trying to avoid federal income taxes by paying out unjustifiably large bonuses to his people. Because Lincoln Electric was a supplier of war material, a congressional committee decided to look into the matter and invited Mr. Lincoln to testify before it. The hearings were covered by the national press and articles in *Time* and *Fortune* made Mr. Lincoln an instant celebrity. A comparison of Lincoln's selling prices against those of its competitors and demonstrations of the kinds of cost reductions Lincoln employees had effected in production processes convinced legislators that Lincoln Electric was doing a good thing. As one writer reported, "They thanked him for coming."[83] The IRS was less cordial. It took a number of years before all its complaints were settled and Mr. Lincoln and his hyperproductive employees were vindicated. (At one point, in the name of the advisory board, Mr. Lincoln sent a wire to Washington asking "How much must we reduce efficiency and raise costs to keep from being penalized?") It was finally settled, however, and The Lincoln Electric Company won its right to treat the year-end bonus as a pretax expense.

Some aspects of the administration of the bonus plan have changed since the early 1940s. Since then, regular wages at Lincoln Electric have been kept on a par with those of comparable jobs in the Cleveland area. Employee representatives serve on a committee which adjusts wage levels. Wages are also adjusted quarterly in line with the rise and fall of the cost of living index. As the company grew, people's immediate supervisors took on greater responsibility for determining their share of the bonus. In the late 1940s, supervisors used a form to rate subordinates, on which a person could be assigned up to 1,000 points. Five hundred were related to the person's qualities as worker in his present job, such as quality of work, quantity of work, and job knowledge. The other 500 were allocated to a person's "potentiality" for growth and development into supervisory capacity. The bonus for Mr. Lincoln's immediate subordinates was determined by him personally and was generally much larger than their base annual salaries.[84] Today, all employees' bonuses, with the exception of the chairman and president, are drawn from the same bonus pool. All employees are rated by their supervisors and department heads on the same four factors twice each year. These are as follows:

1. *Supervision Required:* the ability to supervise oneself, including one's work, safety performance, orderliness, care of equipment, and effectiveness in the use of one's skills.
2. *Workmanship and Attitude Toward Quality:* one's success in eliminating errors and in reducing scrap and waste.
3. *Output:* one's willingness to be productive, not hold back work effort or output, teamwork, and help in meeting emergencies.
4. *Ideas and Cooperation:* initiative and ingenuity in developing new methods to reduce costs, increase output, improve quality,

willingness to help others to do their jobs, and willingness in
making one's knowledge available to others.[85]

In the case of men on the shop floor, the latter three ratings are done
in consultation with the inspection department (workmanship and
quality); the production control department (output); and the methods
and time study department (ideas and cooperation).[86]

Ratings for all employees in a department must average to 100 percent, so all departments are treated equally in their claims on the bonus pool. In cases where an employee should get a rating above 110,
the extra points are awarded by a top-level committee of vice presidents from a supplemental bonus pool, so as not to penalize his
coworkers.

Managers at levels above that of the immediate supervisor responsible for apprising performance take an active role in reviewing all merit ratings. The supervisor informs each subordinate privately what his
score is and posts all scores within his department by number only on
the department's bulletin board. Many employees openly discuss their
scores with each other. Employees are encouraged to discuss their ratings with their department heads if they are dissatisfied or are un-
clear about them.[87]

In summary, the actual dollar size of the bonus an employee receives starts with his or her salary as a base. That base is first adjusted according to the overall size of the bonus pool for that year. That
adjustment is the same for everyone. Then a second adjustment is
made, according to the individual's scores on his or her merit reviews.

Over the last forty years, roughly as much has been paid out to
Lincoln Electric employees in bonuses as in salaries and wages. For
four decades, employees have earned twice as much at Lincoln Electric as they would have in comparable jobs in conventional organizations. Simply because of its enormity, the bonus has been the aspect
of the Lincoln Electric approach to enterprise which has gotten the
most attention of people outside the company. It is also the aspect
which James Lincoln came to feel was the least understood. Many
outsiders, influenced by traditional practices, have tended to look on
the bonus as a huge economic carrot Lincoln management holds out
in front of its people. Lincoln employees work hard—they reason—
they assume responsibility, manage themselves, use their ingenuity
because they want that money. They do it for the dollars. For James
Lincoln, it was not that simple. The conventional explanation
missed the point. People might join The Lincoln Electric Company to
get a crack at that bonus. But once they were part of the team, Lincoln believed, other more powerful forces came into play. Lincoln of-

ten used team sports as a metaphor for the patterns of incentive and work relations which were most likely to lead to high performance in the industrial enterprise. In 1951, he wrote:

> Everyone aspires to a position in which his ability to be a man among men is recognized and developed. He can do this only in an activity which he regards as worthy of his best efforts and under circumstances that recognize his contribution. He wants to be a player in a game that he and all the spectators feel is important. He wants his contribution to victory acknowledged and fair compared to that of the other players. When he has that acknowledgement he will play his head off; not only that he will train, practice, and develop his abilities to make himself the greatest player that his abilities will permit. Organizing the game the players think is important and rewarding them in ways that seem to them just and in accord with their actual contribution—*that is incentive management.*[88]

With high performance came high profits. For people not to feel exploited, Lincoln was convinced, a good share of those profits had to be returned to the people who produced them. Otherwise they would protect themselves from exploitation by not performing. No one wants to be "played for a sucker," he stated plainly.[89] To Lincoln's way of thinking, sharing profits helped eliminate fear of exploitation as a *disincentive* to superior performance. What provided the strongest *incentive,* he believed, was "recognition of our abilities by ourselves and our contemporaries." Time and again Lincoln restated the message in his writings that "recognition is the real incentive," as presented in the statements below:

> It is our sense of achievement and its recognition by others that we desire most. Money is of relatively small importance. Money is an economic necessity. Beyond enough for our real needs, money is valued less for what it will buy than as an evidence of successful skill and achievement.
> Man gauges his success by the opinion of those who know his ability and his work. That is what we strive for, and we hold all else secondary. . . Money as a reward is far less attractive to most of us than the respect of those we know. . . . The greatest incentive that money has, usually is that it is a symbol of success, which gives the successful man status. The resulting status is the real incentive. The ability to gain status by accomplishments, which incidentally bring more income, is of far greater importance to a man than the income itself. Money alone can be an incentive only to the miser.

What, then, is the incentive that causes people to strive so mightily for success . . .? The answer is *recognition of our abilities by our contemporaries and ourselves.* The gaining by our skills of the feeling that we are a man among men. . . . The feeling that we are different in some way or ways that others admire and wish to emulate. The feeling that we are outstanding and are so recognized by our fellows. That is the greatest incentive that is universal. That is the incentive that almost completely determines our efforts in life. . . . We sacrifice all others things to this deep satisfaction that comes from proving our competence and knowing that others recognize it.[90]

Therefore, to Lincoln the bonus and the way it was awarded were equally important. Lincoln drew a parallel between the rating process by which the size of a person's bonus was determined and the "write-ups following a game" in sports.

The man is rated by all those who have accurate knowledge of some phase of his work. . . . The man is rewarded for all the things he does that are of help, and penalized if he does not do as well as others in all these same ways. He is a member of a team and is rewarded or penalized depending on what he can do in all opportunities to win the game.[91]

When this process was managed effectively Lincoln claimed, a "game spirit" could develop in an organization, a spirit of "cooperation and competition within cooperation."

If each person is properly rated on all these things and paid accordingly, there will not only be a fair reward to each worker, but much more important, there will be friendly and exciting competition between the workers, so that each tries to outdistance the others and to contribute more. . . . A spirit of teamwork will prevail, as it does between competing members of a football team.[92]

Three other elements of the Lincoln plan which have to do with the distribution of income within the organization deserve mention. These are the company's use of piece-rate pay, its suggestion program, and its employee stock ownership plan.

Piecework

The majority of the shop-floor people at Lincoln Electric are on piecework. Every production job that can be standardized has a piece rate. Traditionally, piecework plans have been held up by their advocates as a surefire way to kill two birds with one stone: to incite workers to greater effort and to provide management with efficient, accurate data on the real costs of production. In general, however, piecework plans have fallen short on both claims. They are notorious for fostering suspicion and fomenting hostility between workers and managements, and among workers themselves. They have often been most effective at polarizing the organizations to which they have been applied. In piecework organizations, one often sees a good deal of workers' effort going, first, into outwitting engineers into setting loose rates and, second, into campaigning (by means of a vast array of tactics) to get loosened whatever rates the engineers may have succeeded in setting tight in the first place. One hears of little of that kind of activity at Lincoln Electric.

Why that has not happened with piece rates at Lincoln Electric may be explained by how they were initially put in place and how they have been maintained over the years.

One of the first proposals the young James Lincoln set before his newly formed advisory board in 1914 was one that the workers switch from standard base wages to piece-rate pay. Instead of paying people for the hours they worked, Lincoln wanted to pay them for the pieces they produced. To him it made ultimate sense: everything the company bought was priced by the piece; so was everything it sold; so why shouldn't each worker be paid by the piece?

The men were skeptical. Piece rates had already gotten a bad name. They were a key element of this new "scientific management." Unions and others were charging that the introduction of piece rates led to "speed-ups" and rate-cutting, resulting in more work for less pay. In testimony before a congressional committee, Frederick Taylor, the father of scientific management had himself admitted that time-study and piece-rate techniques could be—and already had been—abused in taking unfair advantage of workers. So it is not surprising that Lincoln's workers had a few doubts about his proposal.

Lincoln made a sporting proposition. If they would allow rates to be set on their jobs through time and methods study, they could have the right to challenge any rates they considered unfair. The time-study man could then reset the rate by any method he chose. If the man doing the job objected to that rate, the time-study man would himself work the job for a full day. Whatever rate he demonstrated he could earn would then be the established rate. It might be more, it might be less. But that would be the rate. Lincoln also guaranteed that rates, once set, would not be changed by management as long as a job was not changed in some demonstrably better way (in terms of methods, tools, and techniques). The men decided to give it a try; piece rates went in.[93]

Piece rates can be very helpful in production planning and control. Having a standard against which to measure a day's work can also provide each worker with a convenient measure of, and recognition of, his developing skill. But piecework measures are still rough measures. James Lincoln himself harbored no illusions regarding the precision of piecework measurements. He once wrote

> No ideal application of piecework has ever been made and perhaps never can be made. Piecework cannot be applied that accurately. No one can set prices that will differentiate according to skill, imagination, and effort between workers who are doing various jobs at the same time.[94]

To keep this problem inherent in all piecework systems from becoming an issue among the Lincoln Electric employees, Mr. Lincoln saw the need for administering the system in a way so that workers could see that the company would not willingly treat people unfairly. Three additional features of the Lincoln plan seem to have helped achieve this. First, employee representatives serve on the job evaluation committee which sets the base wage levels on which piece rates are based. Second, any worker whose job is changed in a way that results in a lowering of its rate may request a transfer to a job which pays an equal or higher rate.[95] Third, the company is very selective about the kind of person who carries out the time and methods job. In regards to the latter point, Lincoln issued cautions about the type of man that should fill that role. He warned against the man who would make a small change "of no real importance" in a job, method, or tooling in order to retime it. Lincoln said such a man was "a crook and cannot be trusted to uphold the integrity of the company.... Time-study men doing such a thing should be fired immediately.... No management can pussyfoot here."[96]

Conventional practice has been to appoint young men fresh out of college to the time-study job. At first, that approach seems logical. They have just completed extensive studies of time and motion techniques. Lincoln rejected that approach out of hand. Instead, in Lincoln Electric the methods jobs are staffed by men who have come up through the ranks. Lincoln looked for two kinds of expertise in these men. First, they had to have distinguished themselves as operators in demonstrating originality and skill in developing better work methods in their own jobs. Second, they had to have solid interpersonal skills. According to Lincoln, "The man who is to put piecework into operation must be an expert manufacturer as well as an expert in human relations." The goal of the methods department should be for each man to see it "as made up of experts that are developers of new methods of production that will help him to greater skill."[97] Each year, time and method studies performed by that department number in the thousands. For many years the rate of challenges has been less than 1/2 of 1 percent.[98]

Suggestion Plan

Lincoln Electric's suggestion plan was set up in 1929. Since then, it has provided a systematic way for operations-level employees to put forward ideas for improving methods and reducing costs in all areas of the company's operations. Suggestions are evaluated weekly by a board made up of the top-level managers from each of the company's functional areas. This board receives a steady flow of suggestions, about one in ten of which hits pay dirt.[99]

For many years, extra cash awards for suggestions resulting in new savings were paid out to all employees except engineers, time and methods men, and department heads. (Methods improvements were considered an integral part of their jobs.) An employee received one-half the first year's savings for any idea which was accepted. People sometimes received over $1,000 for a single new idea. A worker on piece rate also had the option of applying his idea to his own job and taking the money instead in increased earnings.[100]

While the suggestion plan continues in operation today, the practice of separate cash awards to individual suggestors has been abandoned. James Lincoln himself came to question the assumption all shop-floor inventions should be treated as individual achievements. In 1951, he wrote:

> the thought that a single mind invents is almost completely wrong. No development ever came about except as a product of the ideas of many people. Actually, invention is generally the outgrowth of ideas and suggestions of others with whom we have come in contact.[101]

As the merit rating process associated with the yearly bonus evolved into its present form, a person's performance in coming up with his own suggestions and in helping others develop theirs became a factor in determining the bonus. Eventually the payment of a separate award for suggestions was abandoned as redundant.[102]

Employee Stock Ownership

The final aspect of the approach Lincoln Electric has taken to the distribution of income is the company's employee stock ownership plan.

James Lincoln established a stock purchase plan for the company's employees in 1925. At that time, Lincoln looked on the plan primarily as a way to allow employees to participate in the company's earnings and, hopefully, thereby to lead them to identify more strongly with the enterprise. Another reason for selling stock to employees emerged after the company adopted its radical bonus plan. That was simply to reduce the threat of interference by outside shareholders who might try to siphon off for themselves a larger share of the operating surplus which made those bonuses possible. Lincoln came to see that possibility as a "constant threat to the organization."[103]

For many years now, the company has restricted sales of stock just to Lincoln Electric employees. The company's growth is financed solely through internally generated funds and internal sale of stock. The company has issued two types of stock: "gold stock," which is voting stock; and "blue stock," which is nonvoting. The gold stock is held primarily by the heirs of John and James Lincoln, their foundations, and the heirs of some of the Lincoln's early associates. A small market for the gold stock exists on the over-the-counter market. The blue stock is sold only to Lincoln Electric employees. Any employee with a year's service or more may purchase up to twenty-five shares of blue stock each year. Because the blue stock is not for sale to the general public, it has no market price. Rather the price of the blue stock is set once each year by the company's board of directors. Generally, the price has been set as a multiple of the previous year's regular dividend, so that the dividend provides a yield roughly equal to that of a high grade bond. In 1978, blue stock sold for $79 and paid a dividend of $7. Gold stock paid the same dividend and what little did change hands on the market sold for around $170. No dividend has been missed on Lincoln stock for over sixty years. The stock has been split several times. If a person leaves the company or retires, LEC has the option of repurchasing his stock at the current price. Not all LEC employees buy stock in the company. The share of LEC employees who own stock has varied over the years between 45 percent and 65 percent.[104]

CRITICISMS OF LINCOLN ELECTRIC'S PRACTICES

The Lincoln Electric Company has not been without its critics. Different people have found fault with various aspects of the company's approach to management and enterprise. Some have questioned whether the company forces people to work too hard, whether the pace required to be as productive as Lincoln employees are might not be good for their health, whether Lincoln employees might not burn themselves out in a matter of years.

On that point, a union leader in Cleveland was quoted over thirty years ago as saying

> They work like dogs out at Lincoln. . . . Personally, I question seriously whether any man can keep up that pace very long. . . . If the day comes when . . . his people decide there is more to life than killing yourself making money, I predict the Lincoln Electric Company is in for trouble.[105]

Lincoln management has had two answers to that criticism. The first is simply that "hard work is healthy." In 1951, Lincoln agreed that a person working under his system would probably "work harder than he ever worked on a production job in his life." "Yet," Lincoln argued, "he would not be fatigued at the end of the day" because "he is developing and showing abilities that make him proud of himself." Rather than leading to "burn out," Lincoln maintained that

> hard work in which we can express our personalities and develop our latent abilities is the one thing that will make us contented, healthy, and long-lived. Loafing or work that does not extend us, and from which we cannot have pride, is a source of danger to our health and lives.[106]

In specific response to the charges set forth by the union leader, Lincoln wrote

> You, of course, understand in the usual 40-hour week a man is working a little less than twenty-five percent of the time. It might be interesting to know that we probably have a great deal greater proportion of people who have been here 25 years, or more, than any company that I know of in this district. Therefore, I doubt very much if they are working themselves to death; as a matter of fact, I rather think the reaction of people here generally is that they are having a good deal better time, they are a good deal longer lived, and a good deal healthier than they are in places where they feel driven to work or in which they object to work.[107]

Lincoln management today takes the same position as that set forth by James Lincoln thirty years ago. Lincoln's impressively low turnover rates, averaging .5 percent monthly—compared to 3.5 percent for the electrical machinery industry in general—and the more than 350 employees in its "Quarter Century Club" tend to support that position.[108]

The second answer is that Lincoln employees are—as a company—so much more productive than others as much or more because they are working *smarter* than they are working harder. Lincoln people do work at a brisk pace. They don't waste a lot of time. But they are not working twice as fast. Far from it. What they are doing is they are carrying out the work of the organization without overloaded layers of management and without bloated staff. That, and their ingenuity in finding more efficient methods, is where their biggest efficiencies come from. Few outsiders have yet to appreciate that aspect of Lincoln Electric.

In another criticism of Lincoln Electric, some have pointed to the effects of LEC's financial and employment practices on its ability to grow. Because so much of the company's earnings go into bonuses, because LEC eschews outside financing, and because of the company's guaranteed employment policy, the company has generally been more conservative in its growth than a more conventional organization might have been. LEC is cautious in adding capacity. As a result, during some periods of market expansion, order backlogs of a year or more have built up on some lines. Customers go elsewhere. For Lincoln's top management, this problem is mostly a question of priorities. The company has simply committed itself to a different set of priorities, one which means that it must act in ways that keep it from getting into a position where a prolonged downturn in the market could force it to renege on its employment guarantees. Lost sales when the market swings up is a price it is willing to pay.

A final criticism some have made of Lincoln Electric is that the company is not as "democratic" as some would like it to be. Although Lincoln's organization is designed and managed in a way to maximize day-to-day self-management at the lower levels of the organization, almost all decisions as to the direction the organization will take are made at the top. Although the company has active advisory boards, there is no question but that the final decisions are in the hands of the top management. In fact, regular contact between top management and lower-level employees on the advisory board can only constrain the prerogatives (and power) available to the company's middle management. According to one Lincoln worker, the company "is like a dictatorship in the fact that the heads of the company completely run it." That worker also went on to say, "But it is not a dictatorship in the fact that the men do have the freedom to have things changed. . . . We can have things changed when we feel they need change."[109]

That describes the way James Lincoln wanted it. Lincoln distrusted full democracy. He was wary of the "ill-considered will of the masses." Lincoln once quoted Madison to the effect that "All democracies destroy the economy and themselves. They are as short in their lives as they are violent in their deaths."[110] Lincoln believed that for an organization not to corrupt itself from within, it had to be lead by a strong leader, who "must have complete power . . . [it] must be a dictatorship . . . not to dominate but to lead."[111]

A MODEL FOR THE FUTURE?

Is The Lincoln Electric Company a good model for the future for U.S. enterprise? Some think so. Howard K. Smith, in a commentary on ABC Evening News several years ago pointed to LEC and said: "In an economy gone wrong, somebody is doing something right: The Lincoln Electric Company of Cleveland, Ohio."[112] But Lincoln Electric has been carrying its story to the business community for years. James Lincoln himself wrote three books about the company's approach to management. The company has welcomed practioners and journalists to make themselves familiar with the Lincoln approach. Up to this time, one has seen little or no diffusion of Lincoln's practices. Why? According to Mitchell Fein, "Managers do not have the courage."[113]
Perhaps the time for courage has come.

NOTES

1. Norman Fast and Norman Berg, "The Lincoln Electric Company," Boston: Harvard Graduate School of Business Administration, 1975, p. 1.
2. Allen Van Cranebrook, "Cost Cutting Ways of Lincoln Electric," *Traffic Management*, May 1966, p. 40.
3. Fast and Berg, pp. 3, 25, 26.
4. Mitchell Fein, *Motivation for Work* , Chicago: Rand McNally & Company, 1971, pp. 55, 56.
5. "Mr. Lincoln's Formula," *Fortune*, XXIX (2), February 1944, p. 145.
6. Charles G. Herbruck, "James Finney Lincoln: A Profile," in James F. Lincoln, *A New Approach to Industrial Economics*, Old Greenwich, Conn.: Devin Adair, 1961, p. 15.
7. Ibid., p. 9.
8. Fast and Berg, p. 32.
9. James F. Lincoln, *A New Approach to Industrial Economics*, Old Greenwich Conn.: Devin Adair, 1961, p. 132.

10. Question and answer session with Don Hastings, LEC's vice president for sales, at the Harvard Business School, June 1, 1979.
11. Van Cranebrook, p. 42.
12. Ibid.
13. Fast and Berg, p. 16.
14. *Fortune*, p. 203.
15. Fast and Berg, p. 13.
16. Ibid., p. 10.
17. Ibid., p. 31.
18. Hastings.
19. James F. Lincoln, *Lincoln's Incentive System,* New York: McGraw-Hill, 1946, p. 117; James F. Lincoln, *Incentive Management, A New Approach to Human Relationships in Industry and Business,* Cleveland: The Lincoln Electric Company, 1951, p. 63.
20. Lincoln, *Incentive System,* p. 107.
21. Fast and Berg, p. 15.
22. Ibid., p. 18.
23. Ibid.
24. Fein, p. 56.
25. "A stockroom with a Built-in Factory," *American Machinist,* undated reprint, p. 3.
26. James F. Lincoln, "What Makes Workers Work?" Cleveland: The Lincoln Electric Company, 1951, pp. 3, 4.
27. A. J. Taylor, "A New-Old Incentive to Employee Productivity," *Production,* June 1971, p. 80.
28. *Time,* XXXIX (23) June 8, 1942, p. 82.
29. Lincoln, *Incentive Management,* p. 17, 58; *New Approach,* p. 128.
30. "Incentive Management in Action: An Interview with William Irrgang, Chief Executive Officer, The Lincoln Electric Company," *Assembly Engineering,* March, 1967, (reprint) p. 2.
31. Fast and Berg, p. 17.
32. John D. Glover and Ralph M. Hower, "Observations on the Lincoln Electric Company," Boston: Harvard Graduate School of Business Administration, 1946, p. 269.
33. Ibid., p. 270.
34. *Fortune*, p. 203.
35. Fast and Berg, p. 13.
36. *Fortune*, p. 203.
37. *American Machinist,* p. 3.
38. Ibid., p. 5.
39. Lincoln, *Incentive Management,* p. 112.
40. Lincoln, *Incentive System,* p. 33.
41. Lincoln, *Incentive Management,* p. 55.
42. Lincoln, *Incentive System,* pp. 40, 101; *New Approach,* p. 72.
43. Lincoln, *Incentive Management,* p. 58.
44. Ibid., p. 101.
45. Ibid.
46. Lincoln, *New Approach,* p. 139.
47. Ibid., p. 129.
48. Ibid., pp. 39, 76.
49. Lincoln, *Incentive System,* p. 162.
50. Lincoln, *New Approach,* p. 36.
51. Ibid., p. 80.

52. Lincoln, *Incentive System,* p. 50.
53. Lincoln, *Incentive Management,* p. 139.
54. Ibid., p. 169.
55. Ibid., p. 108.
56. Ibid., p. 139.
57. Lincoln, *Incentive System,* p. 37.
58. Lincoln, *Incentive Management,* p. 81, 107.
59. Ibid., 128.
60. Ibid., 78.
61. Lincoln, *New Approach,* p. 95.
62. Ibid., p. 72.
63. Lincoln, *Incentive Management,* p. 121.
64. Lincoln, *New Approach,* pp. 247, 271.
65. Lincoln, *Incentive Management.* p. 161.
66. Lincoln, *New Approach,* p. 72.
67. Assembly Engineering, p. 2.
68. Ibid.
69. Fast and Berg, p. 14.
70. *Assembly Engineering,* p. 2.
71. Lincoln, *Incentive system,* p. 51.
72. Glover and Hower, p. 248.
73. Assembly Engineering, p. 3.
74. Fred B. Barton, "They Thanked Him For Coming," *Nation's Business,* XXX (7), August 1942, p. 80.
75. Fast and Berg, p. 21.
76. Lincoln, *Incentive System,* p. 51.
77. Carl Heyel, *The Encyclopedia of Management,* New York: Van Nostrand Reinhart Co., 1963, p. 273. Peter Drucker, *The New Society,* New York: Harper & Row, 1950.
78. Lincoln, *New Approach,* p. 88.
79. Ibid., p. 80.
80. Taylor, "An Old-New Incentive," p. 80.
81. Fast and Berg, p. 17.
82. *Time,* June 8, '42, p. 82.
83. *Fortune,* p. 204.
84. Glover and Hower, pp. 266–67.
85. Carl Heyel, "The Lincoln Incentive Management Plan," in *The Encyclopedia of Management,* Carl Heyel, (ed.), New York: Van Nostrand Reinhart Co., 1973, pp. 436–38.
86. Ibid.
87. Richard I. Henderson, *Compensation Management: Rewarding Performance,* Reston, Vir.: Reston Publishing Company, 1979, p. 357.
88. Lincoln, *Incentive System,* p. 164.
89. Lincoln, *Incentive Management,* p. 81.
90. Ibid., pp. 101–3; *New Approach,* p. 92.
91. *Incentive Management,* p. 109.
92. *Incentive Management,* p. 137; *New Approach,* p. 101.
93. Barton, *Nation's Business,* p. 39.
94. Lincoln, *Incentive Management,* p. 105.
95. Henderson, pp. 375, 377.
96. Lincoln, *Incentive System,* p. 150.

97. Lincoln, *Incentive System,* p. 148; *Incentive Management,* pp. 136, 138.
98. Henderson, p. 377; Charles W. Brennan, *Wage Administration,* Homewood, Ill: Richard D. Irwin, 1959, p. 274.
99. James F. Lincoln, "Intelligent Selfishness and Manufacturing," Cleveland: The Lincoln Electric Company, 1942, Brennan, p. 270; Barton, p. 78.
100. *Fortune,* p. 198.
101. Lincoln, *Incentive System,* p. 101.
102. Taylor, "Old-New Incentive," p. 79.
103. Lincoln, *Incentive Management,* p. 222.
104. Brennan, p. 271; Fast and Berg, p. 3; James F. Lincoln, "Incentive Compensation: The Way to Industrial Democracy," *Advanced Management,* Feb. 1950, p. 18.
105. Glover and Hower, p. 287.
106. Lincoln, *Incentive Management,* pp. 66, 87.
107. Glover and Hower, p. 288.
108. Fast and Berg, pp. 13, 28.
109. Andrew Rooney, "Mr. Rooney Goes to Work," CBS News, Aug. 17, 1977.
110. Lincoln, *Incentive Management,* pp. 160–61.
111. Ibid., p. 228; Lincoln, *Incentive System,* p. 42.
112. ABC Evening News, August 17, 1977.
113. Fein, p. 59.

CHAPTER 14

Work Ethics in an Era of Limited Resources

*Paul E. Tsongas**

The work ethic and related issues are vital to us nationally and personally. Right now this nation is not working as well as it can and must. We are challenged internationally by competitors and predators—nations that have helped push the U.S. standard of living down. Americans have to understand that we must be more productive just to keep pace with our allies and our adversaries. In this era of limited resources, we must work more effectively to safeguard our children's future. Nationally and internationally, we have our work cut out for us.

Work issues are also vital from another vantage—that of the individual worker. Pay is never so high, hours are never so low, that the quality of working life in unimportant. If we get lost in numbers, hung up on output, and if we devalue human dignity in the workplace, the predictable result is an unhappy work force of unproductive people.

We must constantly remember that people are not numbers, but that behind all the interesting data about work are individual men and women. Take just one example of a work-related statistic. Many of you probably think the unemployment rate is a little under 6 percent. Let me suggest that the rate is either 0 percent or 100 percent,

*U.S. Senator, Commonwealth of Massachusetts

depending on whether the recession hits you where you work. And I can't discuss ideals such as quality of working life without mentioning my strong belief that every American has the *right* to a job—every American.

I can't tie two days of panels, workshops, and addresses together in a neat package. (But I do appreciate receiving an advance copy of most of the remarks.) I will talk about the development of workers' rights, and managing the ongoing evolution of new workplace relationships. Then I'll discuss the work ethic and alternative culprits in recent U.S. productivity slow-downs. The two most popular targets are government regulation, and disincentives to investment. I will conclude with some thoughts on the renewed sense of purpose and cooperation that an interdependent world with depleted resources demands.

Much of the challenge of motivating and managing employees in the 1980s is the product of positive developments. Better wages and shorter hours create more opportunities for self-satisfaction and self-definition outside the factory or office. Workers today are better educated. They don't want to work as cogs on a wheel. They don't go for heavy-handed decisions that drop like rocks from the executive suite.

Another bit of progress that comes in a mixed bag of complications for managers is the effort to ensure equal job opportunity. It's what right, and we're headed in the right direction. The perception that certain categories of workers will gain at others' expense is most difficult to manage in times of economic stagnation. When we get the economy growing and producing at a better rate, the mandate for equal employment opportunity will be less divisive.

Increased job-sharing and job switching both indicate an increased assertiveness by workers. More and more, workers stuck in an unsatisfactory work situation will take their job skills and shove off. Employment counselors such as John Crystal and Richard Bolles have strengthened a worker's hand to make the job market work for him or her. *What Color Is Your Parachute?* is still a best-selling trade paperback. *The Three Boxes of Life*—also by Bolles—is an even more complete treatment of the subject.

It's a new day for individual employees—and no way will the 1980s mark a return toward the more rigid, bossy pattern of business. I'm very hopeful for the quality of working life movement. When you back away from the extreme specialization of factory assembly lines, for example, you make a worker's day more fulfilling. Results from the automobile industry, the telephone industry, and elsewhere indicate that it's also good business. Worker-management committees are another good sign that a whole set of attitudes are improving. By itself, a new committee is just window dressing. It must be part of a renewed openness to ideas from all employees, a renewed sense of common interest, and open-minded interaction among employees at all levels.

Basically, I don't believe that the work ethic is wasting away. The easy put-down that "people don't want to work hard anymore" is unfair. But the poll data discussed at this conference indicate that the work ethic is evolving. The changes in process are a challenge to business executives. They are an open invitation to managers to open up nonmaterial sources of job satisfaction—which may eventually pay off in higher productivity.

Changes in the work ethic are not the simple answer for what's happening to American productivity. Indeed, there is no single culprit on productivity . . . just lots of accomplices. The bottom line is that productivity growth has weakened throughout the 1970s, and it stopped last year. This year it is falling.

Some of the causes are demographic. One is the entrance into the job market of younger, less experienced workers who were part of the baby boom. Another is that the large postwar shift from farming into fast-growing highly productive manufacturing is mostly over now. Energy prices also have hurt productivity.

The clear, present dangers of recession and inflation undercut productivity. Every recession creates losses that are never recouped. Inflation hurts productivity by reducing saving and investment, and by increasing the costs and risks in predicting the economy. The circle is vicious, because when productivity falls, it fuels inflation.

A major punching bag on the productivity front is government regulation of business. The cost-effectiveness of regulation is an issue for which contending interests uncover conflicting data. "Output" in the form of cleaner air, safer working conditions, improved health and other "public goods" isn't part of the GNP.

I can't deny that there are instances of regulatory overkill. But they are the predictable, inevitable result of abuses by American business. The private sector has opposed government regulation so indiscriminately that it has suffered a credibility gap. Rising inflation and falling productivity make it vital that business and government work together more responsibly and cooperatively toward regulatory reason that serves the public.

America still leads the world in productivity, but the lead has been slipping. In 1950, it took seven Japanese workers to match the output of one American. Now it takes only two. Most industrial nations have been investing more than the United States—especially since the mid-1970s. From 1966 to 1976 "real nonresidential fixed investment" was 13.5 percent of the U.S. gross domestic product. Japan invested in itself at twice that rate. I am studying the tax system in detail, and intend to support strong measures to encourage capital investment.

In a shrinking, interdependent world, we must strive harder to maintain our technological edge. We must also match the aggressive trade policies of our partners. It's a cop-out to assume that our trade deficit is necessitated by imported oil. Germany is far more dependent on imported energy than the United States, and yet it has a $24 billion balance of trade surplus! We have moved toward a more aggressive policy with the Export Administration Act. But we are still being outhustled by our trading partners. In the automobile, for example, they continue to produce cars for the future. We must do more.

In summary, I would suggest that the new sense of cooperation and common goals involved in revitalizing the work ethic is paralleled on the national level by what the new economic order requires internationally. Workers and management, bureaucrats and industrialists, the various contending interests of our nation must reconfirm their dependence on each other, and their commitment to the national interest. Our economic times are changing, and time does not favor those who drift in a period of sharp challenges.

Discussion

Question: How much time do you think the country has left to adjust its energy demands?

Tsongas: Not long. I don't know how many of you invested in gold four years ago, but those of you who did will agree that the time is very short. There is no rational reason for gold to be at such record levels. These escalating prices are a result of a lack of confidence in the United States and in our economy. Recently, Iran and Liberia raised their oil prices, a step they have taken before and will no doubt take again.

The United States is like an addict who complains about the price charged by the junkie for his addiction. You can only pump out so much of our economy into OPEC before our economy begins to fall apart. I tell you, it is happening right now. The moves of Federal Reserve Chairman Paul Volcker are nothing more than a response to that reality. We must adjust to that reality now! It is not something that we can wait ten years to do. The marketplace is very cruel. If we don't adjust to the reality that's out there, the world is going to make us adjust.

Remember when Kissinger talked about invading Saudi Arabia? His justification was that we could take such steps to secure our oil supplies. That rationale is comparable to someone saying that they are going to invade the United States to secure their wheat supplies. It is a wrong attitude. Today's world is different and we have to admit it. The major problem is the energy issue and our inability to get a handle on it. We are going to pour out $88 billion for a synthetic fuels program. There will be a great to-do about the program and a lot of media attention paid to it. But no one is going to tell the public that we will not derive any energy from synthetic fuels until 1990 when they first begin to penetrate the market.

Congress has passed a $1.2 billion fuel assistance program to help lower-income people pay their winter fuel bills. You know what happens? We pay the states, who give it to low-income people, who give it to the fuel oil dealers, who give it to the oil companies, who give it to OPEC. All we have done is taken $1.2 billion and given it to OPEC through a rather circuitous route. We are going to do that next year and the year after and the year after that.

Look at the Harvard Business School study, *Energy Future*. It states that the only rational short-term approach to the energy situation is to maximize conservation and renewables. It's not the Sierra Club making its usual argument in favor of conservation and renewable energy—it's the Harvard Business School. Every important study done since then arrives at exactly the same conclusion. Unfortunately, however, when it comes to conservation and renewable resources, they don't seem to be very exciting subjects to the media. Let me give you an example. When legislation that I wrote was passed to establish a conservation and solar bank, its passage got little coverage by the Boston media. However, if I say something about a presidential candidate, I can make the front page anyday. When I want to talk about the seriousness of the energy conservation issue, it doesn't make "news." It doesn't grab anyone.

This is a country that put a man on the moon with the Apollo Program and developed the atomic bomb with the Manhattan Project. When the problem is energy, we want something big and dramatic— so we get synthetic fuels. We're going to take Colorado and put it in your gas tank. Yet the only solution that works in the real world is serious conservation and serious approaches to renewables. Congress has approved $20 billion for synthetic fuels. I had to fight from the floor of the Senate to get just $1 billion as an amendment for conservation and renewables. How much time do we have to change our energy habits? Not much.

Question: To push that a step further, I know you've been critical of President Carter in terms of his energy package and you've worked on the Joint Energy Committee. Give us some more specifics about what we ought to be working on in the energy area during the next few years.

Tsongas: The average homeowner can cut his or her fuel oil consumption by between 30-75 percent, depending on the type of home and other factors. It is absurd for any new home to be built in this country without passive solar design techniques. Right now, while we're talking, there are people all over this country building new homes—some of them are all-electric, as is Bentley College. That awareness of where we need to head in the future when it comes to the type of homes we need to build, and the type of energy we should use to run them, just isn't very widespread.

Solar and other renewable resources are the future, and there should be a massive campaign to change building codes to prohibit the construction of new homes that don't achieve certain standards of conservation and the use of the sun. In the debate we had in the Senate about synfuels, Senator Randolph talked about the Germans using synthetic fuel during World War II. That was the age-old process. My response was yes, but they used the sun before Christ was born. Now we are too "sophisticated" for that, and the only way my solar bank and conservation bank are going to pass is because of the Harvard Business School study. It apparently took a Harvard report to legitimize what many of us have been saying for years about conservation and renewables.

Think of all the rivers in this country—flowing out to sea with all that energy never tapped. Think of all the trash we generate in this country; we've got to find a place to put it. What is maddening about the energy crisis is that the technology needed to respond to it is known. What is lacking is leadership. When you come right down to it, we are a presidential system.

Question: Do you anticipate federal legislation for employee rights such as constitutional rights like freedom of speech?

Tsongas: No, I don't think so. It was once said that Houdini used to draw a crowd and charge money to tie himself in knots and get himself out. Congress is pretty much like that except we don't charge money—directly, that is. In an election year, the only things that will pass Congress are those bills that deal with issues that are essential for keeping the government operating. This kind of long-range issue will not pass out of Congress this year. I think most of the emphasis next year will be on energy and a serious attempt to deal with the problem of productivity and capital formation. In terms of workers' rights, that is not in the legislative cards for next year.

Question: What do you see in the long range in this respect?

Tsongas: It depends on who is President. John Connolly isn't exactly going to lead the fight for workers' rights in this nation. I think you really have to depend on who is President. If you own land on Nantucket or if you fish in Georges Bank, you have one view of the Presidential campaign—others would have a different view. We are a Presidential system and I suspect the next eight years will be determined by what will happen in November.

Question: You talked about part of our problem as a "me-first" mentality among the citizens and I think this is led by a "me-first" mentality among congressmen and senators who follow their parties and won't compromise. They are affected by special interest groups and that kind of thing. I wondered what you think of this?

Tsongas: I couldn't agree with you more.

Question: Do you think there's going to be any change?

Tsongas: Will there by any change? Winston Churchill said you get the government you deserve. He was right. Fewer people vote. Fewer people participate. Fewer people contribute. You leave it open to single-issue politics. You leave it open to political action committees to finance elections. What do you expect is going to happen? You have an issue—for example, the energy crisis, and you wonder why the oil lobby has such an impact. If they are the only people on the playing field, of course they're going to have impact. There's a lot to the old expression about the liberty tree having to be watered by blood of patriots every twenty years. Churchill also said that government was like a sausage—you are a lot better off not knowing what goes into it. There's a lot of truth to that as well. But, you have to get in there, participate, and fight, because if you don't, they will. I would rather participate than stand outside and criticize, and I commend people your age who participate in these things—for example, the interns who come to work in my office as opposed to people who simply curse the system and don't participate. When the tide falls and rises, we all go with it. Let's say we make a mistake on the SALT Treaty, we engage in the worst-case scenario, and we and the Soviets are armed to the teeth when some crazy individual eventually does the wrong thing. We have to respond and they have to respond. We obliterate ourselves. It's too late to complain about some politician when those ICBMs are on their way over. You should have replaced him.

Question: You have mentioned overkill with regard to federal control in no particular context. You've also mentioned that it's very difficult for us Americans to impose self-control. I was wondering what the middle ground is that you see.

Tsongas: At the risk of sounding metaphysical, I think that any society has a certain reaction to a perceived sense of drift, in that once people understand that drifting in the current status will lead to chaos, they are willing to make the changes. Part of the Germans' mindset is the chaos they experienced between the two world wars. It's implanted in their psyche and will be there for a long time. The United States will even eventually come to that same conclusion—the awareness that we have no other choice. *When* that comes I think is much more important than *if* it's going to come, because I have no question that it will come. Part of what I have tried to do legislatively is to provide the mechanisms so that when that awareness is there we don't have to start looking for how to finance the charges or how to put them in place. We will have to be prepared. This is a remarkable country. We're very well educated; we have an incredibly well-trained work force. We have a lot going for us. What is missing is the other ingredient that is not a *physical* resource—it's simply leadership. I'm not talking about the president, I'm talking about leadership in all the various sectors of society. That is the easiest attitude to turn around, but you don't have a Pearl Harbor as a sudden stimulus. It's a slower awareness, like any other evolutionary process.

Question: What about business leadership? Can institutions devoted to profit demonstrate a selfless leadership?

Tsongas: I think it's very much like my answer to the last question. There was an article I was told about in the *New York Times* magazine about Reginald Jones's approach to government, the enlightened CEO approach. I think that's where it's going to be. At some point everyone in the business community is going to realize that confrontation is fine in a kind of psychic sense, but that it diminishes our capacity to compete internationally. We're all going to sink or swim together. I think it only arises in times of crisis, and we are rapidly approaching that. There is no way you can guarantee that people in the political process or private sector or academia are going to be any better. We are all human beings with the same instincts. The question is whether, in the interest of common survival, we will adopt certain approaches. Unfortunately, I think we are coming to that point only because of the international crisis in the financial markets. Let me give you an example. There was a senator who said to me privately, "You want me to vote for the Panama Canal Treaty. I voted for the Panama Canal Treaty and I almost got wiped out. Other people got wiped out as well. If I vote for Panama and SALT II, I won't get reelected. Therefore, I'm not going to vote with you on SALT II."

If you analyze this view, there are only two conclusions you can draw: (1) if he is not re-elected, he would be unemployed and therefore must hang on tenaciously; and (2) he honestly believes that it is in the national interest that he be reelected. Most of the people in the Senate share one of these views. The problem is how to get people to do what's necessary and to adopt the view that if they don't get reelected, then so be it.

Senator Hatfield of Montana voted for the Panama Canal Treaty and was criticized by his constituents for the vote. Senator Haskel of Colorado, who knew what he was doing when he voted for the treaty, knew the consequences, and was prepared to vote for the treaty anyway, didn't get reelected. When you see such conviction you have to admire it because you don't see it very often. When I got to the Senate, I didn't expect to find senators so concerned about their next campaign. It was what I saw while serving on the Lowell City Council and it's what I see now in the U.S. Senate. It's a system. It doesn't make any difference who it is, as long as that system—the survival and re-election syndrome—remains in place. When the American people finally say, "My survival is at stake and you're going to do what's right even though it hurts me," that's the point when the spark takes place and you make the transition.

Question: I'm a Canadian and I'd like to know if you think it's any use to pursue a North American energy policy, and if so, whether you think that the attitudes of the Americans, Canadians, and Mexicans might be an insurmountable obstacle.

Tsongas: Well, you have 33 million people and by the year 2000 there will be as many people in Mexico City as there will be in Canada at the current rate of population growth, with the U.S. in between. Can you have a sense of common purpose? I think you can despite those problems, because Canada and Mexico will have producer status, and the U.S. will have consumer status. My hesitation is simply, why is dependence on Canada any better than dependence on Venezuela? In the last analysis, every country will do what's in its self-interest; to expect anything else is absurd. So in the last analysis, the Canadian government will do what is best for Canada and the Mexican government will do what is best for Mexico and we have to do what is best for our country. To understand those limitations and work within those limitations is fine. To somehow expect to repeal those laws of human behavior is an error. I'd rather see this country do everything it can to produce its own resources from renewables and conservation. We can get up to 25 percent of our energy by the year 2000 from those sources. We ought to do it.

About the Editors

W. Michael Hoffman is Director of the Center for Business Ethics and Chair of the Philosophy Department at Bentley College. He received his Ph.D. in philosophy from the University of Massachusetts at Amherst. Dr. Hoffman has published numerous articles in various professional journals and has lectured on metaphysics, philosophy of religion, business ethics, philosophical ecology, and the history of ideas. In addition, he is the author of *Kant's Theory of Freedom: A Metaphysical Inquiry*. Dr. Hoffman has received grants from the National Endowment for the Humanities, the Matchette Foundation, and the Council for Philosophical Studies.

Thomas J. Wyly is Executive Assistant to the President and Assistant Professor of English at Bentley College. He did his undergraduate work at Fordham University and his graduate studies at the University of Pennsylvania. He has taught language, literature, and business communications at the University of Pennsylvania, Hahnemann Medical College, and Bentley College. Mr. Wyly has also held various administrative positions involving strategic planning, program evaluation, and personnel administration with the Office of Economic Opportunity, the Addiction Services Agency of New York City, and the University of Pennsylvania.